Spanish

The Spanish Language Learning Guide for Beginners

© Copyright 2020

All Rights Reserved. No part of this book may be reproduced in any form without permission in writing from the author. Reviewers may quote brief passages in reviews.

Disclaimer: No part of this publication may be reproduced or transmitted in any form or by any means, mechanical or electronic, including photocopying or recording, or by any information storage and retrieval system, or transmitted by email without permission in writing from the publisher.

While all attempts have been made to verify the information provided in this publication, neither the author nor the publisher assumes any responsibility for errors, omissions or contrary interpretations of the subject matter herein.

This book is for entertainment purposes only. The views expressed are those of the author alone, and should not be taken as expert instruction or commands. The reader is responsible for his or her own actions.

Adherence to all applicable laws and regulations, including international, federal, state and local laws governing professional licensing, business practices, advertising and all other aspects of doing business in the US, Canada, UK or any other jurisdiction is the sole responsibility of the purchaser or reader.

Neither the author nor the publisher assumes any responsibility or liability whatsoever on the behalf of the purchaser or reader of these materials. Any perceived slight of any individual or organization is purely unintentional.

Contents

PART 1: SPANISH FOR BEGINNERS 1
A COMPREHENSIVE GUIDE FOR LEARNING THE SPANISH LANGUAGE FAST 1
INTRODUCTION 2
PART I: THE VERY BASICS 4
CHAPTER 1 - THE SPANISH ALPHABET 5
Pronunciation: the vowels 7
The consonants: one letter, one sound 8
The consonants: exceptional cases 13
Exercises 17
CHAPTER 2 - NUMBERS, MONTHS AND DAYS OF THE WEEK 20
Numbers from one to twenty 21
Numbers from twenty-one to ninety-nine: 23
Hundreds, thousands, millions 24
Fractions 26
Ordinal numbers 26
The months of the year 28
The days of the week 29
The hours of the day 30

Exercises *32*
CHAPTER 3 – ARTICLES AND NOUNS 33
Definite articles *35*
Indefinite articles *36*
Exercises *36*
CHAPTER 4 – PRONOUNS 38
CHAPTER 5 – PREPOSITIONS 44
a *45*
ante *46*
bajo *46*
con *46*
de *47*
desde *48*
durante *48*
en *48*
entre *49*
excepto *49*
hacia *49*
hasta *49*
mediante *50*
para *50*
por *50*
salvo *51*
según *51*
sin *52*
sobre *52*
tras *52*
Exercises *53*
CHAPTER 6 – ADJECTIVES 55
Colors *58*
Possessive adjectives *59*
Exercises *61*
CHAPTER 7 – BASIC SPANISH VERBS 64

To be – ser *64*
To be – estar *65*
Regular verbs: present tense *65*
Irregular verbs *67*
Verb haber (impersonal sentences) *71*
Exercises *71*
CHAPTER 8 – NEGATIVE SENTENCES 73
Exercises *74*
CHAPTER 9 – MODAL VERBS 76
Negative modal verbs *79*
Haber que *79*
Exercises *80*
CHAPTER 10 – PRESENT PERFECT 82
Exercises *84*
CHAPTER 11 – SIMPLE PAST 87
Exercises *94*
CHAPTER 12 – IMPERFECTO 96
Exercises *104*
CHAPTER 13 – FUTURE TENSES 106
ir + a + infinitive verb *106*
Simple future *107*
EXERCISES... 114
PART III: CONVERSATION 116
CHAPTER 14 – GREETINGS.. 117
EXERCISES... 120
CHAPTER 15 – INTRODUCING YOURSELF................................. 122
EXERCISES... 127
CHAPTER 16 – FORMING QUESTIONS AND DIALOGUE 128
Exercises *133*
CONCLUSION 135
APPENDIX: VOCABULARY 136
GLOSSARY OF NOUNS 136
GLOSSARY OF ADJECTIVES 140

GLOSSARY OF VERBS..142
EXERCISES: CORRECT ANSWERS 146
CHAPTER 2..146
CHAPTER 3..146
CHAPTER 4..147
CHAPTER 5..148
CHAPTER 6..150
CHAPTER 7..150
CHAPTER 8..151
CHAPTER 9..152
CHAPTER 10..153
CHAPTER 11..154
CHAPTER 12..155
CHAPTER 13..156
CHAPTER 14..157
CHAPTER 15..158
CHAPTER 16..158
PART 2: MASTERING SPANISH WORDS 160
INCREASE YOUR VOCABULARY WITH OVER 3000 SPANISH WORDS IN CONTEXT... 160
INTRODUCTION 161
CHAPTER 1 – WORDS 1-300 163
CHAPTER 2 – WORDS 301-600 184
CHAPTER 3 – WORDS 601-900 208
CHAPTER 4 – WORDS 901-1200 232
CHAPTER 5 – WORDS 1201-1500 257
CHAPTER 6 – WORDS 1501-1800 283
CHAPTER 7 – WORDS 1801-2100 308
CHAPTER 8 – WORDS 2101-2400 333
CHAPTER 9 – WORDS 2401-2700 358
CHAPTER 10 – WORDS 2701-3000.. 383
CONCLUSION 409

Part 1: Spanish for Beginners

A Comprehensive Guide for Learning the Spanish Language Fast

Introduction

Although learning Spanish might seem hard, it is quite a simple language to learn once you know the basics. This is because many Spanish words are similar to English ones (normally, those that derive from Latin). Also, verb conjugation follows a regular pattern for most verbs, which means that once you learn it, you can simply apply it to every regular verb. Lastly, Spanish is not too complex to study because cultures from Latin America and Spain are so rich and interesting that you will find it easy to get lost in them!

This book offers you simple and easy access to the very basics of Spanish, covering pronunciation, basic vocabulary, numbers, prepositions, adjectives, basic verbal tenses—and their present, past, and future conjugations—, greetings, questions, and dialogues.

And even though you will be reading about Spanish grammar, it won't be boring; it will be fun and give you a sense of the soul and music of the Spanish language and culture.

For every subject, a simple explanation and practical examples are given so that you can see the language in action. And, of course, since this is 2020, the content is engaging and up to date—you won't find sentences like "The cat is under the mat." Instead, there are more useful ones, such as "I need an adapter to charge my phone."

A new language is an open door to a whole new culture and experience. After you read this book, you can use your newly acquired knowledge to travel to a Spanish-speaking country, make Spanish-speaking friends, read Spanish books, and so much more.

Enjoy!

PART I: THE VERY BASICS

Chapter 1 – The Spanish Alphabet

Did you know that the Spanish alphabet contains a letter that does not exist in any other major language? The letter *ñ* (pronounced *en-yeh*) might look like an *n* with a diacritic mark, but it is a letter in its own right! It is placed in the Spanish alphabet right after the letter *n*, and before the letter *o*.

So, what does the Spanish alphabet look like? It has 27 letters and goes like this:

a (pronounced *ah*)

b (pronounced *beh*)

c (pronounced *seh*)

d (pronounced *deh*)

e (pronounced *eh*)

f (pronounced *ef-eh*)

g (pronounced *heh*)

h (pronounced *ach-eh*)

i (pronounced *ee*)

j (pronounced *hota*)

k (pronounced *kah*)

l (pronounced *el-eh*)

m (pronounced *em-eh*)

n (pronounced *en-eh*)

ñ (pronounced *en-yeh*)

o (pronounced *oh*)

p (pronounced *peh*)

q (pronounced *cuh*)

r (pronounced *erreh*)

s (pronounced *es-eh*)

t (pronounced *teh*)

u (pronounced *oo*)

v (pronounced *veh* or *uuh-veh*)

w (pronounced *dob-leh-veh* or *dob-leh-uuh* in Latin America and *dob-leh-uuh-veh* in Spain)

x (pronounced *eh-kis*)

y (pronounced *ee-gri-eh-gah*)

z (pronounced *se-tah*)

As you can see, except for the letter *ñ*, it does not look too different from the English alphabet, but some of these letters are indeed pronounced differently.

Luckily, Spanish pronunciation is quite simple: most letters only represent a singular sound. While in English, the letter *a* can sound different in many ways (try saying *cat, angel, water, art*), in Spanish, there is only one correct pronunciation for it: *ah*.

Of course, there are a few exceptions to the 'one letter, one sound' rule, which you will find in the combinations of letters *ci, cc, ch, gui, gue, ll, que, qui,* and the dreaded double *r: rr*.

But first, go over the pronunciation of every letter in the Spanish alphabet and some everyday sentences in which you will find these sounds.

Pronunciation: the vowels

The vowels are *a, e, i, o* and *u*.

The letter **a** is pronounced *ah*, as the *a* in *Alice*. You can find this letter in words such as *ala* (*wing*), *papa* (*potato*), *cantar* (*to sing*).

See these words in the following sentences:

The plane's wing is very large - *El* **ala** *del avión es muy grande*

The potato is an important ingredient in Peru - *La* **papa** *es un ingrediente importante en Perú*

I want to sing a tango - *Quiero* **cantar** *un tango*

The letter **e** is pronounced *eh*, like the *e* in *elephant*. You can find this letter in words such as *estudiar* (*to study*), *equipaje* (*luggage*), and *tenedor* (*fork*).

You could use these words in sentences like the following:

I will go to Spain to study - *Voy a ir a España a* **estudiar**

I don't see my luggage - *No veo mi* **equipaje**

I need a fork to eat this - *Necesito un* **tenedor** *para comer esto*

The letter *i* is always pronounced as *ee*. You can find this sound in words like *insecto* (*insect*), *cima* (*top*), and *niños* (*children*).

See these words in the following sentences:

I had never seen an insect so big! - *¡Nunca vi un* **insecto** *tan grande!*

I want to reach the top of the Aconcagua - *Quiero llegar a la* **cima** *del Aconcagua*

The children are in the park - *Los* **niños** *están en el parque*

The letter *o* is always pronounced as *oh*, like the *o* in *topic*. Some words with *o* in Spanish are *ocaso* (*sunset*), *comprar* (*to buy*), and *teléfono* (*phone*).

See these words in the following sentences:

Let's go see the sunset - *Vamos a ver el* **ocaso**

I am going to buy something to eat - *Voy a comprar algo de* **comer**

Where is my phone? - *¿Dónde está mi* **teléfono**?

Finally, the letter *u* is pronounced as the English *oo*. You can find this letter in the words *música* (*music*), *automóvil* (*car*), and *sueño* (*dream*).

See these words in the following sentences:

The music from Brazil is beautiful - *La* **música** *de Brasil es hermosa*

Where can I rent a car? - *¿Dónde puedo rentar un* **automóvil**?

My dream is to go to Machu Picchu -- *Mi* **sueño** *es ir al Machu Picchu*

The consonants: one letter, one sound

Now, move on to the consonants. In this section, you are going to describe how to pronounce those that represent a single sound in Spanish: *b, d, f, h, j, k, m, n, ñ, p, s, t, v, w, x, z*. The exceptions, those that might sound differently in different situations, are going to be explained in the next section.

The letter *b* is pronounced as a soft English *b*. You can find this letter in words such as *bailar* (*to dance*), *bonito* (*pretty*), and *hablar* (*to talk* or *to speak*).

See these words in the following sentences:

Tonight, we are going to dance - *Esta noche, vamos a* **bailar**

The sky is very pretty - *El cielo es muy* **bonito**

I want to learn to speak Spanish - Quiero aprender a **hablar** en español

The letter *d* is pronounced as a soft English *d*. Some Spanish words with *d* are *dulce* (*sweet*), *llamada* (*call*), and *dorado* (*golden*).

See these words in the following sentences:

The quince is very sweet - El membrillo es muy **dulce**

I am waiting for a call - Estoy esperando una **llamada**

I have a golden watch - Tengo un reloj **dorado**

The letter *f* sounds just like the English *f* in words like *fish*. Some Spanish words with this letter are *fácil* (*easy*), *café* (*coffee*), and *filete* (*steak*).

See these words in the following sentences:

Spanish is easy - El español es **fácil**

Colombia's coffee is the best - El **café** de Colombia es el mejor

Tonight I want to eat a good steak - Esta noche quiero comer un buen **filete**

The letter *j* does not sound like the English *j*. In Spanish, it is used to represent a sound slightly stronger than the English *h* in words like *hello*. You can find this letter in words like *juego* (*game*), *jamón* (*ham*), and *joven* (*young*).

See these words in the following sentences:

If it rains, we can play a game - Si llueve, podemos jugar un **juego**

I came to Spain to eat ham - Vine a España a comer **jamón**

You are very young - Tú eres muy **joven**

The letter *k* sounds like the English *k*. It is not very common in the Spanish language, but you will find it in some words like *kilo* (*kilo*), *kiwi* (*kiwi*), and *kiosko* (*stand*).

See these words in the following sentences:

We need a kilogram of tomatoes - Necesitamos un **kilo** de tomates

I bought a kiwi - Compré un **kiwi**

Where can I find a stand to buy the newspaper? - ¿Dónde puedo encontrar un **kiosko** para comprar el periódico?

The letter **m** sounds just like the English m. You can find this letter in words like *mechero* (*lighter*), *cama* (*bed*), and *amarillo* (*yellow*).

See these words in the following sentences:

Excuse me, do you have a lighter? - Disculpa, ¿tienes un **mechero**?

We need a room with a double bed - Necesitamos una habitación con una **cama** doble

The boat is yellow - El barco es **amarillo**

The letter **n** sounds just like the English n. In Spanish, you will find this letter in words like *nunca* (*never*), *habitación* (*room*), and *desayuno* (*breakfast*).

See these words in the following sentences:

My instinct is never wrong - Mi instinto **nunca** se equivoca

I don't remember my room number - No recuerdo el número de mi **habitación**

Until what time is breakfast served? - ¿Hasta qué hora es el **desayuno**?

The letter **ñ**, as stated at the beginning of the chapter, is unique to the Spanish alphabet. But don't panic! Its sound is very easy: it sounds like an *n* and *i* placed together, or like the *ny* combination in *canyon*. You will find ñ in words like *español* (*Spanish*), *niño* (*kid*), and *año* (*year*).

See these words in the following sentences:

I am learning Spanish - Estoy aprendiendo **español**

*Juan is a very tall kid – Juan es un **niño** muy alto*

*I have been living here for a year – Vivo aquí hace un **año***

The letter **p** in Spanish is slightly softer than the English *p*; actually, it sounds more similar to the English *b*. You will find *p* in words like *perro (dog), playa (beach),* and *apartamento (apartment).*

See these words in the following sentences:

*Back at home, I have a black dog – En casa, tengo un **perro** negro*

*Should we go to the beach? – ¿Vamos a la **playa**?*

*We are renting an apartment – Estamos alquilando un **apartamento***

The letter **s** sounds like the English *s*. You will find this letter in words like *sal (salt), casa (house),* and *reserva (reservation).*

See these words in the following sentences:

*Could you bring me the salt? – ¿Podría traerme la **sal**?*

*We will rent a house on the mountain – Vamos a alquilar una **casa** en la montaña*

*I have a reservation – Tengo una **reserva***

The letter **t** sounds softer than the English *t* in words like *table*. You can find this letter in words like *té (tea), taza (mug/cup),* and *puerta (door).*

See these words in the following sentences:

*I want a chamomile tea, please – Quiero **té** de manzanilla, por favor*

*Could you bring me a cup of coffee from the kitchen? – ¿Podrías traerme una **taza** de café de la cocina?*

*The door is locked – La **puerta** está cerrada*

The letter **v** sounds like the Spanish *b*, which is why it is quite a common mistake for Spanish users to exchange these two letters while writing. It also explains why their names are meant to differentiate them: in some countries, *v* is called *ve corta, ve pequeña* or *ve baja* (*short v, small v, short v*), and *b* is called *be larga, be alta* and *be grande* (*long b, tall b, large b*). In Spain, *v* is called *uve* (because of its resemblance to *u*), and *b* is called *be*.

You can find *v* in words such as *ave* (*bird*), *volcán* (*volcano*), and *ventana* (*window*).

See these words in the following sentences:

*What a colorful bird! - ¡Qué **ave** tan colorida!*

*In Chile, there is an active volcano - En Chile hay un **volcán** activo*

*I want to sit by the window - Quiero sentarme junto a la **ventana***

The letter ***w*** is not a letter usually found in Spanish. Most words that contain this letter are of foreign origin; normally, they are English words. It is pronounced like the English *w*, which means it is also equivalent to a Spanish *u*. You can find *w* in words like *wifi* (*Wi-Fi*), *wafle* (*waffle*), and *show* (*show*).

See these words in the following sentences:

*I need the Wi-Fi password - Necesito la contraseña del **wifi***

*This afternoon, I want to eat a waffle - Esta tarde quiero comer un **wafle***

*Let's go see a salsa show - Vamos a ver un **show** de salsa*

The letter ***x*** is pronounced like the English *x* in words like *next*. It is not very frequent in Spanish, but you will find it in words like *taxi* (*taxi*), *éxito* (*success*), and *conexión* (*connection*).

See these words in the following sentences:

*I will take a taxi to the airport - Tomaré un **taxi** al aeropuerto*

*The hike was a success - La excursión fue un **éxito***

*I lost my Internet connection - Perdí la **conexión** a internet*

The consonants: exceptional cases

This section explains situations where some consonants are pronounced differently depending on where they are placed in a word. Don't worry! You will find this easier than you think; most of these rules also apply to English!

The letter *c*, just as in English, has three different sounds.

The first *c* sound is like a *k*, and it is used when the *c* is placed before consonants or before the vowels *a, o,* and *u*. Some examples are *clase* (*class*), *casi* (*almost*), *cosa* (*thing*), and *cuchara* (*spoon*).

The second *c* sound is like an *s*, and it happens when the *c* is placed before the vowels *e* and *i*. You can find the *ce* and *ci* combination of letters in words like *cena* (*dinner*) and *cita* (*date*).

Finally, when the *c* is placed before an *h*, the sound is like the one for the same combination of letters in the English words *chance* or *choice*. Some Spanish words with the *ch* sound are *chocolate* (*chocolate*), *chiste* (*joke*), and *chico* (*boy*).

The letter *g* has two sounds: a soft sound and a strong sound.

The soft *g* sound is like the English *g* sound in *great* or *gone*. The Spanish *g* sounds like this when it is placed before consonants or the vowels *a, o,* and *u*. You can find this in words like *gracias* (*thanks*), *gato* (*cat*), *gota* (*drop*), and *gusto* (*taste*).

To have a soft *g* before an *e* or *i*, just like in English, a silent *u* is placed between the two letters: *guitarra* (*guitar*), *guerra* (*war*). There are a few rare cases in which this *u* is not meant to be silent, which is indicated with a dieresis over the *u*: *ü*. The most common words in which you will see this are *pingüino* (*penguin*) and *antigüedad* (*antique*).

The strong *g* sound is not like the English sound in *genie*, but like the Spanish *j* sound, which means it is similar to the English *h* in words like *hair*. You will find the *ge* and *gi* combinations in words like *ángel* (*angel*) and *magia* (*magic*).

The letter **h** is the easiest word to pronounce in the Spanish language because it doesn't have a sound! You should never pronounce it unless it is placed after a *c* (as in *chocolate*) or in some words of English origin, where it's placed after an *s* (like *show*). You will find the mute *h* in words like *hola* (*hello*), *hielo* (*ice*), and *almohada* (*pillow*).

See these words in the following sentences:

Hello, do you work here? - **Hola**, *¿trabajas aquí?*

We forgot to buy ice - *Olvidamos comprar* **hielo**

This pillow is very comfortable - *Esta* **almohada** *es muy cómoda*

The letter *l* is pronounced in different ways depending on whether it is a single or double *l*. The single *l* is pronounced like the English *l*, and you will find it in words like *luna* (*moon*), *inglés* (*English*), or *libro* (*book*).

See these words in the following sentences:

The moon is beautiful - *La* **luna** *es hermosa*

Do you speak English? - *¿Hablas* **inglés***?*

I am reading a book - *Estoy leyendo un* **libro**

The double *ll* (and the *y*, as you will see moving on) is a tricky one because it sounds differently depending on the country you visit. There are three possible sounds for this digraph:

-In Spain, and some regions of Mexico and parts of Central and South America, it is pronounced like the English *y* in words like *yellow*.

-In many regions of different Spanish-speaking countries, it is pronounced as a soft English *j*.

-Finally, only in Uruguay and central Argentina, the double *ll* is pronounced as an English *sh*.

Many Spanish words contain the digraph *ll*, such as *llave* (*key*), *llamar* (*to call*), and *lluvia* (*rain*).

See these words in the following sentences:

I can't find the key to our room - *No encuentro la **llave** de nuestra habitación*

I will call the restaurant - *Voy a **llamar** al restaurante*

*I hate the **rain**!* - *¡Odio la **lluvia**!*

The letter *q* is special because it is only used in Spanish in the combinations of letters *que* and *qui*, in which the *u* is silent. These are pronounced *ke* and *ki*, and you can find them in words like *queso* (*cheese*), *quince* (*fifteen*), and *pequeño* (*small*).

See these words in the following sentences:

I love goat cheese - *Amo el **queso** de cabra*

My daughter is fifteen - *Mi hija tiene **quince** años*

The hotel is small - *El hotel es **pequeño***

The letter *r* is quite a challenge for people whose first language is not Spanish. This letter has two sounds: a soft sound and a hard sound.

The hard sound, the 'rolling *r*', happens when the *r* is placed at the beginning of the word, or when there is a double *r*. To produce this sound, you have to place your tongue in the position used when saying the word *throw*. Then, you have to blow hard to make your tongue vibrate and flap against your palate. It should sound similar to a cat's purr. You will find it in words like *regalo* (*gift*), *roto* (*broken*), and *perro* (*dog*).

See these words in the following sentences:

Maria gave me a gift - *María me dio un **regalo***

My phone is broken - *Mi teléfono está **roto***

That dog follows me everywhere - *Ese **perro** me sigue a todos lados*

The soft pronunciation happens when the *r* is not placed at the beginning of the word. The sound is similar to the American

English *d* in *medium* or the *t* in *water*. You will find this sound in words like *pared* (*wall*), *palabra* (*word*), and *transporte* (*transportation*).

See these words in the following sentences:

The wall is green - *La **pared** es verde*

I don't know that word - *No conozco esa **palabra***

We need transportation towards the port - *Necesitamos **transporte** hacia el puerto*

The letter *y* has two sounds. Sometimes it sounds just like a Spanish *i*—like an English *ee* sound. This happens when the *y* is at the end of a word, in cases such as *hoy* (*today*), *hay* (*there is*), and *soy* (*I am*).

See these words in the following sentences:

Today I want to go swimming - ***Hoy** quiero ir a nadar*

There's a spider! - *¡**Hay** una araña!*

I am a school teacher - ***Soy** maestro en una escuela*

The other *y* sound varies depending on the country where you live, and it is normally the same as the double *ll* sound, which means it can sound like an English *y*, as a soft English *j*, or as a *sh*. Some words in which you will find this *y* sound are *mayo* (*May*), *yo* (*I*), and *ya* (*now/already*).

See these words in the following sentences:

In May, I am moving to Madrid - *En **mayo**, me mudaré a Madrid*

I am from England - ***Yo** soy de Inglaterra*

To get there on time, we have to leave right now - *Para llegar a tiempo, tenemos que salir **ya** mismo*

The letter *z* only represents one sound, but its pronunciation depends on the country you visit. While in Latin America this letter is indistinguishable from an *s*, in Spain, it sounds similar to the

English *th* sound in words like *thick*. Some words with *z* are *zanahoria* (*carrot*), *abrazo* (*hug*), and *ajedrez* (*chess*).

See these words in the following sentences:

Do you want some carrot salad? - *¿Quieres ensalada de **zanahoria**?*

I need a hug - *Necesito un **abrazo***

I would like to learn how to play chess - *Me gustaría aprender a jugar al **ajedrez***

Exercises

Now that you know how to pronounce every letter in the Spanish alphabet, practice one more time with these short sentences:

a

The house is tall - La casa es alta

b

The bench is white - El banco es blanco

b

Things are clear - Las cosas son claras

There are a hundred light blue balloons - Hay cien globos celestes

That jacket is very small - Esa chaqueta es muy chica

d

Where is the dice? - ¿Dónde está el dado?

e

Esteban is an electrician - Esteban es electricista

f

Felipe is happy - Felipe está feliz

g

The cat is gray - El gato es gris

Someone is playing the guitar - Alguien toca la guitarra

There are penguins in the south - En el sur hay pingüinos

Solar energy helps people - La energía solar ayuda a la gente

h

Hello, how are you today? - Hola, ¿cómo estás hoy?

i

Irene is very interesting - Irene es muy interesante

j

Juan eats ham - Juan come jamón

k

I want a kilo of kiwis - Quiero un kilo de kiwis

l

The light bugs produce light - Las luciérnagas producen luz

m

My sister is called Mercedes - Mi hermana se llama Mercedes

n

I don't have money - No tengo dinero

ñ

I miss my college years - Extraño mis años en la universidad

o

The balloon is red - El globo es rojo

p

May I try the bread? - ¿Puedo probar el pan?

q

Do you want some cheese? - ¿Quieres un poco de queso?

r

Rafael has a dog - Rafael tiene un perro

To travel, you must have a passport – Para viajar, debes tener un pasaporte

s

We are three friends in Spain – Somos tres amigas en España

t

I have four forks – Tengo cuatro tenedores

u

There are grapes and raspberries – Hay uvas y frambuesas

v

Let's go see Valeria's sailboat – Vamos a ver el velero de Valeria

w

I need Wi-Fi to look up something on the web – Necesito wifi para buscar algo en la web

x

The taxi driver was eccentric – El taxista era excéntrico

y

Today there is nothing to eat – Hoy no hay nada para comer

I do yoga – Yo hago yoga

z

Ezekiel eats a pumpkin – Ezequiel come un zapallo

Chapter 2 – Numbers, Months and Days of the Week

Did you know there are three ways to say *one* in Spanish?

If you have taken a Spanish class before, you might know that Spanish numbers are *uno, dos, tres, cuatro...* However, the indefinite articles *un* and *una* (masculine and feminine) also mean *one*. What is an indefinite article? They are the equivalent to the English *a* or *an*, as in *a duck* or *an apple*.

What is the difference between *un* and *una*? While in English, *a* is used before words that start with consonants and *an* is used before words that start with vowels, *un* and *una* are the masculine and feminine versions of the Spanish indefinite article.

As you might already know, in Spanish (and many other languages), nouns usually have a gender, and masculine and feminine articles and adjectives are meant to match that gender. Overall, you will notice that masculine nouns end in *o* while feminine nouns end in *a* (but there are plenty of exceptions, which you will see in the next chapter). So, when you have to use an indefinite article with a masculine word such as *pato* (*duck*), you should use *un*, and when it is a feminine word, such as *manzana* (*apple*), you should use *una*.

See the indefinite articles *un* and *una* in the following sentences:

There is a duck in the lake - *Hay **un** pato en el lago*

I want to eat an apple - *Quiero comer **una** manzana*

Now you know how *un* and *una* work, but what about *uno*? In which situations should you use this word? *Uno*, and its feminine version *una*, are numerals, which you can use to count, but they also work as pronouns and indefinite pronouns. All this might sound quite technical, but English is the same. Here are some examples:

Uno and *una* as numerals:

To call the police, dial a nine, a one and another one - *Para llamar a la policía, marca un nueve, un **uno** y otro **uno***

I don't have two keys; I have only one - *No tengo dos llaves; tengo solo **una***

Uno and *una* as pronouns:

One of my friends is a musician - ***Uno** de mis amigos es músico*

One of my friends is a musician - ***Una** de mis amigas es música*

Uno and *una* as impersonal pronouns:

One can feel very tired after getting to Machu Picchu - ***Uno** puede sentirse muy cansado después de llegar a Machu Picchu*

One can feel very tired after getting to Machu Picchu - ***Una** puede sentirse muy cansada después de llegar a Machu Picchu*

Numbers from one to twenty

Now that you know all about the number one, you can learn more numbers:

2. two - dos

I have been in Colombia for two days - *Estoy en Colombia hace **dos** días*

3. three - tres

I have three siblings - *Tengo **tres** hermanos*

4. four – cuatro

There are four important cities in the country – Hay **cuatro** ciudades importantes en el país

5. five – cinco

We have to get up at five in the morning – Debemos levantarnos a las **cinco** de la mañana

6. six – seis

Six days are not enough to see this city – **Seis** días no son suficientes para ver esta ciudad

7. seven – siete

We want to book a table for seven people – Queremos reservar una mesa para **siete** personas

8. eight – ocho

There are eight cans of beer in the fridge – Hay **ocho** latas de cerveza en el refrigerador

9. nine – nueve

I will go to Barcelona for nine months – Iré a Barcelona por **nueve** meses

10. ten – diez

I got a ten on my Spanish test! – ¡Obtuve un **diez** en mi examen de español!

11. eleven – once

My daughter is eleven – Mi hija tiene **once** años

12. twelve – doce

Twelve eggs are a dozen – **Doce** huevos son una docena

13. thirteen - trece

They say number thirteen is bad luck – Dicen que el número **trece** es de mala suerte

14. fourteen – catorce

My birthday is on March fourteen – Mi cumpleaños es el **catorce** de marzo

15. fifteen – quince

When girls turn fifteen, they have a big party – Cuando las chicas cumplen **quince** años, hacen una gran fiesta

16. sixteen – dieciséis

The temperature is sixteen degrees – Hace **dieciséis** grados

17. seventeen – diecisiete

You can start driving when you turn **seventeen** – Puedes conducir desde los **diecisiete** años

18. eighteen – dieciocho

My trip will last **eighteen** days in total – Mi viaje durará **dieciocho** días en total

19. nineteen – diecinueve

The plane will take off in nineteen minutes – Faltan **diecinueve** minutos para que despegue el avión

20. twenty – veinte

There are twenty guests in the hostel – Hay **veinte** huéspedes en el hostal

Numbers from twenty-one to ninety-nine:

To form numbers from 21 to 29, you simply need to add *veinti-* to the corresponding numbers from one to nine: **veintiuno** (21), **veintidós** (22), **veintitrés** (23), **veinticuatro** (24), **veinticinco** (25), **veintiséis** (26), **veintisiete** (27), **veintiocho** (28) and **veintinueve** (29).

From 30 onwards, it gets much simpler. First of all, you need to know the tens:

30. thirty – treinta

40. forty – cuarenta

50. fifty – cincuenta

60. sixty – sesenta

70. seventy – setenta

80. eighty – ochenta

90. ninety – noventa

To combine these with other numbers, you have to add the word *y* (*and*) and the corresponding number from one to nine. Here are some examples:

31. thirty-one – treinta y uno

37. thirty-seven – treinta y siete

42. forty-two – cuarenta y dos

55. fifty-five – cincuenta y cinco

83. eighty-three – ochenta y tres

99. ninety-nine – noventa y nuev

Hundreds, thousands, millions

Knowing the hundreds in Spanish will be useful when handling money and buying things while traveling in Spanish-speaking countries. First, you will see what the hundreds are called and then combine them with tens and units to create complex numbers.

100. one hundred – cien (when alone)/*ciento* (when followed by more numbers)

200. two hundred – doscientos

300. three hundred – trescientos

400. four hundred – cuatrocientos

500. five hundred – quinientos

600. six hundred – seiscientos

700. seven hundred – setecientos

800. eight hundred – ochocientos

900. nine hundred – novecientos

Now, try to put complex numbers together:

100. one hundred – cien

105. one hundred and five – ciento cinco

128. one hundred and twenty-eight – ciento veintiocho

230. two hundred and thirty – doscientos treinta

333. three hundred and thirty-three – trescientos treinta y tres

503. five hundred and three – quinientos tres

680. six hundred and eighty – seiscientos ochenta

815. eight hundred and fifteen – ochocientos quince

999. nine hundred and ninety-nine – novecientos noventa y nueve

The number one thousand (1,000) in Spanish is *mil*. To indicate two or more thousand, you simply have to write or say the number of thousands and then the word *mil*, as in the following examples:

2,000. two thousand – dos mil

8,000. eight thousand – ocho mil

12,000. twelve thousand – doce mil

45,000. forty-five thousand – cuarenta y cinco mil

100,000. one hundred thousand – cien mil

560,000. five hundred and sixty thousand – quinientos sesenta mil

Finally, the word *million* in Spanish is *millón*, and to name more than one million, you simply have to indicate the number and then the word *millones* (which is the plural of *millón*): *dos millones* (*two million*), *quince millones* (*fifteen million*), *treinta y dos millones* (*thirty-two million*).

Fractions

Don't worry; this book won't teach you math! In this section, you will briefly go over some simple fractions that might be useful in your day-to-day life in a Spanish-speaking country.

To say *a half* in Spanish, you can say *medio* or *media*. This fraction, unlike others, can be masculine or feminine, depending on the noun it accompanies:

I want half a kilo of tomatoes - *Quiero* **medio** *kilo de tomates*

I ate half an apple - *Comí* **media** *manzana*

To say *a half,* you can also use the expression *la mitad de*, as in the following sentence:

Half of the population lives near the ocean - **La mitad de** *la población vive cerca del mar*

Other fractions you might want to know are:

a quarter - *un cuarto*

a third - *un tercio*

a tenth - *un décimo*

three quarters - *tres cuartos*

two thirds - *dos tercios*

These do not change depending on the gender of the noun they affect.

Ordinal numbers

Finally, you are briefly going to go over the most common ordinal numbers.

These work like adjectives, which means they change according to the gender and number of the noun they affect. For this reason, there are four versions of each ordinal number: single male, single female, plural male, and plural female.

1. first – primero/primera/primeros/primeras
2. second – segundo/segunda/segundos/segundas
3. third – tercero/tercera/terceros/terceras
4. fourth – cuarto/cuarta/cuartos/cuartas
5. fifth – quinto/quinta/quintos/quintas
6. sixth – sexto/sexta/sextos/sextas
7. seventh – séptimo/séptima/séptimos/séptimas
8. eighth – octavo/octava/octavos/octavas
9. ninth – noveno/novena/novenos/novenas
10. tenth – décimo/décima/décimos/décimas

(Additionally, *primero* and *tercero*, only in their single male versions, can lose the final *o* when placed before the noun: **primer** and **tercer**).

Here are some examples with the ordinal numbers you just learned:

Rodriguez was the first to arrive – *Rodríguez fue el **primero** en llegar*

My first day in Lima was excellent – *Mi **primer** día en Lima fue excelente*

Lunch is the second meal of the day – *El almuerzo es la **segunda** comida del día*

It's the third year I come here – *Es el **tercer** año en el que vengo aquí*

Did you read the sixth chapter? – *¿Has leído el **sexto** capítulo?*

My brothers finished seventh in the tournament – *Mis hermanos acabaron **séptimos** en el torneo*

It's the tenth time I say this! – *¡Es la **décima** vez que lo digo!*

And, finally, you could add here the word *last*, which might be used in similar contexts:

last – último/última/últimos/últimas

*Rodriguez was the last to arrive – Rodríguez fue el **último** en llegar*

*Dinner is the last meal of the day – La cena es la **última** comida del día*

*My brothers finished last in the tournament – Mis hermanos acabaron **últimos** en el torneo*

The months of the year

The names of months and days of the week are the kind of things that you might have to learn by heart, but you will continuously use them while traveling. Luckily, most of them are quite similar to English.

January – enero

February – febrero

March – marzo

April – abril

May – mayo

June – junio

July – julio

August – agosto

September – septiembre

October – octubre

November – noviembre

December – diciembre

Now that you have learned numbers and months, you can practice some sentences:

*My flight is scheduled for April 5 – Mi vuelo está programado para el 5 (cinco) de **abril***

*I will be in Colombia from the 20th to the 30th of December - Desde el 20 (veinte) al 30 (treinta) de **diciembre** estaré en Colombia*

*My birthday is on June 15 - Mi cumpleaños es el 15 (quince) de **junio***

The days of the week

Unlike the months, the days of the week in Spanish sound very different than the days of the week in English.

Monday - lunes

Tuesday - martes

Wednesday - miércoles

Thursday - jueves

Friday - viernes

Saturday - sábado

Sunday - domingo

See these words in practical sentences that you might say or hear during a trip through Latin America:

*On Monday, I will start a Spanish class - El **lunes** comenzaré un curso de español*

*I go to the cinema every Tuesday - Todos los **martes** voy al cine*

*See you on Wednesday! - ¡Nos vemos el **miércoles**!*

*I will stay in Buenos Aires until Thursday - Me quedaré en Buenos Aires hasta el **jueves***

*Should we go out for a drink on Friday night? - ¿Vamos a tomar algo el **viernes** por la noche?*

*I have to work on Saturday - El **sábado** tengo que trabajar*

*Sunday is my favorite day of the week - El **domingo** es mi día preferido de la semana*

The hours of the day

Finally, using your knowledge of Spanish numbers, learn how to tell the time.

Just as in English, in Spanish, sometimes you add *in the afternoon* or *in the morning* after saying the time:

noon - mediodía

afternoon - tarde

evening - noche

midnight - medianoche

morning - mañana

Now learn every hour in Spanish. Brackets have been added to the moment of the day that corresponds with every hour:

12 pm - el mediodía/las doce (del mediodía)

1 pm - la una (del mediodía/de la tarde)

2 pm - las dos (de la tarde)

3 pm - las tres (de la tarde)

4 pm - las cuatro (de la tarde)

5 pm - las cinco (de la tarde)

6 pm - las seis (de la tarde)

7 pm - las siete (de la tarde/de la noche)

8 pm - las ocho (de la noche)

9 pm - las nueve (de la noche)

10 pm - las diez (de la noche)

11 pm - las once (de la noche)

12 am - la medianoche/las doce (de la noche)

1 am - la una (de la mañana)

2 am - las dos (de la mañana)

3 am - las tres (de la mañana)

4 am - las cuatro (de la mañana)

5 am - las cinco (de la mañana)

6 am - las seis (de la mañana)

7 am - las siete (de la mañana)

8 am - las ocho (de la mañana)

9 am - las nueve (de la mañana)

10 am - las diez (de la mañana)

11 am - las once (de la mañana)

To combine the hours with the minutes, you simply add the word *y* (which means *and*) and then add the minutes, as in the following examples:

4.15 pm - las cuatro (de la tarde) y cinco (minutos)

6.40 am - las seis (de la mañana) y cuarenta (minutos)

1.20 pm - la una (del mediodía) y veinte (minutos)

Finally, there are other expressions you need to tell the time:

o'clock - en punto

half past - y media

quarter to - menos cuarto

quarter past - y cuarto

ten to - menos diez

ten past - y diez

five to - menos cinco

five past - y cinco

early - temprano

late - tarde

on time - a tiempo

Exercises

Now that you know the names of the days of the weeks, the months, and the hours, practice completing the following sentences with the dates and times. You will find the correct answers at the end of the book.

1. My flight is on October 10 at 10 in the morning - Mi vuelo es el _____ de _____ a las _____

2. My birthday is on September 20 - Mi cumpleaños es el _____ de _____

3. See you on Sunday at 4 in the afternoon - Nos vemos el _____ a las _____

4. I have to go to the dentist on January 9 at 11 in the morning - Tengo que ir al dentista el _____ _____ de _____ a las _____

5. My wedding was on December 19 - Mi boda fue el _____ de _____

Chapter 3 – Articles and Nouns

Did you know that, in Spanish, objects have a gender?

While there are not many gendered nouns in English (with a few exceptions, like words referring to men and women, such as *waiter* and *waitress*), in Spanish, every noun is either masculine or feminine.

Here are some examples of masculine nouns:

the cup - el vaso

the shoe - el zapato

the padlock - el candado

the knife - el cuchillo

And here are some examples of feminine nouns:

the bed - la cama

the door - la puerta

the chair - la silla

the wallet - la cartera

As you can see, an easy way to identify masculine nouns is that they end in *o*, while feminine nouns end in *a*. However, while this is the case for most words, there are plenty of exceptions.

Here are some masculine nouns that do not end in *o*:

the tree - el árbol

the watch/clock - el reloj

the sock - el calcetín

the pencil - el lápiz

the message - el mensaje

the Sun - el sol

And here are some feminine nouns that do not end in *a*:

the cloud - la nube

the reception - la recepción

happiness - la felicidad

the key - la llave

There are even weird cases of masculine nouns that end with *a*:

the map - el mapa

the journalist - el periodista

the day - el día

the problem - el problema

And some feminine nouns that end with *o*:

the photo - la foto

the motorcycle - la moto

the hand - la mano

What makes a noun masculine or feminine? Nothing, really.

When it comes to people (*el niño, la niña*), it is related to the gender of the person. Even so, just as English is leaning towards gender-neutrality, there are attempts in Spanish to introduce gender-neutral nouns when talking about people (*le niñe*). Nonetheless, when it comes to objects, gender has no real meaning, and there are even objects that in some Spanish-speaking countries are feminine, and in others are masculine, such as *sartén* (*pan*).

Definite articles

Knowing the gender of the nouns is important because the articles and adjectives that affect them have to be modified accordingly:

The plate is white – **El** *plato es blanco*

The house is white – **La** *casa es blanca*

As you can see in these two examples, the definite article for masculine nouns is *el*, while the one for feminine nouns is *la*.

Adjectives are discussed more in depth in Chapter 6, but you should also notice that the same adjective (*white*) changes to match the gender: *blanco* is the masculine version and *blanca* is the feminine version.

A few feminine nouns use the masculine articles *el* and *un*. While this might sound a bit too complicated, it makes sense because these are nouns that start with a stressed *a* (or *ha*), and thus they clash with the *a* at the end of *la* or *una*. For this reason, they use the masculine nouns *el* and *un*, but the adjectives and other words remain the same. Some of these words are *agua* (*water*), *alma* (*soul*), *águila* (*eagle*), and *hambre* (*hunger*).

See how these nouns work in the following sentences:

The water tastes better here – **El agua** *es más rica aquí*

Food is the soul of this culture – *La comida es* **el alma** *de esta cultura*

This is a South American eagle – *Esta es* **un águila** *de Sudamérica*

Hunger is a serious problem – **El hambre** *es un problema serio*

Moving forward, while in English there are singular and plural nouns (*the plate, the plates*), the article remains the same: *the*. This is not so in Spanish. While *el* and *la* are the singular definite articles, there are two plural articles: *los* and *las*.

The plates are white - **Los** *platos son blancos*

The houses are white - **Las** *casas son blancas*

Indefinite articles

Then, as mentioned in the previous chapter, the singular indefinite articles in Spanish are *un* and *una*, which can be translated as *a* or *one*.

See these indefinite articles in the following sentences:

I am on a business trip - Estoy en **un** *viaje de negocios*

I have a meeting in fifteen minutes - Tengo **una** *reunión en quince minutos*

A major difference regarding indefinite articles in English and Spanish is that, in Spanish, there are also plural indefinite articles, *unos* and *unas*. You might translate them in English as *some* or *about*.

I have lived here about six months - He vivido aquí **unos** *seis meses*

I have some grapes - Tengo **unas** *uvas*

I have spent some wonderful days in Chile - He pasado **unos** *días maravillosos en Chile*

We have about three hours of travel ahead of us - Tenemos **unas** *tres horas de viaje por delante*

Exercises

Complete the following sentences with the correct definite article:

1. The movie is very long - ___ película es muy larga

2. Where is the toilet? - ¿Dónde está ___ baño?

3. The sandwiches are in your backpack - ___ emparedados están en tu mochila

4. The mountains are snowy - ___ montañas están nevadas

5. The day is cloudy - ___ día está nublado

6. What floor is the reception on? - ¿En qué piso está ___ recepción?

7. Do you have the map? - ¿Tienes ___ mapa?

8. I can't find the key - No encuentro ____ llave

Complete the following sentences with the correct indefinite article:

9. Do you have a minute? - ¿Tienes ___ minuto?

10. I would like to eat a salad - Me apetece comer ____ ensalada

11. I will meet with some friends in Bogotá - Me encontraré con _____ amigos en Bogotá

12. This country has some precious beaches - Este país tiene _____ playas preciosas

13. Could you take a picture of us? - ¿Podrías tomarnos ____ foto?

14. The coffee shop is in front of a large tree - El café está frente a ____ gran árbol

15. Do you have a pencil? - ¿Tienes ___ lápiz?

16. There is a cloud in the sky - Hay ____ nube en el cielo

Chapter 4 – Pronouns

Did you know that there are six ways to say *you* in Spanish?

For the singular *you* (one person), there is *tú* (used in Spain and most of Latin America), *vos* (used in Argentina, Uruguay, and some regions of other Latin American countries), and the formal *usted*.

For the plural *you* (more than one person), there is *vosotros* and its feminine version *vosotras* (used in Spain), and *ustedes* (used in Latin America).

Luckily, this does not happen with the rest of the personal pronouns. These are the personal pronouns in Spanish:

I - yo

you (singular) - tú/vos/usted

he - él

she - ella

we - nosotros/nosotras

you (plural) - vosotros/vosotras/ustedes

they - ellos/ellas

I - yo

As explained in Chapter 1, the pronunciation of the letter *y* in Spanish varies depending on the country. To say it right, it is recommended that you listen carefully to how people pronounce it wherever you go.

See this personal pronoun in the following sentences:

I am a chemistry professor - **Yo** *soy profesor de química*

I want to eat soup - **Yo** *quiero comer sopa*

I will travel to Mexico - **Yo** *viajaré a México*

Unlike English, in Spanish, it is possible to elude the personal pronoun in most cases. As you can see, these sentences also work without the word *yo*:

I am a chemistry professor - *Soy profesor de química*

I want to eat soup - *Quiero comer sopa*

I will travel to Mexico - *Viajaré a México*

You - tú/vos/usted

As mentioned, there are three ways to say *you* while referring to a single person: *you, vos,* and *usted*. The most common one of these three that you should learn is *tú*.

Since it also changes the way verbs are conjugated, it is only recommended that you learn *vos* if you are going to travel or stay for a long time in Uruguay or Argentina. Even so, people in these countries can understand and use *tú* as well.

Regarding *usted*, it is only used in formal situations in some countries. If you are only going to travel to Latin American countries as a tourist, then it might not be necessary for you to learn this pronoun and its conjugations. However, if you are going to travel for business or to study at university, you might want to consider learning it. Luckily, its conjugations are very easy to learn because they are the same as the singular third person (*he/she*).

Now, for you to see the difference between the three, here are some sentences with the three versions:

Could you take a picture of me? - *¿***Tú** *podrías tomarme una foto?*

You are very funny - **Tú** *eres muy divertida*

You have my passport - **Tú** *tienes mi pasaporte*

Could you take a picture of me? - ¿**Vos** *podrías tomarme una foto?*

You are very funny - **Vos** *sos muy divertida*

You have my passport - **Vos** *tenés mi pasaporte*

Could you take a picture of me? - ¿**Usted** *podría tomarme una foto?*

You are very funny - **Usted** *es muy divertida*

You have my passport - **Usted** *tiene mi pasaporte*

He and she - él/ella

He and *she* in Spanish are *él* and *ella*. Here are some examples with *he* and *she*:

He is very tall - **Él** *es muy alto*

He's two years old - **Él** *tiene dos años*

He sings very well - **Él** *canta muy bien*

She's very tall - **Ella** *es muy alta*

She's two years old - **Ella** *tiene dos años*

She sings very well - **Ella** *canta muy bien*

Just as with the other pronouns, you can skip saying *he* or *she* in the sentence. As you will see, in the first sentence, you can identify the gender of the subject because the adjective *alto/alta* varies. In the other two sentences, it is not possible to identify the gender when you elude the pronoun.

He is very tall - Es muy alto

He's two years old - Tiene dos años

He sings very well - Canta muy bien

She's very tall - Es muy alta

She's two years old - Tiene dos años

She sings very well - Canta muy bien

In Spanish, there is no word for *it*. For things, *eso* (literally, *that*) is used instead, or simply avoid the pronoun. For animals, call them either *he* or *she*. Here are some examples:

That's not fair - *Eso no es justo/No es justo*

It's not a goat; it's a sheep - *No es una cabra; es una oveja*

There's something in my pocket; it's my passport! - *Hay algo en mi bolsillo; ¡es mi pasaporte!*

We - nosotros/nosotras

The Spanish word for *we* is *nosotros* or *nosotras*. Just as there are *he* and *she* in English, in Spanish, these two words identify gender in groups. If the group is all-female, you should use *nosotras*, while if the group is all-male or mixed, you should use *nosotros*. This use of the male word when the group is mixed is called "generic masculine".

Here are some examples with *nosotros* and *nosotras*:

We are hungry - **Nosotros** *tenemos hambre*

We don't know each other yet - **Nosotros** *no nos conocemos aún*

We are going to go to Peru - **Nosotras** *vamos a ir a Perú*

We are sisters - **Nosotras** *somos hermanas*

Just as before, these sentences also work without the pronoun:

We are hungry - *Tenemos hambre*

We don't know each other yet - *No nos conocemos aún*

We are going to go to Peru - *Vamos a ir a Perú*

We are sisters - *Somos hermanas*

You - vosotros/vosotras/ustedes

While in Spanish, the plural *you* is *vosotros* or its feminine variation *vosotras*, in Latin America, you will hear the genderless pronoun *ustedes*.

Ustedes is also used in Spain as a formal plural *you*, but in Latin America, it does not have this formal connotation.

The conjugation of *vosotros* and *ustedes* is different. Just as *usted* is conjugated like *he* and *she*, *ustedes* is conjugated like *they*. You will see this in detail in the chapters dedicated to verbs.

Here are some examples with *vosotros* and *vosotras*:

Are you coming to the restaurant? - ¿**Vosotros** venís al restaurante?

You are very good guides - **Vosotros** sois muy buenos guías

Are you going to the music festival? - ¿**Vosotras** vais juntas al festival de música?

You will sleep in room 301 - **Vosotras** dormiréis en la habitación 301 (trescientos uno)

And these are those same sentences, using *ustedes*. As you can see, the conjugation of the verbs changes:

Are you coming to the restaurant? - ¿**Ustedes** vienen al restaurante?

You are very good guides - **Ustedes** son muy buenos guías

Are you going to the music festival? - ¿**Ustedes** van juntas al festival de música?

You will sleep in room 301 - **Ustedes** dormirán en la habitación 301 (trescientos uno)

They - ellos/ellas

Just as with *he* and *she*, *nosotros* and *nosotras*, and *vosotros* and *vosotras*, there are two versions of *they*, a masculine and a feminine one: *ellos* and *ellas*.

Here are some examples:

They are my cousins - **Ellos** son mis primos

They are sleepy - **Ellos** tienen sueño

They are Bolivian - **Ellas** son bolivianas

They are in the museum - **Ellas** están en el museo

Exercises

Complete the following sentences with the appropriate pronoun:

1. I have three weeks of holidays - ___ tengo tres semanas de vacaciones

2. I am very tired - ___ estoy muy cansada

3. Are you my guide? - ¿_____ es mi guía?

4. You are a great cook! - ¡___ eres un excelente cocinero!

5. You are the first client of the day - ____ sos el primer cliente del día

6. He is my brother - ___ es mi hermano

7. She has booked a table - ____ reservó una mesa

8. We want to eat a pizza - _____ queremos comer una pizza

9. We are lawyers - _____ somos abogadas

10. Are you coming to the beach? - ¿_____ venís a la playa?

11. You are very active tourists - _____ sois turistas muy activos

12. Do you have plans for tonight? - ¿_____ tienen planes para esta noche?

13. They are playing the guitar - _____ están tocando la guitarra

14. They are my friends - _____ son mis amigas

Chapter 5 – Prepositions

Prepositions are words that help the coordination of the other elements in a sentence. They indicate origin, procedence, destiny, direction, place, medium, reason, and more.

There are only 20 prepositions in the Spanish language! It might sound like a lot, but there are over 100 prepositions in the English language, which makes Spanish easier in comparison.

Even so, some Spanish prepositions might be a bit tricky, like *por* and *para*, both of which can translate as *for*.

Here are all the Spanish prepositions:

a

ante

bajo

con

de

desde

durante

en

entre

excepto

hacia

hasta

mediante

para

por

salvo

según

sin

sobre

tras

a

The preposition *a* can be used in multiple situations and can be translated as *to, towards,* and *by.* See some of its uses in the following sentences:

Destination: *I will go to Juan's house later* - *Iré **a** la casa de Juan más tarde*

Time: *Check-in is at two in the afternoon* - *El check-in es **a** las dos de la tarde*

Price: *How much is a kilo of tomatoes?* - *¿**A** cuánto está el kilo de tomates?*

Orientation: *The room faces the beach* - *La habitación da **a** la playa*

Periodicity: *I take Spanish classes twice a week* - *Tomo clases de español dos veces **a** la semana*

Location: *The bathroom is on the right* - *El baño está **a** la derecha*

Direct object: *I see Maria* - *Veo **a** María*

Indirect object: *I gave my charger to Roberto* - *Le di mi cargador **a** Roberto*

Way: *I prefer to go by foot* - *Prefiero ir **a** pie*

Future indicator: *Are you going to come?* - *¿Vas **a** venir?*

Imperative: *Let's eat!* - *¡**A** comer!*

Two prepositions, *a* and *de*, form contractions when they are located next to the definite article *el*. In the case of *a*, the contraction that is formed when placed next to *el* is *al*. Here are some examples with *al*:

Should we go to the cinema? - *¿Vamos **al** cine?* (instead of *¿Vamos a el cine?*)

I will see you at noon - *Te veo **al** mediodía* (instead of *Te veo a el mediodía*)

Call the doctor - *Llama **al** doctor* (instead of *Llama a el doctor*)

ante

Ante can be translated as *before*, in situations not related to time, and *in front of*. Here are some examples:

I am in front of a beautiful landscape - *Estoy **ante** un paisaje hermoso*

He puts his family before everything - *Él pone a su familia **ante** todo*

bajo

Bajo means *under* or *underneath*, and it is used to talk about the position of an object in space, and also hierarchies. Here are some examples with *bajo*:

Your wallet is under that book - *Tu cartera está **bajo** ese libro*

I am under my boss' orders - *Estoy **bajo** las órdenes de mi jefe*

con

Con is a very common preposition in Spanish that can be translated as *with*, either to talk about means, company, mode, or motive. Here are some examples:

I like painting with watercolors - *Me gusta pintar **con** acuarelas*

We have to climb very carefully - Debemos subir **con** mucho cuidado

I am traveling with Alicia - Estoy viajando **con** Alicia

With this weather, it's difficult to go out - **Con** este clima, es difícil salir

Just as *a* and *de* form contractions with the article *el*, the preposition *con* forms contractions when placed next to *mí* (*me*) and *ti* (*you*). This means that *with me* is translated as *conmigo*, and *with you* is *contigo*. See these words in the following sentences:

Come with me - Ven **conmigo** (instead of *Ven con mí*)

I will go with you - Iré **contigo** (instead of *Iré con ti*)

de

De is also quite a common preposition in Spanish. It can be translated as *from, of, made of,* and *about*. Here are some uses of *de*:

Procedence: *I am from England* - Soy **de** Inglaterra

Belonging: *This hat belongs to my brother* - Esta gorra es **de** mi hermano

Direction: *I come from the bakery* - Vengo **de** la panadería

Matter: *The sculpture is made of marble* - La escultura es **de** mármol

Subject: *It's a book about local history* - Es un libro **de** historia local

Time: *It's night* - Es **de** noche

Period: *The store opens from eleven to eight* - La tienda abre **de** once a ocho

Mode: *I have been standing all day* - He estado **de** pie todo el día

Just like *a*, the preposition *de* forms a contraction with the article *el*. In this case, the result is *del*, and it means *of the*:

I came out of the ocean at eight at night - *Salí **del** mar a las ocho de la noche* (instead of *Salí de el mar a las ocho de la noche*)

Do you have the hotel's address? - *¿Tienes la dirección **del** hotel?* (instead of *¿Tienes la dirección de el hotel?*)

desde

Desde can be translated as *from* or *since*. In situations where it is translated as *from*, it's interchangeable with *de*, but in situations where it is translated as *since*, *desde* is the only option. Here are some examples:

The store opens from eleven to eight - *La tienda abre **desde** las once hasta las ocho*

I traveled twelve hours from Spain - *Viajé doce horas **desde** España*

I am in this hotel since Tuesday - *Estoy en este hotel **desde** el martes*

durante

Durante means *during* and is used in the same situations. Here are some examples:

I will be here during the summer - *Estaré aquí **durante** el verano*

I studied Spanish during my teenage years - *Estudié español **durante** mi adolescencia*

en

En is a very common preposition in the Spanish language, and it can be translated as *in*, *at*, *on*, and *by*. Here are some examples:

I am at the hotel - *Estoy **en** el hotel*

I came here by bus - *Vine aquí **en** bus*

I can't talk; I am in my car! - *No puedo hablar; ¡estoy **en** mi automóvil!*

I will go to Argentina in March - *Iré a Argentina **en** marzo*

entre

Entre can be translated as *between* or *among*. Here are some examples:

We can leave between two and two-thirty - *Podemos salir **entre** las dos y las dos y media*

The cabin is in between two mountains - *La cabaña está **entre** dos montañas*

I am among very talented people - *Estoy **entre** gente muy talentosa*

excepto

This preposition means *except*, and it is used just like in English. Here are some examples:

I am free every day, except on Thursdays - *Estoy libre todos los días, **excepto** los jueves*

I like everything, except cucumber - *Me gusta todo, **excepto** el pepino*

hacia

Hacia can be translated as *to* and *towards*, but also as *around*, when indicating an imprecise time:

I am going towards the top - *Estoy yendo **hacia** la cima*

Tomorrow we will go to the coast - *Mañana iremos **hacia** la costa*

I will arrive at two in the morning - *Llegaré **hacia** las dos de la mañana*

hasta

Hasta means *until*, *to* or *up to*. Here are some examples:

I work every day until eight - *Todos los días trabajo **hasta** las ocho*

Let's walk to the bar - *Caminemos **hasta** el bar*

mediante

Mediante means *through* or *by means of*. It is not a preposition heard every day, but you might read it in sentences such as the following:

Lucia contacted the company through a lawyer - *Lucía contactó a la empresa **mediante** un abogado*

They chose the president through voting - *Eligieron al presidente **mediante** una votación*

para

Para and *por* are often mistakenly exchanged by non-native Spanish-speakers because their meaning is quite similar (both can be translated as *for*).

The best rule to learn when in doubt is that *para* goes forward, while *por* goes backward, in the sense that *para* normally indicates destination, and *por* indicates origin; and while *para* indicates goal, *por* indicates reason. When talking about time, always use *por* - unless when talking about a deadline, in which case you should use *para*.

Here are some examples:

Destination: *Does this train go to Madrid?* - *¿Este tren va **para** Madrid?*

Goal: *To win, you have to train hard* - ***Para** ganar, debes entrenar duro*

Recipient: *This present is for my mother* - *Este regalo es **para** mi madre*

Deadline: *I have to write an essay for tomorrow* - *Tengo que escribir un ensayo **para** mañana*

por

Now that you know in which situations to use *para*, here are some examples with *por*:

Place: *I went to the lighthouse walking along the coast* - *Fui hasta el faro caminando **por** la costa*

Reason: *I came here for the beautiful beaches* - *Vine aquí **por** las hermosas playas*

Time: *I will travel for six months* - *Viajaré **por** seis meses*

Price: *I sold my car for a lot of money* - *Vendí mi automóvil **por** mucho dinero*

Medium: *I will send you the book by mail* - *Te enviaré el libro **por** correo*

Approximate location: *I will see you around the park* - *Te veo **por** el parque*

Mode: *You won't get to be loved by force* - *No lograrás que te amen **por** la fuerza*

Distribution: *There are two sandwiches per person* - *Hay dos sándwiches **por** persona*

Periodicity: *I take classes twice a week* - *Tomo clases dos veces **por** semana*

salvo

Salvo works just like *excepto*; it indicates exceptions, as you can see in the following sentences:

Except for Martin, we are all staying until the end of the month - ***Salvo** Martín, todos nos quedaremos hasta el final del mes*

I liked everything about the film, except the performances - *Me gustó todo de la película, **salvo** las actuaciones*

según

Según indicates mode and can be translated as *according to* or *as*. Here are some examples:

According to the map, the cabin should be here - ***Según** el mapa, la cabaña debería estar aquí*

According to Manuela, Spanish is more beautiful than Portuguese - **Según** Manuela, el español es más bonito que el portugués

We are moving forward as indicated by the guide - Estamos avanzando **según** nos indicó el guía

sin

Sin means *without*, and in many cases, it is used in the same way as in English. Here are some examples:

I am currently without a job - Actualmente estoy **sin** trabajo

Without a guide, we won't make it far - **Sin** un guía, no llegaremos lejos

Do you have any gluten-free dishes? - ¿Tiene algún plato **sin** gluten?

sobre

Sobre means *on, on top of, above,* and *about*. Here are some examples:

I left the tip on the table - Dejé la propina **sobre** la mesa

The clouds are right above us - Las nubes están justo **sobre** nosotros

I would like to read a book about the city - Me gustaría leer un libro **sobre** la ciudad

What are you talking about? - ¿**Sobre** qué hablan?

tras

Finally, *tras* means *behind* and *after*. It can be used to talk about time or space. Here are some examples:

The electric outlet is behind the sofa - El enchufe está **tras** el sofá

We will go to the museum after the movie - Iremos al museo **tras** la película

Exercises

Complete the following sentences with the appropriate prepositions:

1. The store opens from nine to six - La tienda abre ____ nueve a seis

2. I gave my wallet to Sara - Le di mi cartera ___ Sara

3. Are we going? - ¿Vamos ___ ir?

4. Who is going to the cinema? - ¿Quién va ___ cine?

5. I will meet with my brother at noon - Me encontraré con mi hermano ___ mediodía

6. Climb carefully! - ¡Sube ____ cuidado!

7. I am traveling with a friend - Estoy viajando ____ un amigo

8. Laura is coming with me tonight - Laura vendrá _____ esta noche

9. May I sit with you? - ¿Puedo sentarme _____?

10. I am from Sweden - Soy ___ Suecia

11. This boat belongs to my father - Este bote es ___ mi padre

12. I like food without salt - Me gusta la comida _____ sal

13. It's daytime already! - ¡Ya es ___ día!

14. Check out is at 11 in the morning - El check out es ___ las once de la mañana

15. We are talking about the weather - Estamos hablando _____ el clima

16. What's the hotel's address? - ¿Cómo es la dirección _____ hotel?

17. Under the seawater, there are many rocks - _____ el agua del mar, hay muchas rocas

18. I traveled from Asia to see you - Viajé _____ Asia para verte

19. I am at the park – Estoy ___ el parque

20. The room faces the mountains – La habitación da ___ las montañas

21. I will return home in October – Regresaré a casa ___ octubre

22. Tomorrow we will go towards the East – Mañana iremos _____ el Este

23. I work until 9 at night – Trabajo _____ las nueve de la noche

24. I will walk to the beach – Caminaré _____ la playa

25. Does this bus go to the center? – ¿Este bus va _____ el centro?

26. This is for you – Esto es _____ ti

27. I will travel for a year – Viajaré ____ un año

28. I will go to Pedro's party later – Iré ___ la fiesta de Pedro más tarde

29. Leave the towels on the bed – Deje las toallas _____ la cama

30. I come from the United States – Vengo ___ los Estados Unidos

Chapter 6 – Adjectives

Did you know Spanish adjectives have to match the gender and number of the noun they affect?

In English, you are used to invariable adjectives that do not change, no matter what the number or gender is, and when it comes to objects, you don't even use genders!

For example, in English:

*One melon is **tasty**, and two melons are **tasty***

*One apple is **tasty**, and two apples are **tasty***

As you can see, the adjective does not change in any situation, while in Spanish:

*Un melón es **sabroso** y dos melones son **sabrosos***

*Una manzana es **sabrosa** y dos manzanas son **sabrosas***

The rule is quite simple. Most adjectives that affect plural nouns will add an *s* to the end of the word, and in the feminine form, they will change the *o* for an *a*, while also adding an *s* if they are plural. In short, there are four variations: single male, single female, plural male, and plural female.

Here are some more adjectives:

good – *bueno/buena/buenos/buenas*

new – *nuevo/nueva/nuevos/nuevas*

long – *largo/larga/largos/largas*

wide – ancho/ancha/anchos/anchas
small – pequeño/pequeña/pequeños/pequeñas
short – corto/corta/cortos/cortas
tall – alto/alta/altos/altas
low – bajo/baja/bajos/bajas
little – poco/poca/pocos/pocas
beautiful – hermoso/hermosa/hermosos/hermosas
bad – malo/mala/malos/malas
ugly – feo/fea/feos/feas
angry – enojado/enojada/enojados/enojadas
fast – rápido/rápida/rápidos/rápidas
slow – lento/lenta/lentos/lentas
old – viejo/vieja/viejos/viejas
cold – frío/fría/fríos/frías
broken – roto/rota/rotos/rotas
hard – duro/dura/duros/duras
empty – vacío/vacía/vacíos/vacías
full – lleno/llena/llenos/llenas
dirty – sucio/sucia/sucios/sucias
clean – limpio/limpia/limpios/limpias

Here are some sentences with these adjectives:

*I have good news! – ¡Tengo **buenas** noticias!*

*That's my new car – Ese es mi auto **nuevo***

*Days are very long here – Los días son muy **largos** aquí*

*The river is wide – El río es **ancho***

*My hands are small – Mis manos son **pequeñas***

*The journey is very short – El trayecto es muy **corto***

My brothers are tall – Mis hermanos son **altos**

The tide is low – La marea está **baja**

I have little charge – Tengo **poca** batería

The palm trees are beautiful – Las palmeras son **hermosas**

I think this apple has gone bad – Creo que esta manzana está **mala**

My hotel is very ugly – Mi hotel es muy **feo**

There is an angry customer – Hay un cliente **enojado**

Could we go faster? – ¿Podríamos ir más **rápido**?

The Internet is very slow – Internet es muy **lento**

This magazine is old – Esta revista es **vieja**

The bedroom is very cold – La habitación está muy **fría**

My earplugs are broken – Mis auriculares están **rotos**

The mattresses are hard – Los colchones son **duros**

My pockets are empty – Mis bolsillos están **vacíos**

The car is full – El automóvil está **lleno**

That's my dirty laundry – Esa es mi ropa **sucia**

Could you bring me clean bedsheets? – ¿Podría traerme sábanas **limpias**?

Luckily for you, there are also many adjectives that do not vary according to gender, and they only change according to number:

big – *grande/grandes*

different – *diferente/diferentes*

young – *joven/jóvenes*

important – *importante/importantes*

intelligent – *inteligente/inteligentes*

easy – *fácil/fáciles*

nice – *agradable/agradables*

joyful - *alegre/alegres*

enormous - *enorme/enormes*

strong - *fuerte/fuertes*

weak - *débil/débiles*

hot - *caliente/calientes*

soft - *suave/suaves*

happy - *feliz/felices*

Here are some examples:

That mountain is very big - *Esa montaña es muy **grande***

You look different - *Te ves **diferente***

My parents are young - *Mis padres son **jóvenes***

That is a very important politician - *Ese es un político muy **importante***

Your son is very intelligent! - *¡Tu hijo es muy **inteligente**!*

This game is easy - *Este juego es **fácil***

Your wife is very nice - *Tu esposa es muy **agradable***

What a joyful couple! - *¡Qué pareja **alegre**!*

You have an enormous bag - *Tienes una maleta **enorme***

I am not very strong - *No soy muy **fuerte***

After having a fever, I feel weak - *Después de tener fiebre, me siento **débil***

The soup is hot - *La sopa está **caliente***

The carpet is soft - *La alfombra es **suave***

I am very happy! - *¡Estoy muy **feliz**!*

Colors

Just as with other adjectives, some colors change according to the gender of the noun. Here are the ones that change:

black - *negro/negra/negros/negras*

white – blanco/blanca/blancos/blancas

red – rojo/roja/rojos/rojas

yellow – amarillo/amarilla/amarillos/amarillas

And here are the ones that only change according to number, not gender:

blue – azul/azules

green – verde/verdes

purple – púrpura/púrpuras

gray – gris/grises

Finally, some colors take their names from objects and don't change according to gender or number:

orange – naranja

pink – rosa

violet – violeta

Here are some examples with Spanish colors:

Where are my black shoes? – ¿Dónde están mis zapatos **negros**?

I have a white hat – Tengo un sombrero **blanco**

I like that red car – Me gusta ese coche **rojo**

Have you seen my yellow sandals? – ¿Has visto mis sandalias **amarillas**?

The house is blue – La casa es **azul**

These are my pink trousers – Estos son mis pantalones **rosas**

Are your eyes green? – ¿Tus ojos son **verdes**?

My favourite color is purple – Mi color preferido es el **púrpura**

The sky is gray – El cielo está **gris**

Possessive adjectives

Possessive adjectives are important to indicate ownership of objects.

Just like in English, in Spanish, there is a word for *my* (placed before the noun) and *mine* (placed after the noun), and the same for the other pronouns. The difference is that the first ones change according to number, and the second ones change according to number and gender.

Here are some examples of each:

my - *mi/mis*

mine - *mío/mía/míos/mías*

*That's my book - Ese es **mi** libro*

*Those are my bags - Esas son **mis** maletas*

*That book is mine - Ese libro es **mío***

*That bag is mine - Esa maleta es **mía***

*Those books are mine - Esos libros son **míos***

*Those bags are mine - Esas maletas son **mías***

your - *tu/mis*

yours - *tuyo/tuya/tuyos/tuyas*

*That's your book - Ese es **tu** libro*

*Those are your bags - Esas son **tus** maletas*

*That book is yours - Ese libro es **tuyo***

*That bag is yours - Esa maleta es **tuya***

*Those books are yours - Esos libros son **tuyos***

*Those bags are yours - Esas maletas son **tuyas***

his/her - *su/sus*

his/hers - *suyo/suya/suyos/suyas*

*That's his/her book - Ese es **su** libro*

*Those are his/her bags - Esas son **sus** maletas*

*That book is his/hers - Ese libro es **suyo***

*That bag is his/hers - Esa maleta es **suya***

Those books are his/hers - Esos libros son **suyos**

Those bags are his/hers - Esas maletas son **suyas**

our/ours - nuestro/nuestra/nuestros/nuestras

That's our book - Ese es **nuestro** libro

Those are our bags - Esas son **nuestras** maletas

That book is ours - Ese libro es **nuestro**

That bag is ours - Esa maleta es **nuestra**

Those books are ours - Esos libros son **nuestros**

Those bags are ours - Esas maletas son **nuestras**

your/yours - vuestro/vuestra/vuestros/vuestras

That's your book - Ese es **vuestro** libro

Those are your bags - Esas son **vuestras** maletas

That book is yours - Ese libro es **vuestro**

That bag is yours - Esa maleta es **vuestra**

Those books are yours - Esos libros son **vuestros**

Those bags are yours - Esas maletas son **vuestras**

their/theirs - su/sus/suyo/suya/suyos/suyas

That's their book - Ese es **su** libro

Those are their bags - Esas son **sus** maletas

That book is theirs - Ese libro es **suyo**

That bag is theirs - Esa maleta es **suya**

Those books are theirs - Esos libros son **suyos**

Those bags are theirs - Esas maletas son **suyas**

Exercises

Complete the following sentences with the correct adjective:

1. I have a good backpack - Tengo una _____ mochila

2. Esteban is very tall - Esteban es muy _____

3. This hotel is beautiful - Este hotel es _____

4. I have bad news - Tengo _____ noticias

5. My phone is broken - Mi teléfono está _____

6. My bag is full - Mi maleta está _____

7. You are very young - Eres muy _____

8. He is very strong - Él es muy _____

9. I want to eat something hot - Quiero comer algo _____

10. Do you have red gloves? - ¿Tiene guantes _____?

11. Have you seen a green bike? - ¿Has visto una bicicleta _____?

12. I think that's my charger - Creo que ese es _____ cargador

13. Those sunglasses are mine - Esos lentes de sol son _____

14. Are those your beers? - ¿No son esas _____ cervezas?

15. Where is our taxi? - ¿Dónde está _____ taxi?

PART II: GRAMMAR

Chapter 7 – Basic Spanish Verbs

Did you know that Spanish has two verbs that mean *to be*? Just like other romance languages, these two verbs have different meanings: one is for permanent situations, and the other one is for temporary situations.

Now learn the conjugations of these two verbs and their differences!

To be – ser

Ser means *to be* in situations where the status is permanent or semi-permanent, like your name, profession or personality. Here is the conjugation of *ser*:

I am - yo **soy**

you are - tú **eres**/vos **sos**/usted **es**

he/she is - él/ella **es**

we are - nosotros **somos**

you are - vosotros/vosotras **sois**/ustedes **son**

they are - ellos/ellas **son**

Here are some examples with the different pronouns:

I am a journalist - Yo **soy** periodista

Are you the manager? - ¿**Eres** el gerente?

She's my mother - Ella **es** mi madre

We are boyfriend and girlfriend - **Somos** novios

You are a great team - **Sois** un equipo excelente

They are very hardworking - Ellas **son** muy trabajadoras

To be - estar

Estar is used as *to be* in situations where the status is temporary, such as feelings, location, aspect, and present continuous (next to another verb, to express something that is happening).

Here is the conjugation of *estar*:

I am - yo **estoy**

you are - tú **estás**/vos **estás**/usted **está**

he/she is - él/ella **está**

we are - nosotros **estamos**

you are - vosotros/vosotras **estáis**/ustedes **están**

they are - ellos/ellas **están**

Here are some examples:

I would like to go, but I am tired - Me gustaría ir, pero **estoy** cansado

Are you ready? - ¿**Estás** lista?

Juan is eating - Juan **está** comiendo

We are about to make history - **Estamos** por hacer historia

Are you guys arriving? The plane leaves soon - ¿**Estáis** llegando? El avión sale pronto

My parents are crazy! - ¡Mis padres **están** locos!

Regular verbs: present tense

Now that you know the difference between *ser* and *estar*, next, you will learn the most common Spanish regular verbs and how to conjugate them, so you can do the same with every regular verb you find.

Spanish verbs end in either *ar*, *er*, or *ir*. Just as in English, you can identify an infinitive verb because of the introductory *to* (as in *to iron, to sleep, to go*); in Spanish, infinitive verbs are marked with those three endings.

Here are three examples:

hablar (*to speak*)

comprender (*to understand*)

vivir (*to live*)

To conjugate a regular verb in the present tense, the first step is to take off the *ar*, *er*, or *ir* ending. Then, you end up with the *root* of the verb. In these cases:

habl-

comprend-

viv-

The second step is to add, to that root, the ending corresponding with the conjugation of each pronoun (marked with bold letters in the following examples):

Verbs ending in -ar (to talk - hablar)

*I talk - yo habl**o***

*you talk - tú habl**as**/vos habl**ás**/usted habl**a***

*he/she talks - él/ella habl**a***

*we talk - nosotros habl**amos***

*you talk - vosotros/vosotras habl**áis**/ustedes habl**an***

*they talk - ellos/ellas habl**an***

Verbs ending in -er (to understand - comprender)

*I understand - yo comprend**o***

*you understand - tú comprend**es**/vos comprend**és**/usted comprend**e***

*he/she understands - él/ella comprend**e***

*we understand - nosotros comprend**emos***

*you understand - vosotros comprend**éis**/ustedes comprend**en***

*they understand - ellos/ellas comprend**en***

Verbs ending in -ir (to live - vivir)

*I live - yo viv**o***

*you live - tú viv**es**/vos viv**ís**/usted viv**e***

*he/she lives - él/ella viv**e***

*we live - nosotros viv**imos***

*you live - vosotros/vosotras viv**ís**/ustedes viv**en***

*they live - ellos/ellas viv**en***

Every verb ending in *ar*, *er*, and *ir* will have the same conjugation. Thus, you can take these as models to conjugate every other regular verb.

Here are some examples:

Sometimes, I talk too much - A veces, **hablo** *demasiado*

Do you speak German? - ¿Vosotros **habláis** *alemán?*

I don't understand what you're saying - No **comprendo** *lo que dices*

They don't understand Spanish - Ellos no **comprenden** *español*

I live nearby - Yo **vivo** *cerca de aquí*

Where do you live? - ¿Dónde **vives***?*

You can find a list of Spanish regular verbs in the appendix!

Irregular verbs

In Spanish, there are many irregular verbs. However, they tend to follow a certain regularity.

These irregularities are normally related to little details of losing or adding a consonant or a vowel regarding those exceptional pronunciation cases covered in Chapter 1. For example, verbs ending in -*car* usually change the *c* to a *qu* in some tenses, for it to sound right next to an *e*. Some others change the letter *c* for a *z*, or a *gui* for a *go*.

Some irregular verbs are quite important, like *ser* and *estar*, which you have already learned. Now see some others that you will need in everyday life:

to go - ir

*I go - yo **voy***

*you go - tú **vas**/vos **vas**/usted **va***

*he/she goes - él/ella **va***

*we go - nosotros **vamos***

*you go - vosotros/vosotras **vais**/ustedes **van***

*they go - ellos/ellas **van***

to do - hacer

*I do - yo **hago***

*you do - tú **haces**/vos **hacés**/usted **hace***

*he/she does - él/ella **hace***

*we do - nosotros **hacemos***

*you do - vosotros/vosotras **hacéis**/ustedes **hacen***

*they do - ellos/ellas **hacen***

to read - leer

*I read - yo **leo***

*you read - tú **lees**/vos **leés**/usted **lee***

*he/she reads - él/ella **lee***

*we read - nosotros **leemos***

*you read - vosotros/vosotras **leéis**/ustedes **leen***

*they read - ellos/ellas **leen***

to find – encontrar

I find – yo **encuentro**

you find – tú **encuentras**/*vos* **encontrás**/*usted* **encuentra**

he/she finds – él/ella **encuentra**

we find – nosotros **encontramos**

you find – vosotros/vosotras **encontráis**/*ustedes* **encuentran**

they find – ellos/ellas **encuentran**

to know – saber

I know – yo **sé**

you know – tú **sabes**/*vos* **sabés**/*usted* **sabe**

he/she knows – él/ella **sabe**

we know – nosotros **sabemos**

you know – vosotros/vosotras **sabéis**/*ustedes* **saben**

they know – ellos/ellas **saben**

to give – dar

I give – yo **doy**

you give – tú **das**/*vos* **das**/*usted* **da**

he/she gives – él/ella **da**

we give – nosotros **damos**

you give – vosotros/vosotras **dais**/*ustedes* **dan**

they give – ellos/ellas **dan**

can – poder

I can – yo **puedo**

you can – tú **puedes**/*vos* **podés**/*usted* **puede**

he/she can – él/ella **puede**

we can – nosotros **podemos**

you can – vosotros/vosotras **podéis**/*ustedes* **pueden** *they can - ellos/ellas* **pueden**

to say - decir

I say - yo **digo**

you say - tú **dices**/*vos* **decís**/*usted* **dice**

he/she says - él/ella **dice**

we say - nosotros **decimos**

you say - vosotros/vosotras **decís**/*ustedes* **dicen**

they say - ellos/ellas **dicen**

to see - ver

I see - yo **veo**

you see - tú **ves**/*vos* **ves**/*usted* **ve**

he/she sees - él/ella **ve**

we see - nosotros **vemos**

you see - vosotros/vosotras **veis**/*ustedes* **ven**

they see - ellos/ellas **ven**

to have - tener

I have - yo **tengo**

you have - tú **tienes**/*vos* **tenés**/*usted* **tiene**

he/she has - él/ella **tiene**

we have - nosotros **tenemos**

you have - vosotros/vosotras **tenéis**/*ustedes* **tienen**

they have - ellos/ellas **tienen**

Now, see some sentences with these conjugated verbs:

We do a trip like this every year - **Hacemos** *un viaje como este todos los años*

I read the newspaper every morning - **Leo** *el periódico todas las mañanas*

I can't find my phone - No **encuentro** mi teléfono

They know it's a difficult climb - Ellas **saben** que es una subida difícil

Can you give me three kilos of potatoes, please? - ¿Me **da** tres kilos de papas, por favor?

I can't believe it! - ¡No **puedo** creerlo!

He says that it's the best time to go - Él **dice** que es el mejor momento para ir

Do you see the shore? - ¿**Ves** la costa?

I have a problem - **Tengo** un problema

Do you have change? - ¿**Tienes** cambio?

Verb haber (impersonal sentences)

Haber is used as an auxiliary verb for some tenses (just like *to have* for past tenses in English) and to indicate existence in impersonal sentences.

The use of the auxiliary is detailed in Chapter 10. For now, you will see the impersonal use, which only conjugates the verb for the singular third person: *hay* (*there is/there are*).

There is a problem - **Hay** un problema

There are many fruits in this market - **Hay** muchas frutas en este mercado

Exercises

Complete the following sentences with the appropriate conjugated verb:

1. I am the first one to arrive - _____ el primero en llegar

2. Who are you? - ¿Quién _____ tú?

3. I am tired of walking! - ¡_____ cansada de caminar!

4. Are we lost? - ¿_____ perdidos?

5. I speak Spanish - Yo _____ español

6. I understand - _____

7. She lives on that hill - Ella _____ en esa colina

8. Do we do something tonight? - ¿_____ algo esta noche?

9. I don't read emails during my vacations - No _____ mails durante mis vacaciones

10. I can't find my passport - No _____ mi pasaporte

11. Do you know how to surf? - ¿_____ surfear?

12. My parents give me some money every now and then - Mis padres me _____ algo de dinero a veces

13. Can we go there? - ¿_____ ir allí?

14. She says it's true! - ¡Ella _____ que es cierto!

15. With this fog, I don't see a thing - Con esta niebla, no _____ nada

16. There are only a few hotels in the city - ____ pocos hoteles en la ciudad

17. There is a dog in the garden - ____ un perro en el jardín

Chapter 8 – Negative Sentences

Constructing negative sentences in Spanish is very easy! It is even easier than constructing negative sentences in English for non-natives – since Spanish does not use complex words such as *don't, can't, won't*.

To make a sentence negative in Spanish, you simply need to add the word *no* (pronounced *noh*) right before the verb.

Here are some affirmative and negative examples:

I'm hungry - **Tengo hambre**

I'm not hungry - **No tengo hambre**

I want to go to the beach - **Quiero ir a la playa**

I don't want to go to the beach - **No quiero ir a la playa**

I like seafood - **Me gustan los mariscos**

I don't like seafood - **No me gustan los mariscos**

As you can see in this last example, the *no* is not placed right before the verb, but before the object pronoun *me*. Spanish object pronouns *me, te, se, nos, os, se* are equivalent to *me, you, him, her, us, you*, and *them* in English, and in Spanish, they should always go next to the verb, even in negative sentences.

In addition to *no*, there are some negative words that you can use in specific negative sentences:

nor - ni

nothing - nada

nobody - nadie

never - jamás/nunca

neither - tampoco

none - ningún/ninguno/ninguna

Here are some examples:

I have neither brothers nor sisters - *No tengo hermanos **ni** hermanas*

There's nothing better than taking a nap - ***Nada** es más lindo que dormir la siesta*

Nobody enjoys custom control - ***Nadie** disfruta el control aduanero*

I have never seen a fish so big - *¡**Nunca** he visto un pescado tan grande!*

*I don't feel like surfing **either*** - *Yo **tampoco** tengo ganas de surfear*

You can also use these in double negative sentences, which maintain the negative meaning:

There is nothing else to do - ***No** hay **nada** más que hacer*

Nobody came! - *¡**No** ha venido **nadie**!*

I never heard something like this - ***No** escuché **nunca** una cosa así*

I don't like any room - ***No** me gusta **ninguna** habitación*

Exercises

Construct the negative sentence for the following affirmative sentences:

1. I know the hotel's address - Sé la dirección del hotel

I don't know the hotel's address - _____

2. I have a good job - Tengo un buen trabajo

I don't have a good job - _____

3. I will stay here for a long time - Me quedaré aquí por mucho tiempo

I won't stay here for a long time - _____

4. I like Lila Downs' music - Me gusta la música de Lila Downs

I don't like Lila Downs' music - _____

Complete the following double-negative sentences:

5. I don't like any of the dishes on the menu - _____ me gusta _____ de los platos del menú

6. When it's time to eat, there is no one at the beach - A la hora de comer, _____ hay _____ en la playa

7. My mother never calls - Mi madre _____ me llama _____

8. I don't want to eat anything else; I'm full! - _____ quiero comer _____ más; ¡estoy llena!

Chapter 9 – Modal Verbs

What is a modal verb? In Spanish, some verbs are always accompanied by other verbs. The most common modal verbs are *deber* (*must*), *tener que* (*have to*), *querer* (*want to*), *poder* (*can*), and *soler* (*use to*).

In English, their use is similar, as in *I have to..., I can..., I used to...,* and *I want to...* As you can see, all these are necessarily followed by an infinitive verb.

First of all, you will see the conjugation of each of these verbs, and then see them in sentences next to infinitive verbs.

must – deber

I must – yo **debo**

you must – tú **debes***/vos* **debés***/usted* **debe**

he/she must – él/ella **debe**

we must – nosotros **debemos**

you must – vosotros/vosotras **debéis***/ustedes* **deben**

they must – ellos/ellas **deben**

have to – tener que

I have to – yo **tengo que**

you have to – tú **tienes que***/vos* **tenés que***/usted* **tiene que**

he/she has to – él/ella **tiene que**

we have to – nosotros **tenemos que**

you have to – vosotros/vosotras **tenéis que**/ustedes **tienen que**

they have to – ellos/ellas **tienen que**

want to – querer

I want to – yo **quiero**

you want to – tú **quieres**/vos **querés**/usted **quiere**

he/she wants to – él/ella **quiere**

we want to – nosotros **queremos**

you want to – vosotros/vosotras **queréis**/ustedes **quieren**

they want to – ellos/ellas **quieren**

can – poder

I can – yo **puedo**

you can – tú **puedes**/vos **podés**/usted **puede**

he/she can – él/ella **puede**

we can – nosotros **podemos**

you can – vosotros/vosotras **podéis**/ustedes **pueden**

they can – ellos/ellas **pueden**

use to – soler

This verb does not translate literally into English in the present tense. While in the past tense it translates as *use to* (*I used to go to the park every day* – *Yo solía ir al parque todos los días*), in the present, it can be translated as *I usually + infinitive verb* (*I usually go to the park every day* – *Yo suelo ir al parque todos los días*).

This is the Spanish present conjugation:

I – yo **suelo**

you – tú **sueles**/vos **solés**/usted **suele**

he/she – él/ella **suele**

we – nosotros **solemos**

you – vosotros/vosotras **soléis**/ustedes **suelen**

they – ellos/ellas **suelen**

Here are some examples with these modal verbs:

deber (must) + infinitive verb

I must go to work at eight in the morning – **Debo ir** a trabajar a las ocho de la mañana

When you go to Chile, you must visit Valparaíso – Cuando vayas a Chile, **debes visitar** Valparaíso

My sister must study harder to pass the year – Mi hermana **debe estudiar** más para aprobar el año

tener que (have to) + infinitive verb

I have to make a copy of my keys for my brother – **Tengo que hacer** una copia de mis llaves para mi hermano

We have to walk faster! – ¡**Tenemos que caminar** más rápido!

My parents have to understand that I'm an adult now – Mis padres **tienen que entender** que ahora soy un adulto

querer (want to) + infinitive verb

I want to live in Spain – **Quiero vivir** en España

Do you want to eat Chinese food? – ¿**Quieres comer** comida china?

Do you want to go dancing? – ¿**Queréis salir** a bailar?

poder (can) + infinitive verb

Can I see the rooms? – ¿**Puedo ver** las habitaciones?

You can go play after you eat your food – **Puedes ir** a jugar después de comer tu comida

We can travel by bus or by train – **Podemos viajar** en bus o en tren

soler (use to) + infinitive verb

I usually eat here – **Suelo comer** aquí

*Do you normally travel alone? - ¿**Sueles viajar** sola?*

*Do you usually drink tap water? - ¿**Suelen tomar** agua del grifo?*

Negative modal verbs

To use modal verbs in negative sentences, you simply need to add the word *no* before them:

*I don't want to live in Spain - **No quiero vivir** en España*

*We can't travel by bus nor by train - **No podemos viajar** ni en bus ni en tren*

*I don't usually eat here - **No suelo** comer aquí*

The only exception is the verb *tener que*. As in English, its meaning is not the exact opposite in negative sentences: *no tener que* does not translate as the obligation not to do something but as the possibility of not doing it. To indicate obligation in a negative sentence, the best way is to use the verb *deber*, as in the following example:

*You have to go - **Tienes que ir***

*You do not have to go - **No tienes que ir***

*You must not go - **No debes ir***

Haber que

As explained in Chapter 7, *haber* works as an auxiliary verb and is also used in impersonal sentences to indicate the existence of something. However, *haber* can also work as a modal verb when used together with the word *que*. Just as before, it is only conjugated in the singular third person: *hay*.

This combination of words is used to express obligation in impersonal sentences, which might be translated in English as *it is needed to* or as *we have to, you have to,* or *they have to* - since it is normally used to express something that a group of people has to do.

Here are some examples:

It is necessary to clean the room – **Hay que limpiar** la habitación

One has to take a shower every day – **Hay que bañarse** todos los días

The car has broken! We need to call a mechanic – *¡El automóvil se ha roto!* **Hay que llamar** *a un mecánico*

Exercises

Complete the following sentences with the appropriate modal verbs:

1. You must eat more vegetables – _____ comer más vegetales

2. The government must hire more people with disabilities – El gobierno _____ contratar a más personas con discapacidad

3. We must be more careful – _____ ser más cuidadosos

4. You have to behave – _____ que comportarte

5. My mother has to go to the doctor tomorrow – Mi madre _____ que ir al médico mañana

6. The children want to play in the park – Los niños _____ jugar en el parque

7. I want to swim in the ocean – _____ nadar en el océano

8. Can I use your charger? – ¿_____ usar tu cargador?

9. I usually read here – _____ leer aquí

10. Do you normally travel together? – ¿_____ viajar juntos?

11. I don't want to live in the city – No _____ vivir en la ciudad

12. We can't get a ticket – No _____ conseguir una entrada

13. It is necessary to find the ring - _____ que encontrar el anillo

14. One has to be kind to the local people - _____ que ser amable con la gente local

Chapter 10 – Present Perfect

Past tenses in Spanish are not so different from English past tenses! Even though learning the conjugations might be a bit difficult, the structure and use are basically the same... with one exception. There is a past tense in Spanish called the *imperfecto*, which does not have an English equivalent, but you will learn that one at the end.

Remember how *haber* can be an auxiliary verb? Well, now it is time to use it - since one of the most common Spanish past tenses uses it, just like the English version uses the verb *to have*:

I have gone to Sandra's house many times - **He ido** *a la casa de Sandra muchas veces*

Lucía has gone to the doctor - *Lucía* **ha ido** *al médico*

As you can see in these past examples, the structure is the same as in English: past conjugated auxiliary verb + past participle of action verb.

Now, to learn how to use this past tense, you will see the past conjugation for *haber* and then some of the most common past participles. Remember that, in Spanish, the conjugated verb *haber* is only used as an auxiliary! Do not use it as the verb *to have* (which is *tener*).

to have - haber

*I have - yo **he***

*you have - tú **has**/vos **has**/usted **ha***

*he/she has - él/ella **ha***

*we have - nosotros **hemos***

*you have - vosotros/vosotras **habéis**/ustedes **han***

*they have - ellos/ellas **han***

Past participles

Now, you will learn some of the most common Spanish past participles, and one example for each.

As you will notice, most of them end in *-ado* or *-ido*. The rule to form the past participle of a verb is simply to find the root of the verb (taking off the *-ar*, *-er* or *-ir* ending) and adding *-ado* to the verbs that finish in *-ar*, and *-ido* to the verbs that finish in *-er* and *-ir*.

to go (ir): ido

*I have never gone to the zoo - Jamás **he ido** al zoológico*

to be (ser): sido

*Martin has been a great professor - Martín **ha sido** un gran profesor*

to be (estar): estado

*Juana has been married three times - Juana **ha estado** casada tres veces*

to talk (hablar): hablado

*Have you talked to your mother? - ¿**Has hablado** con tu madre?*

to understand (comprender): comprendido

*We haven't understood what he said - No **hemos comprendido** lo que él dijo*

to live (vivir): vivido

*Have you lived in Spain? - ¿**Has vivido** en España?*

to read (leer): leído

I have read your message - **He leído** *tu mensaje*

to find (encontrar): encontrado

Have they found the keys? - *¿***Han encontrado** *las llaves?*

to give (dar): dado

My boss has given me a raise! - *¡Mi jefa me* **ha dado** *un aumento!*

can (poder): podido

Have you been able to solve the problem? - *¿Ustedes* **han podido** *resolver el problema?*

to have (tener): tenido

My sister has had a son - *Mi hermana* **ha tenido** *un hijo*

However, there are some exceptions to the *-ado* and *-ido* rule, like the following:

to say (decir): dicho

Have you said something? - *¿***Has dicho** *algo?*

to see (ver): visto

We have seen an amazing movie last night - **Hemos visto** *una película increíble anoche*

to do (hacer): hecho

Manuel hasn't done his homework - *Manuel no* **ha hecho** *la tarea*

to write (escribir): escrito

I have written a short story - **He escrito** *un cuento*

to solve (resolver): resuelto

I have solved the problem - **He resuelto** *el problema*

Exercises

Complete the following sentences with the correct conjugated verb or participle:

1. I have gone to the doctor - ___ ido al médico

2. What did you say? - ¿Qué has _____?

3. Have you called a taxi? - ¿Usted ____ llamado un taxi?

4. She is gone - Ella se ____ marchado

5. I couldn't download the file - No he _____ descargado el archivo

6. Have you seen that? - ¿_____ visto eso?

7. They have traveled for many years - Ellas _____ viajado muchos años

8. Have you been to the theater? - ¿____ ido al teatro?

9. Ignacio has never gone to the circus - Ignacio nunca ha _____ al circo

10. I have never been so tired - Jamás he _____ tan cansado

11. Have you found your phone? - ¿Has _____ tu teléfono?

12. Have you talked with the receptionist? - ¿Has _____ con la recepcionista?

13. Have you lived in Spain - ¿Has _____ en España?

14. I have read a Spanish book - He _____ un libro en español

15. We're back! - ¡_____ vuelto!

16. I have given a tip to the waiter - Le he _____ una propina al camarero

17. We had kids already - Ya hemos _____ hijos

18. You have been an amazing friend - Has _____ un amigo increíble

19. They didn't understand - No han _____
20. We have made plans - Hemos _____ planes

Chapter 11 – Simple Past

Just like how in Chapter 7 you learned how to conjugate regular verbs in the present tense, now you will learn how to in the simple past tense (*pretérito perfecto simple*, in Spanish).

Remember: Spanish verbs end in *ar*, *er*, or *ir*. Once more, you will use these verbs as models:

hablar (*to speak*)

comprender (*to understand*)

vivir (*to live*)

Again, to conjugate these regular verbs, you need to take off the *ar*, *er*, or *ir* ending. Once you do that, you will find the *root* of the verb, which in these cases is:

habl-

comprend-

viv-

Now, to conjugate in the past tense, you need to add to that root the ending corresponding to the conjugation of each pronoun (marked with bold letters in the following examples):

Verbs ending in -ar (to talk – hablar)

I talked – yo hablé

you talked – tú hablaste/vos hablaste/usted habló

he/she talked - él/ella habló

we talked - nosotros hablamos

you talked - vosotros/vosotras hablásteis/ustedes hablaron

they talked - ellos/ellas hablaron

Verbs ending in -er (to understand - comprender)

I understood - yo comprendí

you understood - tú comprendiste/vos comprendiste/usted comprendió

he/she understood - él/ella comprendió

we understood - nosotros comprendimos

you understood - vosotros comprendisteis/ustedes comprendieron

they understood - ellos/ellas comprendieron

Verbs ending in -ir (to live - vivir)

I lived - yo viví

you lived - tú viviste/vos viviste/usted vivió

he/she lived - él/ella vivió

we lived - nosotros vivimos

you lived - vosotros/vosotras vivisteis/ustedes vivieron

they lived - ellos/ellas vivieron

Here are some examples:

*Yesterday I talked in Spanish for three hours straight - Ayer **hablé** en español durante tres horas seguidas*

*We already talked to our parents about the wedding - Ya **hablamos** con nuestros padres sobre la boda*

*Did you understand what he said? - ¿**Comprendiste** lo que él dijo?*

I explained it to them, but they didn't understand - *Les expliqué, pero no me* **comprendieron**

I lived with my parents until I was twenty - **Viví** *con mis padres hasta los veinte años*

My cousins lived in Sweden for some time - *Mis primos* **vivieron** *un tiempo en Suecia*

Since these are regular verbs, every verb ending in *ar*, *er*, and *ir* will have the same conjugation. Remember that there is a list of Spanish regular verbs in the appendix!

Irregular verbs

Now, you will go over the conjugation of some common irregular verbs, and some examples for each.

to be - ser

I was - yo **fui**

you were - tú **fuiste**/*vos* **fuiste**/*usted* **fue**

he/she was - él/ella **fue**

we were - nosotros **fuimos**

you were - vosotros/vosotras **fuisteis**/ *ustedes* **fueron**

they were - ellos/ellas **fueron**

I never was a good student - *Nunca* **fui** *un buen estudiante*

My grandmother was a famous photographer - *Mi abuela* **fue** *una famosa fotógrafa*

They were a couple for a long time - *Ellos* **fueron** *pareja durante mucho tiempo*

to be - estar

I was - yo **estuve**

you were - tú **estuviste**/*vos* **estuviste**/*usted* **estuvo**

he/she was - él/ella **estuvo**

we were - nosotros **estuvimos**

you were - vosotros/vosotras **estuvisteis**/ustedes **estuvieron**

they were - ellos/ellas **estuvieron**

I was lost for ten minutes until I found the guide - **Estuve** perdido durante diez minutos hasta que encontré al guía

We were traveling for a month around the Caribbean - **Estuvimos** viajando un mes por el Caribe

Have you been in Barcelona? - ¿Ustedes **estuvieron** en Barcelona?

to go - ir

I went - yo **fui**

you went - tú **fuiste**/vos **fuiste**/usted **fue**

he/she went - él/ella **fue**

we went - nosotros **fuimos**

you went - vosotros/vosotras **fuisteis**/ustedes **fueron**

they went - ellos/ellas **fueron**

I went to university in Buenos Aires - **Fui** a la universidad en Buenos Aires

She went to the cinema with me - Ella **fue** al cine conmigo

My brothers went to Brazil - Mis hermanos **fueron** a Brasil

to do - hacer

I did - yo **hice**

you did - tú **hiciste**/vos **hiciste**/usted **hizo**

he/she did - él/ella **hizo**

we did - nosotros **hicimos**

you did - vosotros/vosotras **hicisteis**/ustedes **hicieron**

they did - ellos/ellas **hicieron**

Did you do the homework? - ¿**Hiciste** la tarea?

My mother-in-law made a cake - Mi suegra **hizo** un pastel

We did a trip to Ecuador - **Hicimos** *un viaje a Ecuador*

to read – leer

I read - *yo* **leí**

you read - *tú* **leíste**/*vos* **leíste**/*usted* **leyó**

he/she read - *él/ella* **leyó**

we read - *nosotros* **leímos**

you read - *vosotros/vosotras* **leísteis**/*ustedes* **leyeron**

they read - *ellos/ellas* **leyeron**

I read many books during this trip - **Leí** *muchos libros durante este viaje*

Did you read the message I sent you last night? - *¿***Leíste** *el mensaje que te envié anoche?*

They read the menu - *Ellos* **leyeron** *el menú*

to find – encontrar

I found - *yo* **encontré**

you found - *tú* **encontraste**/*vos* **encontraste**/*usted* **encontró**

he/she found - *él/ella* **encontró**

we found - *nosotros* **encontramos**

you found - *vosotros/vosotras* **encontrasteis**/*ustedes* **encontraron**

they found - *ellos/ellas* **encontraron**

I found my keys - **Encontré** *mis llaves*

Laura found a ring - *Laura* **encontró** *un anillo*

Did you find that restaurant I recommended? - *¿***Encontraron** *ese restaurante que les recomendé?*

to know – saber

I knew - *yo* **supe**

you knew - *tú* **supiste**/*vos* **supiste**/*usted* **supo**

he/she knew - *él/ella* **supo**

we knew – nosotros **supimos**

you knew – vosotros/vosotras **supisteis**/ustedes **supieron**

they knew – ellos/ellas **supieron**

I never knew how to ride a bike – Nunca **supe** montar en bicicleta

He knew how to win my heart – Él **supo** ganarse mi corazón

They never knew what happened with their travel bag – Ellos nunca **supieron** qué sucedió con su maleta

to give – dar

I gave – yo **di**

you gave – tú **diste**/vos **diste**/usted **dio**

he/she gave – él/ella **dio**

we gave – nosotros **dimos**

you gave – vosotros/vosotras **disteis**/ustedes **dieron**

they gave – ellos/ellas **dieron**

Did you already give me the invitation? – ¿Ya me **diste** la invitación?

My best friend gave me a present for Christmas – Mi mejor amiga me **dio** un regalo por Navidad

We gave my old phone to our kid – Le **dimos** mi teléfono viejo a nuestro hijo

can – poder

I could – yo **pude**

you could – tú **pudiste**/vos **pudiste**/usted **pudo**

he/she could – él/ella **pudo**

we could – nosotros **pudimos**

you could – vosotros/vosotras **pudisteis**/ustedes **pudieron**

they could – ellos/ellas **pudieron**

I couldn't understand what he said to me – No **pude** entender lo que me dijo

Could you get there on time? – ¿**Pudiste** llegar a tiempo?

They could do more than they had planned – **Pudieron** hacer más de lo que habían planeado

to say – decir

I said – yo **dije**

you said – tú **dijiste**/vos **dijiste**/usted **dijo**

he/she said – él/ella **dijo**

we said – nosotros **dijimos**

you said – vosotros/vosotras **dijisteis**/ustedes **dijeron**

they said – ellos/ellas **dijeron**

I told her yesterday on the phone – Ya se lo **dije** ayer por teléfono

She said that she is waiting for us – Ella **dijo** que nos espera

Did you say something? – ¿**Dijisteis** algo?

to see – ver

I saw – yo **vi**

you saw – tú **viste**/vos **viste**/usted **vio**

he/she saw – él/ella **vio**

we saw – nosotros **vimos**

you saw – vosotros/vosotras **visteis**/ustedes **vieron**

they saw – ellos/ellas **vieron**

I watched the film you recommended – **Vi** la película que me recomendaste

Did you see Julieta? – ¿**Viste** a Julieta?

Last night we saw a wonderful theater play – Anoche **vimos** una obra de teatro maravillosa

to have – tener

*I had – yo **tuve***

*you had – tú **tuviste**/vos **tuviste**/usted **tuvo***

*he/she had – él/ella **tuvo***

*we had – nosotros **tuvimos***

*you had – vosotros/vosotras **tuvisteis**/ustedes **tuvieron***

*they had – ellos/ellas **tuvieron***

*I had some problems with my visa – **Tuve** algunos problemas con mi visa*

*We had three dogs – **Tuvimos** tres perros*

*My cousin and her wife had a son last week – Mi prima y su esposa **tuvieron** un hijo la semana pasada*

Exercises

Complete the following sentences with the correct conjugated verb:

1. Did you talk with your parents? – ¿_____ con tus padres?

2. I never had problems in this hotel – Nunca _____ problemas en este hotel

3. I lived in Latin America for more than ten years – _____ en América Latina por más de diez años

4. What did you say? – ¿Qué _____?

5. We were in Peru during several months – _____ durante varios meses en Perú

6. My parents gave me everything I have – Mis padres me _____ todo lo que tengo

7. We did everything we could – _____ todo lo que pudimos

8. We read your article! – ¡_____ tu artículo!

9. Yesterday I went to some friends' house - Ayer _____ a la casa de unos amigos

10. We didn't find the bag - No _____ la maleta

11. I never knew what to do with my life - Nunca _____ qué hacer con mi vida

12. She was a terrible student during her whole life - Ella _____ una pésima estudiante durante toda su vida

13. Could she take the plane? - ¿_____ tomar el avión?

14. I never understood why that is so important - Jamás _____ por qué eso es tan importante

15. Yesterday I saw an amazing film - Ayer ____ una película genial

Chapter 12 – Imperfecto

While this past tense, as mentioned, does not have an exact equivalent in English, it is not hard to learn.

The *imperfecto* is used for past events or actions that happened with a certain frequency or continuity – in opposition to the simple past, which is used for concrete actions that are already concluded.

Here are some examples:

We used to have lunch together every Thursday - **Comíamos** *juntos todos los jueves*

I used to go to my grandparents' house every summer - *Yo* **iba** *a la casa de mis abuelos todos los veranos*

Around that time, I was studying in university - *En aquella época, yo* **estudiaba** *en la universidad*

I walked, he ran - *Yo* **caminaba**, *él* **corría**

As you can see, sometimes this past tense can be translated to English as simple past, past continuous, or *used to + infinitive verb*.

This tense is also ideal to stress a contrast between continuous actions and punctual actions:

While we were eating, someone opened the door - *Cuando* **comíamos**, *alguien abrió la puerta*

Agustina slept quietly, until her phone rang - *Agustina* **dormía** *tranquilamente, hasta que su teléfono sonó*

The imperfect tense is also used to tell the time, date, and age in the past:

It was two in the morning - **Eran** *las dos de la mañana*

I think it was May 10 - *Creo que* **era** *el diez de mayo*

I was six - **Tenía** *seis años*

Regular verbs

Just as in the simple past tense, to conjugate regular verbs in *imperfect,* you will use the following verbs as models:

hablar (to speak)

comprender (to understand)

vivir (to live)

To conjugate these regular verbs, you have to take off the *ar, er,* or *ir* ending. Once you do it, you will find the root of the verb:

habl-

comprend-

viv-

Now, to conjugate in the *imperfecto* tense, you need to add to that root the ending corresponding to the conjugation of each pronoun:

Verbs ending in -ar (to talk - hablar)

I talked - *yo hablaba*

you talked - *tú hablabas/vos hablabas/usted hablaba*

he/she talked - *él/ella hablaba*

we talked - *nosotros hablábamos*

you talked - *vosotros/vosotras hablabais/ustedes hablaban*

they talked - *ellos/ellas hablaban*

Verbs ending in -er (to understand - comprender)

I understood - *yo comprendía*

you understood - *tú comprendías/vos comprendías/usted comprendía*

he/she understood - *él/ella comprendía*

we understood - *nosotros comprendíamos*

you understood - *vosotros comprendíais/ustedes comprendían*

they understood - *ellos/ellas comprendían*

Verbs ending in -ir (to live - vivir)

I lived - *yo vivía*

you lived - *tú vivías/vos vivías/usted vivía*

he/she lived - *él/ella vivía*

we lived - *nosotros vivíamos*

you lived - *vosotros/vosotras vivíais/ustedes vivían*

they lived - *ellos/ellas vivían*

Here are some examples:

I wanted to sleep, but Juana was talking non-stop - *Yo quería dormir, pero Juana* **hablaba** *sin parar*

I explained everything slowly, but he didn't understand anything that I was saying - *Yo le explicaba todo lentamente, pero él no* **comprendía** *nada de lo que yo decía*

Until my graduation, I lived with my parents - *Hasta mi graduación, yo* **vivía** *con mis padres*

Since these are regular verbs, every verb ending in *ar*, *er*, and *ir* will have the same conjugation. Once more, remember that there is a list of Spanish regular verbs in the appendix. You can practice conjugating those verbs according to these models.

Irregular verbs

Now, you will go over the conjugation of some common irregular verbs, and some examples for each.

to be – ser

*I was – yo **era***

*you were – tú **era**/vos **eras**/usted **era***

*he/she was – él/ella **era***

*we were – nosotros **éramos***

*you were – vosotros/vosotras **erais**/ustedes **eran***

*they were – ellos/ellas **eran***

*I was a good student – Yo **era** un buen estudiante*

*My grandmother was a famous photographer – Mi abuela **era** una famosa fotógrafa*

*They were a couple, but then they broke up – Ellos **eran** pareja, pero después rompieron*

to be – estar

*I was – yo **estaba***

*you were – tú **estabas**/vos **estabas**/usted **estaba***

*he/she was – él/ella **estaba***

*we were – nosotros **estábamos***

*you were – vosotros/vosotras **estabais**/ustedes **estaban***

*they were – ellos/ellas **estaban***

*I was lost, but then I found the guide – **Estaba** perdido, pero luego encontré al guía*

*You didn't find us at home because we were traveling – No nos encontraste en casa porque **estábamos** viajando*

*You were also in Barcelona at that time? – ¿Ustedes también **estaban** en Barcelona en ese momento?*

to go – ir

*I went – yo **iba***

*you went – tú **ibas**/vos **ibas**/usted **iba***

he/she went – él/ella **iba**

we went – nosotros **íbamos**

you went – vosotros/vosotras **ibais**/ustedes **iban**

they went – ellos/ellas **iban**

I used to go to university in Buenos Aires – Yo **iba** a la universidad en Buenos Aires

She used to go with me everywhere – Ella **iba** a todos lados conmigo

My parents used to go dancing every weekend – Mis padres **iban** a bailar todos los fines de semana

to do – hacer

I did – yo **hacía**

you did – tú **hacías**/vos **hacías**/usted **hacía**

he/she did – él/ella **hacía**

we did – nosotros **hacíamos**

you did – vosotros/vosotras **hacíais**/ustedes **hacían**

they did – ellos/ellas **hacían**

Were you doing your homework? – ¿**Hacías** tu tarea?

My mother-in-law was making a cake and I was watching TV – Mi suegra **hacía** un pastel, y yo miraba la tele

Around that time, we were traveling around Ecuador – Por esa época, **hacíamos** un viaje por Ecuador

to read – leer

I read – yo **leía**

you read – tú **leías**/vos **leías**/usted **leía**

he/she read – él/ella **leía**

we read – nosotros **leíamos**

you read – vosotros/vosotras **leíais**/ustedes **leían**

they read - *ellos/ellas* **leían**

Alicia was reading all the time - *Alicia* **leía** *todo el tiempo*

While we were reading, someone rang the bell - *Mientras* **leíamos**, *alguien tocó el timbre*

They were reading the menu - *Ellos* **leían** *el menú*

to find - encontrar

I found - *yo* **encontraba**

you found - *tú* **encontrabas**/*vos* **encontrabas**/*usted* **encontraba**

he/she found - *él/ella* **encontraba**

we found - *nosotros* **encontrábamos**

you found - *vosotros/vosotras* **encontrabais**/*ustedes* **encontraban**

they found - *ellos/ellas* **encontraban**

Isidro always found the things that I lost - *Isidro siempre* **encontraba** *las cosas que yo perdía*

How did you find the time to study and work at the same time? - *¿Cómo* **encontrabas** *el tiempo para trabajar y estudiar al mismo tiempo?*

Laura couldn't find her ring - *Laura no* **encontraba** *su anillo*

to know - saber

I knew - *yo* **sabía**

you knew - *tú* **sabías**/*vos* **sabías**/*usted* **sabía**

he/she knew - *él/ella* **sabía**

we knew - *nosotros* **sabíamos**

you knew - *vosotros/vosotras* **sabíais**/*ustedes* **sabían**

they knew - *ellos/ellas* **sabían**

The kid didn't know how to ride a bike - *El niño no* **sabía** *montar en bicicleta*

He knew that he had to win my heart – Él **sabía** que debía ganarse mi corazón

They didn't know what was happening with their travel bag – Ellos no **sabían** qué sucedía con su maleta

to give – dar

I gave – yo **daba**

you gave – tú **dabas**/vos **dabas**/usted **daba**

he/she gave – él/ella **daba**

we gave – nosotros **dábamos**

you gave – vosotros/vosotras **dabais**/ustedes **daban**

they gave – ellos/ellas **daban**

Every Friday, my dad used to give me some money – Todos los viernes, mi padre me **daba** algo de dinero

My best friend gave me a present every Christmas – Mi mejor amiga me **daba** un regalo todas las Navidades

We used to give our old phones to our kids – Les **dábamos** nuestros teléfonos viejos a nuestros hijos

can – poder

I could – yo **podía**

you could – tú **podías**/vos **podías**/usted **podía**

he/she could – él/ella **podía**

we could – nosotros **podíamos**

you could – vosotros/vosotras **podíais**/ustedes **podían**

they could – ellos/ellas **podían**

I couldn't understand what he was saying to me – No **podía** entender lo que me decía

He could never arrive on time – Él nunca **podía** llegar a tiempo

They could do more, but they didn't want to – **Podían** hacer más, pero no querían

to say - decir

I said - yo **decía**

you said - tú **decías**/*vos* **decías**/*usted* **decía**

he/she said - él/ella **decía**

we said - nosotros **decíamos**

you said - vosotros/vosotras **decíais**/*ustedes* **decían**

they said - ellos/ellas **decían**

I told everyone that I was leaving soon, but I stayed here to live - Yo le **decía** *a todo el mundo que me iría pronto, pero me quedé a vivir*

She used to say lots of lies - Ella **decía** *muchas mentiras*

What were you saying? - ¿Vosotros qué **decíais***?*

to see - ver

I saw - yo **veía**

you saw - tú **veías**/*vos* **veías**/*usted* **veía**

he/she saw - él/ella **veía**

we saw - nosotros **veíamos**

you saw - vosotros/vosotras **veíais**/*ustedes* **veían**

they saw - ellos/ellas **veían**

I watched every film he recommended - Yo **veía** *todas las películas que él me recomendaba*

*Did you see Julieta very often? - ¿***Veías** *a Julieta muy seguido?*

Every Saturday, we saw a theater play - Todos los sábados **veíamos** *una obra de teatro*

to have - tener

I had - yo **tenía**

you had - tú **tenías**/*vos* **tenías**/*usted* **tenía**

he/she had - él/ella **tenía**

we had – nosotros **teníamos**

you had – vosotros/vosotras **teníais**/ustedes **tenían**

they had – ellos/ellas **tenían**

I had some problems with my visa – **Tenía** algunos problemas con mi visa

We used to have three dogs – **Teníamos** tres perros

My cousin and her wife had a big house, but they sold it – Mi prima y su esposa **tenían** una casa grande, pero la vendieron

Exercises

Complete the following sentences with the correct conjugated verb:

1. Who were you talking to? – ¿Con quién _____?

2. Laura didn't have pets – Laura no _____ mascotas

3. I used to live in England, but now I live in Spain – Yo _____ en Inglaterra, pero ahora vivo en España

4. You were saying something very interesting last night – Usted _____ algo muy interesante anoche

5. Yesterday I didn't go out because I was very tired – Ayer no salí porque _____ muy cansada

6. In Colombia, we used to go to the market every day – En Colombia, todos los días _____ al mercado

7. I couldn't believe that the landscape was so beautiful – No _____ creer que el paisaje fuera tan bello

8. When I was little, I used to read a lot – Cuando era pequeña, _____ mucho

9. I was worried because I couldn't find my passport – Estaba preocupada porque no _____ mi pasaporte

10. What was Antonia doing at my sister's house? – ¿Qué _____ Antonia en la casa de mi hermana?

11. I didn't know that you two were brothers - No _____ que ustedes dos eran hermanos

12. I used to give lessons in a primary school - Yo _____ clases en una escuela primaria

13. I was a lawyer, but now I am a writer - Yo _____ abogado, pero ahora soy escritor

14. During the first days traveling, we didn't understand a thing - Durante los primeros días de viaje, no _____ nada

15. From where I was, I couldn't see the show very well - Desde donde estaba, no _____ bien el espectáculo

Chapter 13 – Future Tenses

There are two main ways to construct the future with Spanish.

One of them is very simple – since it only consists of using the present-tense conjugation of the verb *ir* (*to go*) plus the preposition *a*, plus the infinitive verb.

The second option, the proper simple future tense, implies learning a new conjugation, the future conjugation.

Now, you will see them both!

ir + *a* + infinitive verb

This is similar to the *I am going to* construction in English – since it is a present conjugation of the verb *ir* (*to go*) plus the preposition *a* (*to*), plus one non-conjugated action verb.

Before seeing some examples, here is a reminder of the present-tense conjugation for the verb *ir*:

I go - *yo* **voy**

you go - *tú* **vas**/*vos* **vas**/*usted* **va**

he/she goes - *él/ella* **va**

we go - *nosotros* **vamos**

you go - *vosotros/vosotras* **vais**/*ustedes* **van**

they go - *ellos/ellas* **van**

Now, here are some examples of combining these with infinitive verbs. You can combine this structure with any verb, even with the verb *ir*:

When I finish high school, I am going to go to university - Cuando termine la escuela, **voy a ir** a la universidad

Are you going to buy something? - ¿**Vas a comprar** algo?

Marina will be a great lawyer - Marina **va a ser** una gran abogada

Tomorrow we are going to eat pasta - Mañana **vamos a comer** pasta

You two are going to sleep in room 301 - Vosotros dos **vais a dormir** en la habitación 301

Manuel and Lucía are going to get married in April - Manuel y Lucía **van a casarse** en abril

Simple future

Although the version just explained is simpler, there is a proper future-tense conjugation, the simple future. Now you will see, as you did for the past-tense verbs, how to conjugate this tense for regular verbs, and how to do it for some common irregular verbs.

Just as before, to conjugate regular verbs in the simple future tense, you will use the verbs *hablar* (*to speak*), *comprender* (*to understand*), and *vivir* (*to live*).

To conjugate these, you have to take off the *ar*, *er*, or *ir* ending. Once you do it, you will find the *root* of the verb:

habl-

comprend-

viv-

Now, to conjugate them, you need to add to that root the ending corresponding to the conjugation of each pronoun:

Verbs ending in -ar (to talk – hablar)

*I will talk - yo habl*aré

you will talk - *tú hab***larás**/*vos hab***larás**/*usted hab***lará*

he/she will talk - *él/ella hab***lará**

we will talk - *nosotros hab***laremos**

you will talk - *vosotros/vosotras hab***laréis**/*ustedes hab***larán**

they will talk - *ellos/ellas hab***larán**

Verbs ending in -er (to understand - comprender)

I understood - *yo comprend***eré**

you understood - *tú comprend***erás**/*vos comprend***erás**/*usted comprend***erá**

he/she understood - *él/ella comprend***erá**

we understood - *nosotros comprend***eremos**

you understood - *vosotros comprend***eréis**/*ustedes comprend***erán**

they understood - *ellos/ellas comprend***erán**

Verbs ending in -ir (to live - vivir)

I lived - *yo viv***iré**

you lived - *tú viv***irás**/*vos viv***irás**/*usted viv***irá**

he/she lived - *él/ella viv***irá**

we lived - *nosotros viv***iremos**

you lived - *vosotros/vosotras viv***iréis**/*ustedes viv***irán**

they lived - *ellos/ellas viv***irán**

Here are some examples:

I will talk to my brother tomorrow - *Mañana* **hablaré** *con mi hermano*

My parents will never understand me - *Mis padres jamás me* **comprenderán**

My sister will live in Australia for one year - *Mi hermana* **vivirá** *por un año en Australia*

Since these are regular verbs, every verb ending in *ar*, *er*, and *ir* will have the same conjugation. You can practice using the list of Spanish regular verbs in the appendix.

Irregular verbs

Now, you will go over the conjugation of some common irregular verbs, and some examples for each.

to be – ser

I will be – yo **seré**

you will be – tú **serás**/*vos* **serás**/*usted* **será**

he/she will be – él/ella **será**

we will be – nosotros **seremos**

you will be – vosotros/vosotras **seréis**/*ustedes* **serán**

they will be – ellos/ellas **serán**

I will be a good student – Yo **seré** *un buen estudiante*

My daughter will be a famous actress – Mi hija **será** *una famosa actriz*

Someday, they will be boyfriend and girlfriend – Algún día, ellos **serán** *novios*

to be – estar

I will be – yo **estaré**

you will be – tú **estarás**/*vos* **estarás**/*usted* **estará**

he/she will be – él/ella **estará**

we will be – nosotros **estaremos**

you will be – vosotros/vosotras **estaréis**/*ustedes* **estarán**

they will be – ellos/ellas **estarán**

I will be fine, don't worry – **Estaré** *bien, no te preocupes*

You won't find us at home because we will be traveling – No nos encontrarás en casa porque **estaremos** *viajando*

You will also be in Barcelona? - ¿*Ustedes también* **estarán** *en Barcelona?*

to go - ir

I will go - yo **iré**

you will go - tú **irás**/*vos* **irás**/*usted* **irá**

he/she will go - él/ella **irá**

we will go - nosotros **iremos**

you will go - vosotros/vosotras **iréis**/*ustedes* **irán**

they will go - ellos/ellas **irán**

I will go to university in Buenos Aires - **Iré** *a la universidad en Buenos Aires*

She will go to the theater tonight - Ella **irá** *al teatro esta noche*

We will go travel around the world - **Iremos** *a viajar por el mundo*

to do - hacer

I will do - yo **haré**

you will do - tú **harás**/*vos* **harás**/*usted* **harás**

he/will do - él/ella **hará**

we will do - nosotros **haremos**

you will do - vosotros/vosotras **haréis**/*ustedes* **harán**

they will do - ellos/ellas **harán**

Will you do your homework? - ¿**Harás** *tu tarea?*

My mother-in-law will make a cake - Mi suegra **hará** *un pastel*

Around that time, we will do a trip around Ecuador - Por esa época, **haremos** *un viaje por Ecuador*

to read - leer

I will read - yo **leeré**

you will read - tú **leerás**/*vos* **leerás**/*usted* **leerá** *he/she will read* – él/ella **leerá**

we will read – nosotros **leeremos**

you will read – vosotros/vosotras **leeréis**/ustedes **leerán**

they will read – ellos/ellas **leerán**

I will not read anything during the trip – No **leeré** nada durante el viaje

Will you read my emails some day? – ¿Algún día **leerás** mis correos?

We will read the menu carefully before deciding – **Leeremos** el menú tranquilamente antes de decidir

to find – encontrar

I will find – yo **encontraré**

you will find – tú **encontrarás**/vos **encontrarás**/usted **encontrará**

he/she will find – él/ella **encontrará**

we will find – nosotros **encontraremos**

you will find – vosotros/vosotras **encontraréis**/ustedes **encontrarán**

they will find – ellos/ellas **encontrarán**

I will never find the time to do everything I want – Nunca **encontraré** el tiempo para hacer todo lo que quiero

Will you find your passport before take off? – ¿**Encontrarás** tu pasaporte antes de la partida del avión?

We will not find seats if we go too late – No **encontraremos** sitio si vamos muy tarde

to know – saber

I will know – yo **sabré**

you will know – tú **sabrás**/vos **sabrás**/usted **sabrá**

he/she will know – él/ella **sabrá**

we will know – nosotros **sabremos**

you will know – vosotros/vosotras **sabréis**/ustedes **sabrán**

they will know – ellos/ellas **sabrán**

I will never know everything you know – Nunca **sabré** todo lo que sabes tú

We will never know what happened – Jamás **sabremos** qué sucedió

With time, they will know what to do – Con el tiempo, **sabrán** qué hacer

to give – dar

I will give – yo **daré**

you will give – tú **darás**/vos **darás**/usted **dará**

he/she will give – él/ella **dará**

we will give – nosotros **daremos**

you will give – vosotros/vosotras **daréis**/ustedes **darán**

they will give – ellos/ellas **darán**

I will give my best friend a present for Christmas – Le **daré** un regalo a mi mejor amigo por Navidad

We will give our old phones to our kids – Les **daremos** nuestros teléfonos viejos a nuestros hijos

My parents will give me some money – Mis padres me **darán** algo de dinero

can – poder

I will be able to – yo **podré**

you will be able to – tú **podrás**/vos **podrás**/usted **podrá**

he/she will be able to – él/ella **podrá**

we will be able to – nosotros **podremos**

you will be able to – vosotros/vosotras **podréis**/ustedes **podrán**

they will be able to – ellos/ellas **podrán**

I feel I won't be able to understand people - Siento que no **podré** comprender a la gente

If she does not study, she will not pass the year - Si no estudia, no **podrá** pasar de año

They won't be able to do much to help us - No **podrán** hacer mucho para ayudarnos

to say - decir

I will say - yo **diré**

you will say - tú **dirás**/vos **dirás**/usted **dirá**

he/she will say - él/ella **dirá**

we will say - nosotros **diremos**

you will say - vosotros/vosotras **diréis**/ustedes **dirán**

they will say - ellos/ellas **dirán**

I will tell the truth! - ¡**Diré** la verdad!

She will never tell a lie to her parents - Ella jamás **dirá** una mentira a sus padres

Will you tell María about the party at my house on Friday? - ¿Le **diréis** a María sobre la fiesta en mi casa este viernes?

to see - ver

I will see - yo **veré**

you will see - tú **verás**/vos **verás**/usted **verá**

he/she will see - él/ella **verá**

we will see - nosotros **veremos**

you will see - vosotros/vosotras **veréis**/ustedes **verán**

they will see - ellos/ellas **verán**

I will watch every film you have recommended - **Veré** todas las películas que me recomendaste

Will you go see your family when you get back? - ¿**Verás** a tu familia cuando vuelvas?

We'll see what to do when we're there - Ya **veremos** qué hacer cuando estemos ahí

to have - tener

I will have - yo **tendré**

you will have - tú **tendrás**/vos **tendrás**/usted **tendrá**

he/she will have - él/ella **tendrá**

we will have - nosotros **tendremos**

you will have - vosotros/vosotras **tendréis**/ustedes **tendrán**

they will have - ellos/ellas **tendrán**

I will surely have problems with my credit card - Seguramente **tendré** problemas con mi tarjeta de crédito

Will you feel like going out tonight? - ¿**Tendrás** ganas de salir esta noche?

We will have two kids and a big house - **Tendremos** dos hijos y una casa grande

Exercises

Complete the following sentences with the correct verb:

1. Will you go to the cinema with us tonight? - ¿_____ a ir al cine con nosotros esta noche?

2. Will you make something to eat tonight? - ¿_____ algo de comer esta noche?

3. Are you going to go to the new restaurant in the Gothic Quarter - ¿_____ a ir al nuevo restaurante del barrio Gótico?

4. They will travel with me - Ellas _____ a viajar conmigo

5. You will be allowed to go play when we all finish our meal - _____ ir a jugar cuando terminemos de comer

6. I will talk with the receptionist - Yo _____ con la recepcionista

7. You will understand Latin culture when you're there - _____ la cultura latina cuando estés allí

8. She will live in Venezuela for some time - Ella _____ en Venezuela por algún tiempo

9. He will see his mistake someday - Él _____ su error algún día

10. We are going to get married in three months - _____ a casarnos en tres meses

11. We will be good guests: we will not make a lot of noise at night - _____ buenos huéspedes: no haremos mucho ruido por la noche

12. Will you be fine in this room? - ¿_____ bien en esta habitación?

13. I will go to walk for a while - _____ a caminar un rato

14. I will climb that mountain today - _____ a escalar esa montaña hoy

15. Do you think your boss will read my CV? - ¿Crees que tu jefe _____ mi currículum?

16. We will not find the hotel without the address - No _____ el hotel si no tenemos la dirección

17. Will they know how to get here? - ¿Ellos _____ cómo llegar hasta aquí?

18. I will give you a clue - Te _____ una pista

19. I will tell you everything when we're alone - Te _____ todo cuando estemos solos

20. I will study Economics; she will study Law - Yo _____ a estudiar Economía; ella _____ a estudiar Derecho

PART III: CONVERSATION

Chapter 14 – Greetings

Now that you know the Spanish basics and grammar, it is time to work on your conversation!

In this chapter, you will go over the many ways of saying *hello, how are you, see you later*, and *goodbye*!

Saying hello

First of all, here are some common ways of saying *hello*:

Hello - Hola

Good morning - Buen día/Buenos días

Good afternoon - Buenas tardes

Good evening/Good night - Buenas noches

It's a pleasure to meet you - Es un placer conocerte

It's a pleasure to meet you - Un gusto

Greetings - Saludos

Asking how someone is feeling

Now see the different ways to ask *how are you*. Some of these may vary from country to country.

For example, in some countries, the formal *usted* is more widely used, while in some others, it is quite unusual. You should do some quick research on formalities in the country where you are going before getting there.

Additionally, the slang for *what's up* should vary from place to place. Hear what people say and copy it!

How are you? - *¿Cómo estás?* (informal)

How are you? - *¿Cómo está?* (formal)

How are you? - *¿Cómo estáis?* (plural, *vosotros*)

How are you? - *¿Cómo están?* (plural, *ustedes*)

How are you? - *¿Cómo te encuentras?* (informal)

How are you? - *¿Cómo se encuentra?* (formal)

How have you been - *¿Cómo has estado?* (informal, past)

How is it going? - *¿Cómo te va?* (informal)

What's up? - *¿Qué tal?* (informal)

What's up? - *¿Qué pasa?* (informal)

What's up? - *¿Qué hubo?* (informal)

How's it going? - *¿Cómo va?* (informal)

Hey! - *¡Oye!* (informal)

Now, here are some options to answer these questions:

I'm fine - *Estoy bien*

I'm very well - *Estoy muy bien*

All good - *Todo bien*

And you? - *¿Y tú?*

I'm great! - *¡Estoy genial!*

Everything perfect - *Todo perfecto*

Not so well - *No muy bien*

Could be better - *Podría estar mejor*

I'm very bad - *Estoy muy mal*

I'm not well at all - *No estoy nada bien*

Saying goodbye

Now, see how to say *goodbye*:

Bye - Chau

Goodbye - Adiós

See you later! - ¡Nos vemos luego!

See you later! - ¡Hasta luego!

See you soon! - ¡Hasta pronto!

Good luck! - ¡Mucha suerte!

Basic politeness

Here are some words that will take you far! Never forget to use them - since being polite can open many doors for you:

please - por favor

thank you - gracias

thank you very much - muchas gracias

you're welcome - de nada/no hay de qué/no hay por qué

excuse me - permiso

excuse me - disculpe (formal)

excuse me - disculpa (informal)

I'm sorry - lo lamento/perdón/lo siento

welcome - bienvenido/bienvenida/bienvenidos/bienvenidas

Talking on the phone

The following are some ways of answering the phone if a Spanish-speaker calls you:

¿Hola?

¿Aló?

¿Sí?

¿Bueno?

Diga

Writing an email

If you make friends in a Spanish-speaking country or if you go there for work or to study, eventually you will need to write an email in Spanish. Here are some useful words, sentences, and expressions:

Dear... - Estimado... (formal, masculine)

Dear... - Estimada... (formal, feminine)

Dear... - Estimado/a... (formal, when you don't know the gender of the person you are addressing)

Dear... - Querido... (informal, masculine)

Dear... - Querida... (informal, feminine)

I am writing to... - Le escribo para... (formal)

I am writing to... - Te escribo para... (informal)

I have a question about... - Tengo una duda sobre...

Could you please... - Podría, por favor... (formal)

Could you please... - Podrías, por favor... (informal)

Thank you in advance for your help - Gracias desde ya por su ayuda (formal)

Looking forward to your reply - Espero su respuesta (formal)

Looking forward to your reply - Espero tu respuesta (informal)

Kind regards - Saludos cordiales

Kind regards - Atentamente

Exercises

1. Complete the following informal conversation:

Hello, Marta. How are you? - _____, Marta. ¿Cómo _____?

I'm very well, Lucas. I'm going to class. How are you? - Estoy muy _____, Lucas. Estoy yendo a clase. ¿_____ estás _____?

I could be better, actually. I have a Spanish test and I don't think I'm ready - Realmente, podría _____ _____. Tengo un examen de español y creo que no estoy listo.

Everything will be fine! Good luck! - ¡Todo irá bien! ¡Mucha _____!

OK, see you soon - Vale, nos _____ luego.

Bye! - ¡_____!

2. Complete the following formal conversation:

Good morning, professor. How are you? - _____, profesor. ¿Cómo _____?

I'm very well, thank you. How are you? - Estoy muy _____, gracias. ¿_____ está _____?

I am fine... a little worried about the test - Estoy _____ ... un poco preocupado por el examen

You are a good student, Mr García. You'll be fine - _____ es un buen estudiante, señor García. Estará _____.

I hope so! Thank you very much, sir - ¡Eso espero! _____ gracias, señor

You're welcome - _____ hay de qué

Chapter 15 – Introducing Yourself

Now that you know how to say *hello*, you need to know how to talk about yourself and how to make questions about others when having conversations and meeting people.

Saying your name

My name is - Me llamo...

My name is - Mi nombre es...

I am... - Soy

My last name is... - Mi apellido es...

Everyone calls me... - Todos me dicen...

Here are some example sentences:

Hello, my name is Sofia - Hola, me llamo Sofia

My name is Patrick, but you can call me Pat - Mi nombre es Patrick, pero puedes decirme Pat

I am Susan, and you? - Soy Susan, ¿y tú?

My last name is Martinez - Mi apellido es Martínez

My name is Sandra, but everyone calls me Sandy - Me llamo Sandra, pero todos me dicen Sandy

Asking people's names

What's your name? - ¿Cómo se llama? (formal)

What's your name? - ¿Cómo te llamas? (informal)

What's your name? - ¿Cómo es su nombre? (formal)

What's your name? - ¿Cómo es tu nombre? (informal)

What's your last name? - ¿Cómo es su apellido? (formal)

What's your last name? - ¿Cómo es tu apellido? (informal)

Who are you? - ¿Quién es usted? (formal)

Who are you? - ¿Quién eres tú? (informal)

What's your nickname? - ¿Cómo te dicen?

Talking about your profession

Now see some words, expressions, and sentences that might be useful to talk about your job and studies:

I am a... - Soy...

I work as a... - Trabajo de...

I work at a... - Trabajo en...

I study... - Estudio...

I study at... - Estudio en...

I want to be a... - Quiero ser...

See these in the following sentences:

I am an architect - Soy arquitecta

I work as a salesperson in a store - Trabajo de vendedor en una tienda

I work at a very big company - Trabajo en una empresa muy grande

I study Medicine - Estudio Medicina

I study at the University of Madrid - Estudio en la Universidad de Madrid

I want to be an Engineer – *Quiero ser ingeniera*

Asking about people's profession

What do you do for a living? – *¿A qué te dedicas?*

What do you do? – *¿Qué haces?*

Do you work? – *¿Trabajas?*

Do you study? – *¿Estudias?*

Where do you work – *¿Dónde trabajas?*

What do you study? – *¿Qué estudias?*

Are you here for work? – *¿Estás aquí por trabajo?*

Did you come here to study? – *¿Has venido aquí para estudiar?*

Talking about your family and friends

Now learn some words, expressions, and sentences to use to tell others about your loved ones.

mother – madre

father – padre

husband – esposo

wife – esposa

boyfriend – novio

girlfriend – novia

partner – pareja

brother – hermano

sister – hermana

children – hijos

son – hijo

daughter – hija

cousin – primo/prima

grandfather – abuelo

grandmother - abuela

friend - amigo/amiga

acquaintance - conocido/conocida

colleague - colega

pet - mascota

See these words in the following sentences:

*My mother is a doctor - Mi **madre** es médica*

*I am traveling with my father - Estoy viajando con mi **padre***

*He's Juan, my husband - Él es Juan, mi **esposo***

*My wife is very tired - Mi **esposa** está muy cansada*

*I don't have a boyfriend - No tengo **novio***

*Is she your girlfriend? - ¿Ella es tu **novia**?*

*My partner went to buy some beers - Mi **pareja** fue a comprar unas cervezas*

*I have three brothers - Tengo tres **hermanos***

*I'm sharing a room with my sister - Estoy compartiendo una habitación con mi **hermana***

*I don't have children - No tengo **hijos***

*He's my son - Él es mi **hijo***

*My daughter is nine - Mi **hija** tiene nueve años*

I am traveling with some friends - Estoy viajando con algunas **amigas**

Talking about your origins

While traveling, it is normal to explain to people where you come from and where you were born. Now see how to do it.

I am from... - Soy de...

I come from... - Vengo de...

I live in... - Vivo en...

I was born in... – Nací en...

My family is from... – Mi familia es de...

I am part... and part... – Soy parte... y parte...

I speak... – Hablo...

Now see how to use these expressions in everyday sentences:

I am from England – Soy de Inglaterra

I come from Belgium, but I was born in Spain – Vengo de Bélgica, pero nací en España

I live in Mexico, but I am from the Netherlands – Vivo en México, pero soy de los Países Bajos

I was born in Russia, but now I live in Argentina – Nací en Rusia, pero ahora vivo en Argentina

My family is from Peru, but I grew up in the United States – Mi familia es de Perú, pero yo crecí en Estados Unidos

I am part Spanish and part French – Soy parte español y parte francés

I speak Spanish and English – Hablo español e inglés

Talking about yourself

Finally, here are some words and sentences to describe yourself:

I am ... years old – Tengo ... años

I am young – Soy joven

I am old – Soy viejo/vieja

I am tall – Soy alto/alta

I am short – Soy bajo/baja

I am shy – Soy tímido/tímida

I am outgoing – Soy extrovertido/extrovertida

I like traveling – Me gusta viajar

I work a lot – Trabajo mucho

I like art - Me gusta el arte

I like nature - Me gusta la naturaleza

I like music - Me gusta la música

Exercises

Complete the following informal conversation:

Hello, my name is Samuel, what's your name? - Hola, me _____ Samuel, ¿cómo _____ llamas tú?

My name is Patricia, but they call me Pato - Mi _____ es Patricia, pero me _____ Pato

It's a pleasure to meet you, Pato. So... what do you do? - Un gusto conocerte, Pato. Entonces... ¿____ qué _____ dedicas?

I am a writer, and you? - Yo _____ escritora, ¿y tú?

I am a student. I study Architecture - Yo soy estudiante. _____ Arquitectura

Where do you study? - ¿_____ estudias?

At the University of Barcelona, but I'm not from here, I was born in Valencia - En la Universidad de Barcelona, pero no soy de aquí, _____ en Valencia

Oh, you came here to study. Did you come alone? - Oh, has venido para _____. ¿Has venido solo?

No, I came with my brother - No, vine con mi _____

Chapter 16 – Forming Questions and Dialogue

You are almost ready to start speaking Spanish! It might be a bit difficult at first, but the more you practice, the simpler it will become. In this final chapter, you're going to go over some everyday situations, with sentences and vocabulary that you will definitely need.

As you probably noticed, in Spanish, you don't only have to use a closing question mark, but also an opening question mark: ¿..?

Unlike in English, to transform a regular affirmative sentence into a question, you don't need to move the elements of the sentence around:

Adrian is hungry - Adrián tiene hambre

Is Adrian hungry? - ¿Adrián tiene hambre?

However, of course, most questions are not like regular sentences. To ask things, you need these words:

what - qué

why - por qué

how - cómo

where - dónde

who - quién/quiénes

which – cuál/cuáles

how much – cuánto/cuántos

Here are some examples:

What are you doing? – ¿**Qué** haces?

Why is the door open? – ¿**Por qué** la puerta está abierta?

How did you get here so fast? – ¿**Cómo** llegaste aquí tan rápido?

Where were you? – ¿**Dónde** estabas?

Who is that guy? – ¿**Quién** es ese chico?

Who are those two? – ¿**Quiénes** son esos dos?

Which one is your car? – ¿**Cuál** es tu automóvil?

Which shoes do you want to buy? – ¿**Cuáles** zapatos quieres comprar?

How much money do we have? – ¿**Cuánto** dinero tenemos?

How many days of vacations do you have left? – ¿**Cuántos** días de vacaciones te quedan?

Everyday dialogue and questions

Now that you know how to form basic questions, see some basic vocabulary and sentences for everyday settings:

At the restaurant, cafe or bar:

menu – menú

dish – plato

chair – silla

table – mesa

reservation -- reserva

food – comida

hot – caliente

cold – frío

coffee – café

tea – té

milk – leche

water – agua

hot chocolate – chocolate caliente

beer – cerveza

wine – vino

tip – propina

Could you bring us a menu? – ¿Podría traernos un menú?

Do you have some salt? – ¿Tiene sal?

Could you heat this up? – ¿Podría calentar esto?

Everything is very good – Está todo muy rico

We need some water – Necesitamos agua

The check, please – La cuenta, por favor

One coffee, please – ¡Un café, por favor!

We want two coffees, one with milk – Queremos dos cafés, uno con leche

Do you have today's newspaper? – ¿Tiene el periódico de hoy?

Do you have chamomile tea? – ¿Tiene té de manzanilla?

Two beers, please! – ¡Dos cervezas, por favor!

Could you bring me some ice, please? – ¿Podría traerme hielo, por favor?

Do you have sugar or sweetener? – ¿Tiene azúcar o edulcorante?

Shopping:

store – tienda

price – precio

credit card – tarjeta de crédito

cash – efectivo

change – cambio/vuelta

cheap – barato

expensive – caro

clothes – ropa

Do you have lettuce? – *¿Tiene lechuga?*

Could you give me two kilos of potatoes, please? – *¿Podría darme dos kilos de papas, por favor?*

How much are the strawberries? – *¿Cuánto cuestan las fresas?*

How much is this? – *¿Cuánto cuesta esto?*

Do you have a bigger size – *¿Tiene una talla más grande?*

May I try this on? – *¿Puedo probarme esto?*

What are these plates made with? – *¿De qué material son estos platos?*

Asking for directions:

left – izquierda

right – derecha

straight – recto

street – calle

to turn – girar

to cross – cruzar

north – norte

south – sur

east – este

west – oeste

Where is the Prado Museum? – *¿Dónde está el Museo del Prado?*

How can I get to the Cathedral – *¿Cómo puedo llegar a la Catedral?*

Walk three blocks and then turn to the right – Camine tres calles y luego gire hacia la derecha

Go south for about two hundred meters – Vaya hacia el sur por unos doscientos metros

Turn left and then keep going straight until you see the museum – Doble a la izquierda y luego siga recto hasta ver el museo

At the airport:

luggage – equipaje

passport – pasaporte

visa – visa

bag – mochila

seat – asiento

plane – avión

flight – vuelo

gate – puerta de embarque

terminal – terminal

boarding pass – tarjeta de embarque

Are you going to check in any luggage? – ¿Va a facturar equipaje?

Do I have to check in this bag? – ¿Tengo que facturar esta mochila?

I have the boarding pass on my phone – Tengo la tarjeta de embarque en mi teléfono

My flight is departing at quarter past three – Mi vuelo sale a las tres y cuarto

Our seats are 20A and 20B – Nuestros asientos son el 20A y el 20B

We have to walk up to terminal 2 – Tenemos que caminar hasta la terminal 2

In nature:

nature – naturaleza

ocean – océano

landscape – paisaje

sky – cielo

jungle – selva/jungla

tree – árbol

animals – animales

gear – equipamiento

camera – cámara de fotos

hat – sombrero

bug repellent – repelente

sunscreen – loción solar

Did you bring the camera? – ¿Has traido la cámara?

Will these shoes be good enough for the hike? – ¿Estos zapatos servirán para la excursión?

Do we need to bring water? – ¿Tenemos que llevar agua?

Should we buy bug repellent? – ¿Es necesario comprar repelente?

Look at that landscape! – ¡Mira ese paisaje!

I need a break – Necesito un descanso

Exercises

Complete the following sentences:

1. This needs more salt – Esto necesita más _____

2. Did you bring milk? – ¿Has traído _____?

3. Where is the police station? – ¿_____ está la estación de policía?

4. Can we drink the tap water? - ¿Podemos beber el _____ del grifo?

5. I want a black coffee, please - Un _____ negro, por favor

6. Could you hand me the menu? - ¿Podrías alcanzarme el _____?

7. How much is the beer? - ¿_____ cuesta la _____?

8. How much are these trousers? - ¿Cuánto _____ estos pantalones?

9. Do you have your boarding pass? - ¿Tiene su _____ de embarque?

10. How can I get to the university - ¿Cómo _____ llegar a la universidad?

11. Where is your luggage? - ¿Dónde está su _____?

12. Do you have tomatoes? - ¿_____ tomates?

13. How much are the carrots? - ¿_____ cuestan las zanahorias?

14. I will lose my flight! - ¡Perderé mi _____!

15. Where is the camera? - ¿_____ está la _____ de fotos?

16. Go north - Vaya _____ el norte

17. The fish is very good - El pescado está _____ rico

18. The check, please - La cuenta, por _____

Conclusion

You made it! See? Spanish isn't that hard.

Now that you have reached this point, you can understand Spanish sentences, introduce yourself, talk about your family, order, shop, and travel around Latin America. Of course, you are not an expert - yet -, but you have learned the basics to keep on learning and immerse yourself in the fascinating world of the Spanish language.

What's next? Challenge yourself! Listen to Spanish music, watch Spanish films (maybe with subtitles at first), try to read a Spanish book. And, of course, travel to Spain and Latin America to start practicing.

If you keep learning Spanish, it might open doors for you to new work, academic and personal opportunities, international connections, new people, and, naturally, new cultures and landscapes.

Good luck with your Spanish adventures! And don't hesitate to come back to this book to practice more, go over some chapters, and confirm how much you have learned.

¡Chau!

APPENDIX: VOCABULARY

Glossary of nouns

door - puerta

window - ventana

table - mesa

chair - silla

couch - sofá/sillón

bed - cama

pillow - almohada

lamp - lámpara

fridge - refrigerador

oven - horno

microwave - microondas

knife - cuchillo

fork - tenedor

spoon - cuchara

tub - bañera

head - cabeza

neck - cuello

shoulders – hombros
arms – brazos
hands – manos
fingers – dedos
chest – pecho
belly – barriga
waist – cintura
hips – cadera
legs – piernas
feet – pies
face – rostro/cara
hair – pelo/cabello
eyes – ojos
nose – nariz
mouth – boca
chin – mentón
ears – orejas
food – comida
potato – papa
ingredient – ingrediente
coffee – café
steak – filete
plane – avión
wing – ala
luggage – equipaje
car – automóvil
children – niños

man – hombre
woman – mujer
person – persona
people – gente
crowd – multitud
group – grupo
lawyer – abogado/abogada
cook – cocinero/cocinera
writer – escritor/escritora
doctor – médico/médica
student – estudiante
president – presidente/presidenta
politician – político/política
journalist – periodista/reportero/reportera
programmer – programador/programadora
accountant – contable
teacher – maestro/maestra
translator – traductor/traductora
artist – artista
musician – músico/música
dancer – bailarín/bailarina
actor – actor/actriz
director – director/directora
hairdresser – peluquero/peluquera
the dog – el perro
the cat – el gato
the elephant – el elefante

the insect - *el insecto*

the sky - *el cielo*

the earth - *la tierra*

the water - *el agua*

the grass - *el césped/el pasto*

the wind - *el viento*

the top - *la cima*

sunset - *ocaso*

the computer - *la computadora/el computador/el ordenador*

the phone - *el teléfono*

the call - *la llamada*

the watch/the clock - *el reloj*

the park - *el parque*

the beach - *la playa*

the hotel - *el hotel*

the street - *la calle*

Spanish - *español*

English - *inglés*

French - *francés*

Italian - *italiano*

Russian - *ruso*

Chinese - *chino*

Spain - *España*

Dominican Republic - *República Dominicana*

Argentina - *Argentina*

Peru - *Perú*

Chile - *Chile*

Mexico - México
Colombia - Colombia
freedom - libertad
intelligence - inteligencia
peace - paz
passion - pasión
love - amor
friendship - amistad
happiness - felicidad

Glossary of adjectives

good - bueno/buena/buenos/buenas
new - nuevo/nueva/nuevos/nuevas
long - largo/larga/largos/largas
wide - ancho/ancha/anchos/anchas
small - pequeño/pequeña/pequeños/pequeñas
short - corto/corta/cortos/cortas
tall - alto/alta/altos/altas
short - bajo/baja/bajos/bajas
little - poco/poca/pocos/pocas
beautiful - hermoso/hermosa/hermosos/hermosas
bad - malo/mala/malos/malas
ugly - feo/fea/feos/feas
right - correcto/correcta/correctos/correctas
happy - contento/contenta/contentos/contentas
angry - enojado/enojada/enojados/enojadas
fast - rápido/rápida/rápidos/rápidas

slow - lento/lenta/lentos/lentas
old - viejo/vieja/viejos/viejas
cold - frío/fría/fríos/frías
broken - roto/rota/rotos/rotas
hard - duro/dura/duros/duras
empty - vacío/vacía/vacíos/vacías
full - lleno/llena/llenos/llenas
dirty - sucio/sucia/sucios/sucias
clean - limpio/limpia/limpios/limpias
big - grande/grandes
different - diferente/diferentes
young - joven/jóvenes
important - importante/importantes
smart - inteligente/inteligentes
easy - fácil/fáciles
nice - agradable/agradables
happy - alegre/alegres
enormous - enorme/enormes
strong - fuerte/fuertes
weak - débil/débiles
hot - caliente/calientes
soft - suave/suaves
black - negro/negra/negros/negras
white - blanco/blanca/blancos/blancas
red - rojo/roja/rojos/rojas
yellow - amarillo/amarilla/amarillos/amarillas
blue - azul/azules

orange – naranja/naranjas
green – verde/verdes
purple – violeta/violetas/morado/morados/púrpura/púrpuras
gray – gris/grises
brown – café/cafés/marrón/marrones
pink – rosa/rosas/rosado/rosada/rosados/rosadas
golden – dorado/dorada/dorados/doradas
light blue – celeste/celestes
Argentinian – argentino/argentina
Bolivian – boliviano/boliviana
Brazilian – brasileño/brasileña
Chilean – chileno/chilena
Colombian – colombiano/colombiana
Paraguayan – paraguayo/paraguaya
Peruvian – peruano/peruana
Uruguayan – uruguayo/uruguaya

Glossary of verbs

to answer – contestar
to pass – pasar
to arrive – llegar
to pay – pagar
to ask a question – preguntar
to believe – creer
to present – presentar
to annoy – molestar
to break – romper

to promise – prometer
to read – leer
to buy – comprar
to receive – recibir
to call – llamar
to respond – responder
to change – cambiar
to rest – descansar
to clean – limpiar
to return – regresar
to go up – subir
to check – revisar
to run – correr
to see – ver
to cook – cocinar
to sell – vender
to cry – llorar
to send – mandar/enviar
to dance – bailar
to share – compartir
to deliver – entregar
to sing – cantar
to wish – desear
to draw – dibujar
to drink – beber/tomar
to drive – manejar/conducir
to speak/to talk – hablar

to eat – comer
to end – terminar/acabar
to spend – gastar
to enter – entrar
to take out – sacar
to put away – guardar
to fill – llenar
to study – estudiar
to fix – arreglar
to get off – bajar
to go down – bajar
to swim – nadar
to give a gift – regalar
to take care of – cuidar
to greet – saludar
to take – tomar
to have dinner – cenar
to take/carry – llevar
to help – ayudar
to hide – esconder
to hug – abrazar
to teach/to show – enseñar
to touch – tocar
to kiss – besar
to know – saber
to travel – viajar
to last – durar

to leave – dejar

to turn off – apagar

to lend – prestar

to use – usar

to listen – escuchar

to live – vivir

to look at – mirar

to visit – visitar

to watch – mirar

to wait – esperar

to look for – buscar

to walk – andar

to need – necesitar

to wash – lavar

to win – ganar

to open – abrir

to earn – ganar (dinero)

to work – trabajar

to paint – pintar

to write – escribir

EXERCISES: CORRECT ANSWERS

Chapter 2

1. My flight is on October 10 at ten in the morning – Mi vuelo es el _diez_ de _octubre_ a las _diez de la mañana_.

2. My birthday is on September 20 – Mi cumpleaños es el _veinte_ de _septiembre_.

3. See you on Sunday at four in the afternoon – Nos vemos el _domingo_ a las _cuatro de la tarde_.

4. I have to go to the dentist on January 9 at eleven in the morning – Tengo que ir al dentista el _nueve_ de _enero_ a las _once de la mañana_.

5. My wedding was on December 19 – Mi boda fue el _diecinueve_ de _diciembre_.

Chapter 3

1. The movie is very long – _La_ película es muy larga

2. Where is the toilet? – ¿Dónde está _el_ baño?

3. The sandwiches are in your backpack – _Los_ emparedados están en tu mochila

4. The mountains are snowy - _Las_ montañas están nevadas

5. The day is cloudy - _El_ día está nublado

6. What floor is the reception on? - ¿En qué piso está _la_ recepción?

7. Do you have the map? - ¿Tienes _el_ mapa?

8. I can't find the key - No encuentro _la_ llave

9. Do you have a minute? - ¿Tienes _un_ minuto?

10. I would like to eat a salad - Me apetece comer _una_ ensalada

11. I will meet with some friends in Bogota - Me encontraré con _unos_ amigos en Bogotá

12. This country has some precious beaches - Este país tiene _unas_ playas preciosas

13. Could you take a picture of us? - ¿Podrías tomarnos _una_ foto?

14. The coffee shop is in front of a large tree - El café está frente a _un_ gran árbol

15. Do you have a pencil? - ¿Tienes _un_ lápiz?

16. There is a cloud in the sky - Hay _una_ nube en el cielo

Chapter 4

1. I have three weeks of holidays - _Yo_ tengo tres semanas de vacaciones

2. I am very tired - _Yo_ estoy muy cansada

3. Are you my guide? - ¿_Usted_ es mi guía?

4. You are a great cook! - ¡_Tú_ eres un excelente cocinero!

5. You are the first client of the day - _Vos_ sos el primer cliente del día

6. He is my brother - _Él_ es mi hermano

7. She has booked a table - _Ella_ reservó una mesa

8. We want to eat a pizza - <u>Nosotros/Nosotras</u> queremos comer una pizza

9. We are lawyers - <u>Nosotras</u> somos abogadas

10. Are you coming to the beach? - ¿<u>Vosotros/Vosotras</u> venís a la playa?

11. You are very active tourists - <u>Vosotros</u> sois turistas muy activos

12. Do you have plans for tonight? - ¿<u>Ustedes</u> tienen planes para esta noche?

13. They are playing the guitar - <u>Ellos/Ellas</u> están tocando la guitarra

14. They are my friends - <u>Ellas</u> son mis amigas

Chapter 5

1. The store opens from nine to six - La tienda abre <u>de</u> nueve a seis

2. I gave my wallet to Sara - Le di mi cartera <u>a</u> Sara

3. Are we going? - ¿Vamos <u>a</u> ir?

4. Who is going to the cinema? - ¿Quién va <u>al</u> cine?

5. I will meet with my brother at noon - Me encontraré con mi hermano <u>al</u> mediodía

6. Climb carefully! - ¡Sube <u>con</u> cuidado!

7. I am traveling with a friend - Estoy viajando <u>con</u> un amigo

8. Laura is coming with me tonight - Laura vendrá <u>conmigo</u> esta noche

9. May I sit with you? - ¿Puedo sentarme <u>contigo</u>?

10. I am from Sweden - Soy <u>de</u> Suecia

11. This boat belongs to my father - Este bote es <u>de</u> mi padre

12. I like food without salt - Me gusta la comida <u>sin</u> sal

13. It's daytime already! - ¡Ya es *de* día!

14. Check out is at 11 in the morning - El check out es *a* las once de la mañana

15. We are talking about the weather - Estamos hablando *sobre* el clima

16. What's the hotel's address? - ¿Cómo es la dirección *del* hotel?

17. Under the seawater, there are many rocks - *Bajo* el agua del mar hay muchas rocas

18. I traveled from Asia to see you - Viajé *desde* Asia para verte

19. I am at the park - Estoy *en* el parque

20. The room faces the mountains - La habitación da *a/hacia* las montañas

21. I will return home in October - Regresaré a casa *en* octubre

22. Tomorrow we will go towards the East - Mañana iremos *hacia* el Este

23. I work until 9 at night - Trabajo *hasta* las nueve de la noche

24. I will walk to the beach - Caminaré *hacia* la playa

25. Does this bus go to the center? - ¿Este bus va *hacia* el centro?

26. This is for you - Esto es *para* ti

27. I will travel for a year - Viajaré *por* un año

28. I will go to Pedro's party later - Iré *a* la fiesta de Pedro más tarde

29. Leave the towels on the bed - Deje las toallas *sobre* la cama

30. I come from the United States - Vengo *de/desde* los Estados Unidos

Chapter 6

1. I have a good backpack – Tengo una _buena_ mochila

2. Esteban is very tall – Esteban es muy _alto_

3. This hotel is beautiful – Este hotel es _hermoso_

4. I have bad news – Tengo _malas_ noticias

5. My phone is broken – Mi teléfono está _roto_

6. My bag is full – Mi maleta está _llena_

7. You are very young – Eres muy _joven_

8. He is very strong – Él es muy _fuerte_

9. I want to eat something hot – Quiero comer algo _caliente_

10. Do you have red gloves? – ¿Tiene guantes _rojos_?

11. Have you seen a green bike? – ¿Has visto una bicicleta _verde_?

12. I think that's my charger – Creo que ese es _mi_ cargador

13. Those sunglasses are mine – Esos lentes de sol son _míos_

14. Are those your beers? – ¿No son esas _tus_ cervezas?

15. Where is our taxi? – ¿Dónde está _nuestro_ taxi?

Chapter 7

1. I am the first one to arrive – _Soy_ el primero en llegar

2. Who are you? – ¿Quién _eres_ tú?

3. I am tired of walking! – ¡_Estoy_ cansada de caminar!

4. Are we lost? – ¿_Estamos_ perdidos?

5. I speak Spanish – Yo _hablo_ español

6. I understand – _Comprendo_

7. She lives on that hill – Ella _vive_ en esa colina

8. Do we do something tonight? – ¿_Hacemos_ algo esta noche?

9. I don't read emails during my vacations – No *leo* mails durante mis vacaciones

10. I can't find my passport – No *encuentro* mi pasaporte

11. Do you know how to surf? – ¿*Sabes* surfear?

12. My parents give me some money every now and then – Mis padres me *dan* algo de dinero a veces

13. Can we go there? – ¿*Podemos* ir allí?

14. She says it's true! – ¡Ella *dice* que es cierto!

15. With this fog, I don't see a thing – Con esta niebla, no *veo* nada

16. There are only a few hotels in the city – *Hay* pocos hoteles en la ciudad

17. There is a dog in the garden – *Hay* un perro en el jardín

Chapter 8

1. I know the hotel's address – Sé la dirección del hotel

I don't know the hotel's address – *No sé la dirección del hotel*

2. I have a good job – Tengo un buen trabajo

I don't have a good job – *No tengo un buen trabajo*

3. I will stay here for a long time – Me quedaré aquí por mucho tiempo

I won't stay here for a long time – *No me quedaré aquí por mucho tiempo*

4. I like Lila Downs' music – Me gusta la música de Lila Downs

I don't like Lila Downs' music – *No me gusta la música de Lila Downs*

5. I don't like any of the dishes on the menu – *No* me gusta *ninguno* de los platos del menú

6. When it's time to eat, there is no one at the beach – A la hora de comer, _no_ hay _nadie_ en la playa

7. My mother never calls – Mi madre _no_ me llama _nunca_

8. I don't want to eat anything else; I'm full! – _No_ quiero comer _nada_ más; ¡estoy llena!

Chapter 9

1. You must eat more vegetables – _Debes/debés/debe/debéis/deben_ comer más vegetales

2. The government must hire more people with disabilities – El gobierno _debe_ contratar a más personas con discapacidad

3. We must be more careful – _Debemos_ ser más cuidadosos

4. You have to behave – _Tienes/tenés_ que comportarte

5. My mother has to go to the doctor tomorrow – Mi madre _tiene_ que ir al médico mañana

6. The children want to play in the park – Los niños _quieren_ jugar en el parque

7. I want to swim in the ocean – _Quiero_ nadar en el océano

8. Can I use your charger? – ¿_Puedo_ usar tu cargador?

9. I usually read here – _Suelo_ leer aquí

10. Do you normally travel together? – ¿_Soléis/suelen_ viajar juntos?

11. I don't want to live in the city – No _quiero_ vivir en la ciudad

12. We can't get a ticket – No _podemos_ conseguir una entrada

13. It is necessary to find the ring – _Hay_ que encontrar el anillo

14. One has to be kind to the local people – _Hay_ que ser amable con la gente local

Chapter 10

1. I have gone to the doctor - *He* ido al médico

2. What did you say? - ¿Qué has *dicho*?

3. Have you called a taxi? - ¿Usted *ha* llamado un taxi?

4. She is gone - Ella se *ha* marchado

5. I couldn't download the file - No he *podido* descargar el archivo

6. Have you seen that? - ¿*Has/ha/habéi/han* visto eso?

7. They have traveled for many years - Ellas *han* viajado muchos años

8. Have you been to the theater? - ¿*Has/ha/habéis/han* ido al teatro?

9. Ignacio has never gone to the circus - Ignacio nunca ha *ido* al circo

10. I have never been so tired - Jamás he *estado* tan cansado

11. Have you found your phone? - ¿Has *encontrado* tu teléfono?

12. Have you talked with the receptionist? - ¿Has *hablado* con la recepcionista?

13. Have you lived in Spain - ¿Has *vivido* en España?

14. I have read a Spanish book - He *leído* un libro en español

15. We're back! - ¡*Hemos* vuelto!

16. I have given a tip to the waiter - Le he *dado* una propina al camarero

17. We had kids already - Ya hemos *tenido* hijos

18. You have been an amazing friend - Has *sido* un amigo increíble

19. They didn't understand - No han *comprendido*

20. We have made plans - Hemos *hecho* planes

Chapter 11

1. Did you talk with your parents? - ¿*Hablaste* con tus padres?

2. I never had problems in this hotel - Nunca *tuve* problemas en este hotel

3. I lived in Latin America for more than ten years - *Viví* en América Latina por más de diez años

4. What did you say? - ¿Qué *dijiste/dijo*?

5. We were in Peru during several months - *Estuvimos* durante varios meses en Perú

6. My parents gave me everything I have - Mis padres me *dieron* todo lo que tengo

7. We did everything we could - *Hicimos* todo lo que pudimos

8. We read your article! - ¡*Leímos* tu artículo!

9. Yesterday I went to some friends' house - Ayer *fui* a la casa de unos amigos

10. We didn't find the bag - No *encontramos* la maleta

11. I never knew what to do with my life - Nunca *supe* qué hacer de mi vida

12. She was a terrible student during her whole life - Ella *fue* una pésima estudiante durante toda su vida

13. Could she take the plane? - ¿*Pudo* tomar el avión?

14. I never understood why that is so important - Jamás *comprendí* por qué eso es tan importante

15. Yesterday I saw an amazing film - Ayer *vi* una película genial

Chapter 12

1. Who were you talking to? - ¿Con quién *hablabas*?

2. Laura didn't have pets - Laura no *tenía* mascotas

3. I used to live in England, but now I live in Spain - Yo *vivía* en Inglaterra, pero ahora vivo en España

4. You were saying something very interesting last night - Usted *decía* algo muy interesante anoche

5. Yesterday I didn't go out because I was very tired - Ayer no salí porque *estaba* muy cansada

6. In Colombia, we used to go to the market every day - En Colombia, todos los días *íbamos* al mercado

7. I couldn't believe that the landscape was so beautiful - No *podía* creer que el paisaje fuera tan bello

8. When I was little, I used to read a lot - Cuando era pequeña, *leía* mucho

9. I was worried because I couldn't find my passport - Estaba preocupada porque no *encontraba* mi pasaporte

10. What was Antonia doing at my sister's house? - ¿Qué *hacía* Antonia en la casa de mi hermana?

11. I didn't know that you two were brothers - No *sabía* que ustedes dos eran hermanos

12. I used to give lessons in a primary school - Yo *daba* clases en una escuela primaria

13. I was a lawyer, but now I am a writer - Yo *era* abogado, pero ahora soy escritor

14. During the first days traveling, we didn't understand a thing - Durante los primeros días de viaje, no *comprendíamos* nada

15. From where I was, I couldn't see the show very well - Desde donde estaba, no *veía* bien el espectáculo

Chapter 13

1. Will you go to the cinema with us tonight? - ¿_Vas/va/vais/van_ a ir al cine con nosotros esta noche?

2. Will you make something to eat tonight? - ¿_Harás_ algo de comer esta noche?

3. Are you going to go to the new restaurant in the Gothic Quarter? - ¿_Vas/va/vais/ van_ a ir al nuevo restaurante del barrio Gótico?

4. They will travel with me - Ellas _van_ a viajar conmigo

5. You will be allowed to go play when we all finish our meal - _Podrás/podréis/ podrán_ ir a jugar cuando terminemos de comer

6. I will talk with the receptionist - Yo _hablaré_ con la recepcionista

7. You will understand Latin culture when you're there - _Comprenderás_ la cultura latina cuando estés allí

8. She will live in Venezuela for some time - Ella _vivirá_ en Venezuela por algún tiempo

9. He will see his mistake someday - Él _verá_ su error algún día

10. We are going to get married in three months - _Vamos_ a casarnos en tres meses

11. We will be good guests: we will not make a lot of noise at night - _Seremos_ buenos huéspedes: no haremos mucho ruido por la noche

12. Will you be fine in this room? - ¿_Estaréis/Estarán_ bien en esta habitación?

13. I will go to walk for a while - _Iré/Voy_ a caminar un rato

14. I will climb that mountain today - _Voy_ a escalar esa montaña hoy

15. Do you think your boss will read my CV? - ¿Crees que tu jefe *leerá* mi currículum?

16. We will not find the hotel without the address - No *encontraremos* el hotel si no tenemos la dirección

17. Will they know how to get here? - ¿Ellos *sabrán* cómo llegar hasta aquí?

18. I will give you a clue - Te *daré* una pista

19. I will tell you everything when we're alone - Te *diré* todo cuando estemos solos

20. I will study Economics; she will study Law - Yo *voy* a estudiar Economía; ella *va* a estudiar Derecho

Chapter 14

1.

Hello, Marta. How are you? - *Hola*, Marta. ¿Cómo *estás*?

I'm very well, Lucas. I'm going to class. How are you? - Estoy muy *bien*, Lucas. Estoy yendo a clase. ¿*Cómo* estás *tú*?

I could be better, actually. I have a Spanish test and I don't think I'm ready - Realmente, podría *estar mejor*. Tengo un examen de español y creo que no estoy listo.

Everything will be fine! Good luck! - ¡Todo irá bien! ¡Mucha *suerte*!

OK, see you soon - Vale, nos *vemos* luego.

Bye! - ¡*Chau*!

2.

Good morning, professor. How are you? - *Buen día*, profesor. ¿Cómo *está*?

I'm very well, thank you. How are you? - Estoy muy *bien*, gracias. ¿*Cómo* está *usted*?

I am fine... a little worried about the test - Estoy *bien*... un poco preocupado por el examen

You are a good student, Mr García. You'll be fine - *Usted* es un buen estudiante, señor García. Estará *bien*.

I hope so! Thank you very much, sir - ¡Eso espero! *Muchas* gracias, señor

You're welcome - *No* hay de qué

Chapter 15

Complete the following informal conversation:

Hello, my name is Samuel, what's your name? - Hola, me *llamo* Samuel, ¿cómo *te* llamas tú?

My name is Patricia, but they call me Pato - Mi *nombre* es Patricia, pero me *dicen* Pato

It's a pleasure to meet you, Pato. So... what do you do? - Un gusto conocerte, Pato. Entonces... ¿*a* qué *te* dedicas?

I am a writer, and you? - Yo *soy* escritora, ¿y tú?

I am a student. I study Architecture - Yo soy estudiante. *Estudio* Arquitectura

Where do you study? - ¿*Dónde* estudias?

At the University of Barcelona, but I'm not from here, I was born in Valencia - En la Universidad de Barcelona, pero no soy de aquí, *nací* en Valencia

Oh, you came here to study. Did you come alone? - Oh, has venido para *estudiar*. ¿Has venido solo?

No, I came with my brother - No, vine con mi *hermano*

Chapter 16

1. This needs more salt - Esto necesita más *sal*

2. Did you bring milk? - ¿Has traído *leche*?

3. Where is the police station? - ¿_Dónde_ está la estación de policía?

4. Can we drink the tap water? - ¿Podemos beber el _agua_ del grifo?

5. I want a black coffee, please - Un _café_ negro, por favor

6. Could you hand me the menu? - ¿Podrías alcanzarme el _menú_?

7. How much is the beer? - ¿_Cuánto_ cuesta la _cerveza_?

8. How much are these trousers? - ¿Cuánto _cuestan_ estos pantalones?

9. Do you have your boarding pass? - ¿Tiene su _tarjeta_ de embarque?

10. How can I get to the university - ¿Cómo _puedo_ llegar a la universidad?

11. Where is your luggage? - ¿Dónde está su _equipaje_?

12. Do you have tomatoes? - ¿_Tiene/tienes_ tomates?

13. How much are the carrots? - ¿_Cuánto_ están las zanahorias?

14. I will lose my flight! - ¡Perderé mi _vuelo_!

15. Where is the camera? - ¿_Dónde_ está la _cámara_ de fotos?

16. Go north - Vaya _hacia_ el norte

17. The fish is very good - El pescado está _muy_ rico

18. The check, please - La cuenta, por _favor_

Part 2: Mastering Spanish Words

Increase Your Vocabulary with Over 3000 Spanish Words in Context

Introduction

How many words do we use when we speak?

According to some publications, while a two-year old baby uses around two hundred words, a beginner in any language needs around two thousand to communicate. And an expert user can employ up to forty thousand!

But knowing words and their meanings is hardly enough.

If you want to learn Spanish to actually use it, be it for travelling, working or studying, you need to really *master* your vocabulary: you need to know synonyms, you need to know which prepositions are used next to which verbs and how words change their meaning in different contexts.

Do you want an example? Look at the Spanish word *sal*, which is both a noun (*salt*) and the imperative form of verb *salir* (*to go out*). That is, the word *salt* changes its meaning completely in sentences such as "¡Sal de aquí!" ("Get out of here!") and "Pásame la sal" ("Hand me the salt").

In this book we offer a comprehensive list of the 3.000 most frequent words of the Spanish language, according to the Real Academia Española, Spain's official royal institution dedicated to the Spanish language.

We did not just include the words and their meanings, but also eventual indications for you to understand the use of the word, since translations are otherwise incomplete. For example, we indicate if it's a masculine or feminine word, if it's a plural word and if it belongs to a verbal tense that does not translate literally into English (such as the subjunctive mode or the imperfect past tense). Additionally, we indicate if the word has more than one meaning, as in the *salt* example, so you can avoid confusion.

And, of course, for each word we include a practical example, a sentence that in a few words tells a story and helps you understand how the word is used in the real Spanish-speaking world.

We encourage you to read these sentences out loud, to copy them, to use them in conversations until you can really grasp their use and meaning in context. By the time you're finished with this book, your vocabulary will be comparably better, richer and wider.

Ready to give it a go? Start right away! You'll feel the difference... and everyone else will notice too!

Chapter 1 – Words 1-300

1. de - of / from
Vengo de España - I come from Spain
2. la - the (feminine, singular)
La cama es grande - The bed is big
3. que - that, which
El recepcionista me dijo que la habitación está lista - The receptionist told me that the room is ready
4. el - the (masculine, singular)
El hotel está frente a la playa - The hotel is in front of the beach
5. en - in / on / at
María está en el parque - María is at the park
6. y - and
Esta ciudad es interesante y linda - This city is interesting and pretty
7. a - to
Esta noche iré a una fiesta - Tonight I will go to a party
8. los - the (masculine or mixed group, plural)
Los taxis son amarillos - The taxis are yellow
9. del - of the / from the
Vengo del centro de la ciudad - I come from the city center
10. las - the (feminine, plural)
Las flores son azules - The flowers are blue
11. un - a (masculine, singular)
Tengo un problema - I have a problem

12. por - for / because of

¡Hazlo por mí! - Do it for me!

13. con - with

Iré a Colombia con mi hermano - I will go to Colombia with my brother

14. no - no, not

No tengo hambre todavía - I'm not hungry yet

15. una - a (feminine, singular)

Quiero comer una empanada - I want to eat an empanada

16. su - his / her / their (singular object)

Marcos ama a su perro - Marco loves his dog

17. para - for / to

Este regalo es para mi madre - This present is for my mother

18. es - is

Pedro es mi primo - Pedro is my cousin

19. al - to the

¿Vamos al parque? - Should we go to the park?

20. lo - the (neutral)

Lo mejor del viaje fue la comida - The best part of the trip was the food

21. cómo - how

¿Cómo estás? - How are you?

22. más - more / plus

¿Quieres más sal? - Do you want more salt?

23. o - or

¿Quieres cerveza o vino? - Do you want beer or wine?

24. pero - but

Quiero comprarlo, pero no tengo efectivo - I want to buy it, but I don't have any cash

25. sus - his / her/ their (plural object)

Marcos ama a sus perros - Marco loves his dogs

26. le - him / her

Le compré un regalo - I bought her a present

27. ha - has (auxiliary)
Laura ha perdido su vuelo - Laura has lost her flight
28. me - me
Mi madre me prestó su coche - My mother lent me her car
29. si - if
Si salimos ahora, llegaremos a tiempo - If we leave now, we'll get there on time
30. sin - without
Quiero una bebida sin alcohol - I want a drink without alcohol
31. sobre - about / above / on top of
Estoy leyendo un libro sobre esta ciudad - I'm reading a book about this city
32. este - this (masculine)
Este es mi coche - This is my car
33. ya - now / already / yet
¿Ya has ido al banco? - Have you gone to the bank yet?
34. entre - between / among
La tienda está entre el casino y el hotel - The store is between the casino and the hotel
35. cuándo - when
¿Cuándo sale el barco? - When is the boat leaving?
36. todo - all / everything
¡Ya está todo listo! - Everything is ready!
37. esta - this (feminine)
Esta es mi cama - This is my bed
38. ser - to be
Quiero ser abogada - I want to be a lawyer

39. son - they are
Mis padres son mexicanos - My parents are Mexican
40. dos - two
Tengo dos hijos - I have two children
41. también - also / too / as well
Yo también estoy cansado - I am also tired

42. fue - was

Mi abuela fue una importante arquitecta - My grandmother was an important architect

43. había - there was / there were

Había mucha gente en la playa - There were a lot of people at the beach

44. era - he was / she was / it was

El hotel era muy bueno - The hotel was very good

45. muy - very

Juana es muy alta - Juana is very tall

46. años - years

Tengo veinticinco años - I am twenty-five years old

47. hasta - until

Estaré aquí hasta el sábado - I will be here until Saturday

48. desde - from

He venido en bus desde Chile - I have come by bus from Chile

49. está - is

El perro está durmiendo - The dog is sleeping

50. mi - my

Mi familia vive en Estados Unidos - My family lives in the US

51. porque - because

Llegué tarde porque había mucho tránsito - I was late because there was a lot of traffic

52. qué - what

¿Qué quieres hacer hoy? - What do you want to do today?

53. solo - only / alone / just

Hoy solo quiero descansar - Today I just want to rest

54. han - they have (auxiliary)

Mis amigos han salido a comer - My friends have gone out to eat

55. yo - I

Yo soy cocinero - I am a cook

56. hay - there is / there are

Hay muchos restaurantes en esta zona - There are many restaurants in this area

57. *vez - time*
Hice surf una sola vez - I surfed only one time
58. *puede - he can / she can / it can*
El clima puede cambiar - The weather can change
59. *todos - all / everyone*
Todos vamos a ir a la reunión - We are all going to the meeting
60. *así - like this / like that/ this way*
¿Puedes bailar así? - Can you dance like this?
61. *nos - us*
Amanda nos envió un paquete - Amanda sent us a package
62. *ni - nor*
No tengo hambre ni sueño - I'm not hungry nor sleepy
63. *parte - a part of / some of the*
Parte del grupo se fue - A part of the group left
64. *tiene - he has / she has / it has*
Ese hombre tiene mucho dinero - That man has a lot of money
65. *él - he*
Él es Manuel - He's Manuel
66. *uno - one*
Uno de esos chicos es mi novio - One of those guys is my boyfriend
67. *dónde - where*
¿A dónde quieres ir ahora? - Where do you want to go now?
68. *bien - well / good*
Estoy bien, ¿y tú? - I am well, and you?
69. *tiempo - time / weather*
Tenemos algo de tiempo antes del vuelo - We have some time before the flight
70. *mismo - same (masculine)*
Siempre tenemos el mismo problema - We always have the same problem
80. *ese - that (masculine)*
Ese plato está muy rico - That dish is very good

81. ahora - now

¿Tienes que irte ahora? - Do you have to leave now?

82. cada - each

Hay un sándwich para cada uno de nosotros - There is a sandwich for each one of us

83. e - and (before i)

Clara e Inés son mis hermanas - Clara and Inés are my sisters

84. vida - life

En toda mi vida no vi un paisaje así - In my whole life I haven't seen such a view

85. otro - other / another / another one (masculine)

Quiero otro trago - I want another drink

86. después - after

Después del museo, podemos ir al mercado - After the museum, we can go to the market

87. te - you

¡Te amo! - I love you!

88. otros - others / other (plural)

¿Tienes otros planes? - Do you have other plans?

89. aunque - even though / even if

Quiero continuar, aunque estoy cansada - I want to continue, even if I'm tired

90. esa - that (feminine)

Esa es mi mochila - That is my backpack

91. eso - that (neutral)

¡Eso no es cierto! - That's not true!

92. hace - It's been / ago

Hace tres años vine de vacaciones - Three years ago I came on my holidays

93. otra - another / other / another one (feminine)

¿Hay otra carretera para llegar allí? - Is there another road to get there?

94. gobierno - government

El gobierno es muy activo - The government is very active

95. tan - so

Estoy tan cansado que dormiré una siesta - I am so tired that I will take a nap

96. durante - during

No enfermé durante el viaje - I didn't get sick during the trip

97. siempre - always

Siempre te recordaré - I will always remember you

98. día - day

¿Qué día es hoy? - What day is it today?

99. tanto - so much

¡Tengo tanto que hacer! - I have so much to do!

100. ella - she

Ella es mi esposa - She's my wife

101. tres - three

Estoy en Madrid hace tres días - I have been in Madrid for three days

102. sí - yes

Sí, quiero ir - Yes, I want to go

103. dijo - said

El camarero dijo que no hay sopa - The waiter said that there is no soup

104. sido - been

Javier ha sido un gran compañero de viaje - Javier has been a great travelling companion

105. gran - big (before noun)

¡Es una gran ciudad! - It's a big city!

106. país - country

Amo este país - I love this country

107. según - according to

Según el guía, debemos beber mucha agua - According to the guide, we have to drink a lot of water

108. menos - less

¡Hagan menos ruido, por favor! - Please, make less noise!

109. mundo - world

Quiero viajar por todo el mundo - I want to travel around the world

110. año - year

El año que viene, cumpliré treinta años - Next year, I'll turn thirty

111. antes - before

Antes de ir al cine, vayamos a la tienda - Before going to the cinema, let's go to the store

112. estado - state / status

En este estado, eso es ilegal - In this state, that's illegal

113. contra - against

Estoy contra las corridas de toros - I'm against bullfighting

114. sino - but

No lo haré por él, sino por mis amigos - I won't do it for him, but for my friends

115. forma - shape

¡Mira la forma de esa nube! - Look at the shape of that cloud!

116. caso - case

En este caso, es diferente - In this case, it's different

117. nada - nothing

No tengo nada mejor que hacer - I have nothing better to do

118. hacer - to do

¿Qué quieres hacer hoy? - What do you want to do today?

119. general - general

En general, mi español es muy bueno - In general, my Spanish is very good

120. estaba - I was / he was / she was / it was

No fui porque estaba cansado - I didn't go because I was tired

121. poco - a little / little

Tengo un poco de hambre - I'm a little hungry

122. estos - these

Estos son mis zapatos - These are my shoes

123. presidente - President

¡El presidente renunció! - The President quit!

124. mayor - bigger / older

Este es Rafael, mi hermano mayor - This is Rafael, my older brother

125. ante - before / in the face of

Ante esa situación, no supe qué hacer - In the face of that situation, I didn't know what to do

126. unos - some / a few (masculine)

¿Tienes unos minutos? - Do you have a few minutes?

127. les - them

Yo les di el libro - I gave them the book

128. algo - something

¡Tengo algo para ti! - I have something for you!

129. hacia - to / towards

Ahora debemos ir hacia el Este - Now we have to go towards the east

130. casa - house

Hemos alquilado una casa muy bonita - We have rented a very pretty house

131. ellos - they (masculine or mixed group)

Ellos son mis padres - They are my parents

132. ayer - yesterday

Ayer escalé esa montaña - Yesterday, I climbed that mountain

133. hecho - done / fact

¡Es un hecho! - It's a fact!

134. primera - first (feminine)

Es la primera vez que viajo sola - It's my first time travelling alone

135. mucho - a lot of (masculine)

Tengo mucho trabajo hoy - I have a lot of work today

136. mientras - while

Mientras tú te duchas, iré de compras - While you shower, I'll go shopping

137. además - also / other than

¿Qué debo comprar, además de tomates? - What should I buy, other than tomatoes?

138. quien - who / whoever

Este sandwich es para quien lo quiera - This sandwich is for whoever wants it

139. momento - moment

¡Espera un momento! - Wait a moment!

140. millones - millions

Laura dice millones de mentiras - Laura says millions of lies

141. esto - this (neutral)

Esto es nuevo - This is new

142. queso - cheese

Quiero un emparedado de queso - I want a cheese sandwich

143. hombre - man

Adrián es un hombre muy callado - Adrián is a very quiet man

144. están - they are

Mis hermanos están casados - My siblings are married

145. pues - well / since / then

¿No quieres venir? Pues no vengas - You don't want to come? Well, don't come

146. hoy - today

Hoy es mi cumpleaños - Today is my birthday

147. lugar - place

¡Amo este lugar! - I love this place!

148. nacional - national

¿Cuál es el plato nacional? - What's the national dish?

149. trabajo - work / job

Tengo que sacar fotos, es mi trabajo - I have to take pictures, it's my job

150. otras - others / other (feminine, plural)

Tengo otras cosas que hacer - I have other things to do

151. mejor - better / best
Lo mejor será que esperemos un taxi - It will be best for us to wait for a taxi

152. nuevo - new
Compré un cuaderno nuevo - I bought a new notebook

153. decir - to say
¿Quieres decir algo? - Do you want to say something?

154. algunos - some (masculine or mixed group)
Algunos turistas son muy maleducados - Some tourists are very rude

155. entonces - then / so
Entonces, ¿qué hacemos esta noche? - So, what do we do tonight?

156. todas - all / everyone (feminine, plural)
Todas mis amigas estudian Psicología - All my friends study Psychology

157. días - days
El clima fue bueno en los últimos días - The weather was good in the last few days

158. debe - has to / must
¡El show debe continuar! - Show must go on!

159. política - politics / policy
No entiendo la política de este país - I don't understand this country's politics

160. cómo - how
¿Cómo has estado? - How have you been?

161. casi - almost
Tengo casi veintiocho años - I'm almost 28 years old

162. toda - all (feminine)
Pasé toda la tarde leyendo - I spent the whole afternoon reading

163. tal - such
Nunca había visto tal ignorancia - I had never seen such ignorance

164. luego - later

¡Nos vemos luego! - See you later!

165. pasado - past

En el pasado, las cosas eran distintas - In the past, things were different

166. primer - first (before noun, masculine)

Hoy es el primer día de mi viaje - Today is the first day of my trip

167. medio - half (masculine)

El miércoles tengo medio día libre - On Wednesday I have half a day off

168. va - he goes / she goes / it goes

Marta va a bailar todos los viernes - Marta goes dancing every Friday

169. estas - these (feminine)

¿Estas zapatillas son tuyas? - Are these shoes yours?

170. sea - I am / he/she/it is (subjunctive)

Cuando sea grande, quiero ser piloto - When I'm older, I want to be a pilot

171. tenía - I/he/she/it had / used to have

Yo tenía un perro parecido a ese - I used to have a dog similar to that one

172. nunca - never

Nunca pensé que me enamoraría de ti - I never thought I'd fall in love with you

173. poder - can / to be able to / power

¡Vas a poder hacerlo! - You will be able to do it!

178. aquí - here

Estaré aquí cuando vuelvas - I will be here when you return

179. ver - to see

¿Puedes ver ese arcoiris? - Can you see that rainbow?

180. veces - times

Fui a España varias veces - I went to Spain many times

181. sin embargo - however

Tengo hambre; sin embargo, esperaré - I'm hungry; however, I'll wait

182. partido - game / match

Vamos a ver el partido a un bar - We're going to watch the game at a bar

183. personas - people

¿Cuántas personas duermen en la habitación? - How many people sleep in the room?

184. grupo - group

Hemos formado un lindo grupo de trabajo - We have formed a nice working group

185. cuenta - the check / the bill

La cuenta, por favor - The check, please

186. pueden - they can

No pueden escalar sin un guía - They can't climb without a guide

187. tienen - they have

Mis padres tienen un amigo en Costa Rica - My parents have a friend in Costa Rica

188. misma - same (feminine)

Mira, ¡tengo la misma mochila que tú! - Look, I have the same backpack as you!

189. nueva - new (feminine)

Esta es mi nueva mochila - This is my new backpack

190. cual - which / that

Su perro, el cual había estado perdido, regresó - His dog, which had been lost, returned

191. fueron - they were

Mis amigos fueron irresponsables anoche - My friends were irresponsible last night

192. mujer - woman

Tu hermana es una mujer muy atlética - Your sister is a very athletic woman

193. frente - in front of / front / facing
La tienda está frente al banco - The store is in front of the bank
194. tras - behind
¡Hay una cucaracha tras el refrigerador! - There is a cockroach behind the refrigerator!
195. cosas - things
Hay cosas que no entiendo - There are things that I don't understand
196. fin - end
Es el fin de nuestro viaje - It is the end of our trip
197. ciudad - city
Me gustan las ciudades grandes - I like big cities
198. he - I have (auxiliary)
He comprado lasaña - I have bought lasagna
199. social - social
Mi vida social es muy activa - My social life is very active
200. manera - way
¿Hay alguna manera de solucionar esto? - Is there any way to solve this?
201. tener - to have
Quiero tener una casa grande - I want to have a big house
202. sistema - system
Su sistema de gobierno es distinto al nuestro - Their government system is different from ours
203. será - he will be / she will be / it will be
Mi hija será cineasta - My daughter will be a filmmaker
204. historia - story / history
Esta historia tiene un final feliz - This story has a happy ending
205. muchos - a lot of / many
Tengo muchos amigos - I have a lot of friends
206. tipo - kind / type
¿Qué tipo de café es este? - What kind of coffee is this?
207. cuatro - four
Tengo cuatro hermanos - I have four brothers

208. dentro - inside / within
La botella de agua está dentro de mi mochila - The water bottle is inside my backpack

209. nuestro - our (masculine)
Nuestro padre es ingeniero - Our father is an engineer

210. punto - point / dot / period / stop
Es mi decisión... ¡y punto! - It's my decision ... period!

211. dice - he says / she says / it says
Ana dice que cocinará esta noche - Ana says she will cook tonight

212. ello - it
No te preocupes por ello - Do not worry about it

213. cualquier - any (before noun)
Podemos ir al cine cualquier día - We can go to the cinema any day

214. noche - night
Esta noche iremos a un bar - Tonight we will go to a bar

215. aún - yet / still
Aún no he recibido noticias - I have not received news yet

216. agua - water
¡No olviden llevar agua! - Don't forget to bring water!

217. parece - it seems / he seems / she seems
Parece que hoy será un día lluvioso - It seems that today will be a rainy day

218. haber - to exist / to be (only infinitive)
Va a haber muchos problemas - There are going to be many problems

219. situación - situation
Esta es una situación incómoda - This is an awkward situation

220. fuera - outside / out
Esto está fuera de nuestro presupuesto - This is out of our budget

221. bajo - under / underneath
Tus zapatillas están bajo la cama - Your shoes are under the bed

222. grandes - big (plural)

Tengo grandes planes para el futuro - I have big plans for the future

223. nuestra - our (feminine)

Esta es Helena, nuestra hija - This is Helena, our daughter

224. ejemplo - example

¿Podrías darme un ejemplo? - Could you give me an example?

225. de acuerdo - agree / in agreement / according to / alright

Estoy de acuerdo contigo - I agree with you

226. usted - you (formal)

¿Usted es el profesor González? - Are you Professor González?

227. estados - states

¿Cuántos estados hay en Estados Unidos? - How many states are there in the US?

228. hizo - he did / she did / it did

Mi padre hizo un pastel - My father made a cake

229. nadie - nobody / no one

Nadie sabe cómo llegar allí - Nobody knows how to get there

230. países - countries

¿Cuántos países visitarás? - How many countries will you visit?

231. horas - hours

Mañana viajaremos diez horas en bus - Tomorrow we will travel ten hours by bus

232. posible - possible

¿Es posible que tardemos tanto en llegar? - Is it possible that we take so long to get there?

233. tarde - late

Es tarde, me voy a dormir - It's late, I'm going to sleep

234. ley - law

¡Es la ley de la selva! - It is the law of the jungle!

235. importante - important

Tengo algo importante que decirte - I have something important to tell you

236. guerra - war
Este país no está en guerra - This country is not at war

237. desarrollo - development
La educación es fundamental para el desarrollo - Education is essential for development

238. proceso - process
El proceso de adaptación es largo - The adaptation process is long

239. realidad - reality
En la realidad, las cosas no son tan sencillas - In reality, things are not so simple

240. sentido - sense
En ese sentido, tienes razón - In that sense, you're right

241. lado - side
¿De qué lado estás? - What side are you on?

242. mí - me
¿Este regalo es para mí? - Is this gift for me?

243. tu - your
¿Me prestas tu cargador? - Could I borrow your charger?

244. cambio - change
Aquí tienes tu cambio - Here's your change

245. allí - there
Mi automóvil está por allí - My car is over there

246. mano - hand
¡Tu mano es muy grande! - Your hand is very big!

247. eran - they were
Mis abuelos eran franceses - My grandparents were French

248. estar - to be
Quiero estar en mi casa - I want to be at home

249. número - number
¿Cuál es tu número de teléfono? - What's your phone number?

250. sociedad - society
Esta es una sociedad muy compleja - This is a very complex society

251. unas - some (feminine)

¿Tienes hambre? Tengo unas ricas manzanas - Are you hungry? I have some delicious apples

252. centro - center / downtown

Vamos caminando al centro - Let's walk downtown

253. padre - father

Mi padre y yo somos muy buenos amigos - My father and I are really good friends

254. gente - people

Hay gente muy interesante en este hostel - There are very interesting people in this hostel

255. final - final / end / ending

El final de la película me pareció bueno - I thought the ending of the movie was good

256. relación - relation / relationship

Estoy en una relación desde hace cuatro años - I have been in a relationship for four years

257. cuerpo - body

Mi cuerpo está cansado después de la caminata de ayer - My body is tired after yesterday's walk

258. obra - play / work / site

Vimos una obra de teatro maravillosa - We saw a wonderful play

259. incluso - even

Es una bella ciudad, incluso cuando llueve - It's a beautiful city, even when it rains

260. a través - through

El sonido pasa a través de las paredes - The sound goes through the walls

261. último - last

Es mi último día de vacaciones - It is the last day of my holidays

262. madre - mother

Mi madre es médica - My mother is a doctor

263. mis - my (plural)

Mis padres viven en España - My parents live in Spain

264. modo - mode / way

¡De ningún modo! - No way!

265. problemas - problems

No tendremos problemas para llegar - We won't have problems to get there

266. cinco - five

Vivo aquí desde hace cinco años - I've lived here for five years

267. hombres - men

Este es el baño de hombres - This is the men's toilet

268. información - information

¿Dónde hay una oficina de información? - Where is there an information office?

269. ojos - eyes

¿Tus ojos son verdes? - Are your eyes green?

270. muerte - death

La muerte del poeta fue muy triste - The poet's death was very sad

271. nombre - name

¿Cómo es tu nombre? - What's your name?

272. algunas - some (feminine)

Algunas habitaciones tienen aire acondicionado - Some rooms have air conditioning

273. público - public / audience

El público ama el drama - The audience loves drama

274. mujeres - women

Esta habitación es solo para mujeres - This room is for women only

275. siglo - century

Este lugar se habitó durante el siglo pasado - This place was inhabited during the last century

276. todavía - still

¿Todavía tienes el mapa? - Do you still have the map?

277. meses - months
¿Por cuántos meses viajarás? - For how many months will you travel?

278. mañana - morning / tomorrow
Nos vemos mañana por la mañana - See you tomorrow morning

279. esos - those (masculine)
Esos libros son muy buenos - Those books are very good

280 - nosotros - we / us
Nosotros vivimos en Canadá - We live in Canada

281. hora - time / hour
¿Qué hora es? - What time is it?

282. muchas - many / a lot of (feminine)
Tengo muchas dudas - I have many doubts

283. pueblo - people / town
Este es un pueblo tranquilo - This is a quiet town

284. alguna - some (feminine)
¿Tienen alguna fruta? - Do you have any fruit?

285. dar - to give
Mi madre me va a dar su coche - My mother will give me her car

286. problema - problem
Tenemos un pequeño problema - We have a small problem

287. da - he gives / she gives / it gives
Mi abuela me da comida - My grandmother gives me food

288. tú - you (informal)
¿Tú tienes el sacacorchos? - Do you have the corkscrew?

289. derecho - right / straight
Tengo el derecho de saberlo - I have the right to know

290. verdad - truth
¿Esa es la verdad? - Is that the truth?

291. unidos - together / united
Mi padre y yo estamos muy unidos - My father and I are very close

292. podría - I could / he could / she could / it could (conditional)

Este podría ser mi mejor viaje - This could be my best trip

293. sería - I would be / he would be / she would be / it would be

Sería peligroso ir sin un guía - It would be dangerous to go without a guide

294. junto - next to / together with

Quiero sentarme junto a ti - I want to sit next to you

295. cabeza - head

¡Me golpeé la cabeza! - I hit my head!

296. aquel - that (masculine)

Aquel restaurante es muy bueno - That restaurant is very good

297. en cuanto - as soon as / regarding

En cuanto llegue Andrea, partiremos - As soon as Andrea arrives, we will depart

298. tierra - earth / ground / soil / dirt

Tengo tierra en mis zapatos - There's dirt in my shoes

299. equipo - team

Mi equipo perdió un partido importante - My team lost an important game

300. segundo - second

Dame un segundo, por favor - Give me a second please

Chapter 2 – Words 301-600

301. director - director

Mi hermano es director de una empresa - My brother is the director of a company

302. dicho - said / told

Le he dicho a todos que es una buena película - I've told everyone it's a good movie

303. cierto - true / a certain

¡No puede ser cierto! - It can't be true!

304. casos - cases / situations

En algunos casos, es mejor estar callado - In some cases, it is better to be silent

305. manos - hands

¡Arriba las manos! - Hands up!

306. nivel - level

Es un restaurante de muy alto nivel - It is a very high level restaurant

307. podía - I could / he could / she could / it could (past)

Antes de mi lesión, podía correr muy rápido - Before my injury, I could run very fast

308. familia - family

Mi familia es muy grande - My family is very large

309. largo - long (masculine)

¡Este libro es demasiado largo! - This book is too long!

310. partir - to split / to depart

¿Puedes partir esa galleta en dos? - Can you split that biscuit in two?

311. falta - it misses / it lacks / how long until...

¿Cuánto falta para que salga el avión? - How long until the plane takes off?

312. llegar - to arrive

¡Quiero llegar a Ecuador! - I want to get to Ecuador!

313. propio - of one's own / own (masculine)

Mi propio hijo me traicionó - My own son betrayed me

314. ministro - minister

Falleció el ministro de Economía - The Minister of Economy passed away

315. cosa - thing

¿Qué es esa cosa? - What is that thing?

316. primero - first (masculine)

Mi hermano fue el primero en graduarse en mi familia - My brother was the first one to graduate in my family

317. seguridad - security

La seguridad del hostel es bastante buena - The hostel's security is pretty good

318. hemos - we have (auxiliary)

Hemos ido dos veces al museo - We have gone to the museum twice

319. mal - bad / wrong

Me siento mal - I feel bad

320. trata - he/she/it tries to (indicative) / you try to (imperative)

Trata de estudiar más - Try to study harder

321. algún - some / any (masculine, before noun)

Algún día me lo agradecerás - Some day you will thank me

322. tuvo - he had / she had / it had

Marcela tuvo un problema al cruzar la frontera - Marcela had a problem while crossing the border

323. respeto - respect

Tengo mucho respeto por Matilde - I have a lot of respect for Matilde

324. semana - week

Me quedaré en esta ciudad toda la semana - I will stay in this city all week

325. varios - various / several / some

Tengo varios amigos en España - I have several friends in Spain

326. real - real

¿Esto es real? - Is this real?

327. sé - I know

¡Ya sé qué podemos cocinar! - I know what we can cook!

328. voz - voice

Esta cantante tiene una voz fenomenal - This singer has a phenomenal voice

329. paso - step / passage

Debemos ir paso a paso - We have to go step by step

330. señor - sir / mister

Señor, ¿qué hora es? - Sir, what time is it?

331. mil - a thousand

Tengo como mil llamadas perdidas - I have about a thousand missed calls

332. quienes - who (plural)

Quienes quieran pizza pueden tomar una porción - Those who want pizza can grab a slice

333. proyecto - project

Estoy trabajando en un nuevo proyecto - I'm working on a new project

334. mercado - market

¿Quieres ir al mercado conmigo? - Do you want to go to the market with me?

335. mayoría - most of / majority

La mayoría de la población es bilingüe - The majority of the population is bilingual

334. luz - light
¿Puedes encender la luz? - Can you turn on the light?

335. claro - light / clear
El problema es muy claro - The problem is very clear

336. iba - I/he/she/it used to go / went
Cuando era pequeña, iba a la playa todos los veranos - When I was little, I used to go to the beach every summer

337. orden - order
Hay que poner esta casa en orden - We have to put this house in order

338. español - Spanish
¿Hablas español? - Do you speak Spanish?

339. buena - good (feminine)
Esta tarta está muy buena - This cake is very good

340. quiere - he wants / she wants / it wants
¿Quién quiere una porción? - Who wants a portion?

341. aquella - that (feminine)
Aquella tienda tiene unos helados riquísimos - That store has some delicious ice cream

342. programa - program / show
Lo vi en un programa de televisión - I saw it on a television show

343. palabras - words
No hay palabras para describir lo que siento - There are no words to describe what I feel

344. internacional - international
Iremos a un festival internacional de cine - We will go to an international film festival

345. van - they go
Mis hijos van a la escuela todos los días - My children go to school every day

346. esas - those (feminine)
Esas botas están muy sucias - Those boots are very dirty

347. segunda - second (feminine)

Es mi segunda vez en Sudamérica - It's my second time in South America

348. empresa - enterprise / company

Trabajo en una gran empresa - I work in a big company

349. puesto - position / post / place / stall

Me ofrecieron un puesto mejor - I was offered a better position

350. ahí - there

¿Estás ahí? - Are you there?

351. propia - of one's own / own (feminine)

Algún día tendré mi propia casa - Someday I will have my own house

352. libro - book

Tengo ganas de leer un libro - I feel like reading a book

353. igual - same / equal / too

Mi camiseta es igual que la tuya - My shirt is the same as yours

354. político - politic / political

Este no es un asunto político - This is not a political issue

355. persona - person

Eres una persona muy inteligente - You are a very smart person

356. últimos - last (masculine, plural)

Estos son los últimos días de mi viaje - These are the last days of my trip

357. ellas - they (feminine)

Ellas son mis primas - They are my cousins

358. total - total

Dividiremos el total de las ganancias entre nosotros cuatro - We will split the total earnings among the four of us

359. creo - I think / I believe

Creo que deberíamos esperar a que deje de llover - I think we should wait until it stops raining

360. tengo - I have

Tengo un pequeño problema - I have a small problem

361. española - *Spanish (feminine)*
Amo la tortilla española - I love Spanish omelette

362. condiciones - *conditions*
¿Cómo son las condiciones climáticas? - What are the weather conditions?

363. fuerza - *strength*
No tengo mucha fuerza física - I don't have much physical strength

364. único - *unique / only (masculine)*
El martes es mi único día libre - Tuesday is my only day off

365. acción - *action*
¿Están listos para la acción? - Are you ready for action?

366. amor - *love*
Vine a España para encontrar el amor - I came to Spain to find love

367. policía - *police*
¿Crees que deberíamos llamar a la policía? - Do you think we should call the police?

368. puerta - *door*
Abre la puerta - Open the door

369. pesar - *to weight*
Si sigo comiendo así, voy a pesar mucho más cuando regrese a casa - If I keep on eating like this, I will weigh much more when I return home

370. zona - *zone / area*
¿Hay algún supermercado en esta zona? - Is there a supermarket in this area?

371. sabe - *he knows / she knows / it knows*
Mi madre sabe todo - My mother knows everything

372. calle - *street*
Sobre esta calle hay una heladería - There is an ice cream shop on this street

373. *interior - interior / inside / within*
En el interior de mi mochila hay una botella de agua - Inside my backpack there is a bottle of water

374. *tampoco - neither / nor*
No tengo dinero, ni tampoco tiempo para ir al cine - I don't have the money nor the time to go to the movies

375. *música - music*
¿Escuchamos música? - Should we go listen to some music?

376. *ningún - no / none*
No tengo ningún problema con él - I have no problem with him

377. *vista - view*
Desde mi ventana, la vista es muy bella - From my window, the view is very beautiful

378. *campo - countryside / field*
Mañana vamos a pasar el día al campo - Tomorrow we will spend the day in the countryside

379. *buen - good (before noun)*
Pasamos un buen día - We had a good day

380. *hubiera - I/he/she/it would have*
Hubiera sido mejor si no hubiera llovido tanto - It would have been better if it hadn't rained so much

381. *saber - to know*
Quiero saber todo sobre esta cultura - I want to know everything about this culture

382. *obras - works / plays / construction sites*
Hay muchas obras en construcción en este barrio - There are many construction sites in this neighborhood

383. *razón - reason*
¿Por qué razón sucede esto? - What's the reason for this?

384. *niños - children / kids*
Es un lugar ideal para los niños - It is an ideal place for children

385. *presencia - presence*
Tu presencia es realmente relajante - Your presence is really soothing

386. tema - subject / theme / topic

No hay muchos libros sobre este tema - There are not many books on this topic

387. dinero - money

No tengo más dinero - I have no more money

388. servicio - service

El servicio es realmente excelente - The service is really excellent

389. hijo - son

Tengo un hijo de tres años - I have a three year old son

390. última - last (feminine)

Es mi última parada antes de volver a casa - It is my last stop before returning home

391. ciento - a hundred and...

Tengo ciento cincuenta pesos - I have a hundred and fifty pesos

392. estoy - I am

Estoy aburrida - I am bored

393. hablar - to talk / to speak

¿Puedes hablar en español? - Can you speak Spanish?

394. dio - he gave / she gave / it gave

Mi novio me dio un regalo - My boyfriend gave me a present

395. minutos - minutes

Nuestro taxi llegará en cinco minutos - Our taxi will arrive in five minutes

396. producción - production

Carlos trabaja en la producción de soja - Carlos works in soy production

397. camino - road

¡No salgas del camino! - Don't get out of the way!

398. seis - six

Ella ha escrito seis libros - She has written six books

399. quién - who

Who are you? - ¿Quién eres tú?

400. fondo - back / background

Sentémonos en el fondo - Let's seat in the back

401. dirección - address / direction
¿Conoces la dirección del hotel? - Do you know the address of the hotel?

402. papel - paper / role
Necesito un papel y un lápiz - I need a piece of paper and a pencil

403. demás - other / the rest / the others
Juan y Laura van al parque; los demás van al museo - Juan and Laura are going to the park; the rest are going to the museum

404. idea - idea
Tengo una idea brillante - I have a brilliant idea

405. especial - special
Este es un momento especial - This is a special moment

406. diferentes - different (plural)
Mis ambiciones son diferentes de las tuyas - My ambitions are different from yours

407. dado - given
Le hemos dado un regalo a Celeste - We have given Celeste a gift

408. base - base / foundation / basis
La comunicación es la base de una buena relación - Communication is the basis of a good relationship

409. capital - capital
Llegaremos a la capital en cinco horas - We will arrive in the capital in five hours

410. ambos - both
¿Mis padres? Ambos son dentistas - My parents? Both of them are dentists

411. libertad - freedom / liberty
La libertad es un derecho humano - Freedom is a human right

412. relaciones - relationships / relations
He tenido relaciones buenas y relaciones malas - I've had good and bad relationships

413. espacio - space

Me gustaría ir al espacio - I would like to go to space

414. medios - media / means / mediums

Hay muchos medios de transporte - There are several means of transport

415. ir - to go

¿Quieres ir a pescar conmigo? - Do you want to go fishing with me?

416. actual - current

La situación actual no es peligrosa - The current situation is not dangerous

417. población - population

La población está disminuyendo - Population is decreasing

418. empresas - companies

La mayor parte de las empresas son estatales - Most of the companies belong to the State

419. estudio - study / studying

Debo concentrarme en el estudio - I must concentrate on studying

420. salud - health

Me gustaría trabajar en el sector de la salud - I would like to work in the health sector

421. servicios - services

Hay un área de servicios a menos de un kilómetro - There is a service area less than a kilometer away

422. haya - I/he/she/it have (subjunctive auxiliary)

Cuando haya comido, me sentiré mejor - When I have eaten, I will feel better

423. principio - beginning / principle / start

El principio de la novela es muy atrapante - The beginning of the novel is very captivating

424. siendo - being

Mis gafas están siendo reparadas - My glasses are being repaired

425. cultura - culture

Para comprender la cultura, debes hablar con la gente - To understand the culture, you must talk to the people

426. anterior - previous

En nuestro viaje anterior, llovió todo el tiempo - On our previous trip, it rained all the time

427. alto - tall (masculine)

Ese árbol es muy alto - That tree is very tall

428. media - a half of / half a (feminine)

¿Me das media manzana? - Can you give me half an apple?

429. mediante - through / by means of

Contacté con ellos mediante su línea de asistencia - I contacted them through their helpline

430. primeros - first (masculine, plural)

Seremos los primeros en llegar - We will be the first ones to arrive

431. arte - art

Me gusta mucho el arte precolombino - I really like pre-Columbian art

432. paz - peace

Este paisaje me da mucha paz - This landscape gives me a lot of peace

433. sector - sector

Este sector de la ciudad es muy tranquilo - This sector of the city is very quiet

434. imagen - picture / image

He visto una imagen impactante en las noticias - I've seen a shocking image in the news

435. medida - measure / measurement / action

Debemos tomar una medida urgente - We must take urgent action

436. deben - they must/should / you must/should (plural)

Mis padres deben viajar más - My parents should travel more

437. datos - data

El conocimiento real se basa en los datos - Real knowledge is based on data

438. consejo - advise / council

Mi madre me dio un consejo - My mother gave me some advice

439. personal - personal

Tuve un problema personal - I had a personal problem

440. interés - interest

No tengo interés en la historia - I have no interest in history

441. julio - July

Estoy viajando desde julio - I have been traveling since July

442. grupos - groups

Subiremos a la cima en tres grupos - We will climb to the top in three groups

443. miembros - members

Este salón es solo para miembros del club - This room is only for club members

444. ninguna - no / none (feminine)

No me queda ninguna duda - I have no doubt left

445. existe - it exists

¡El Chupacabras no existe! - The Chupacabras does not exist!

446. cara - face

Tu cara está roja - Your face is red

447. edad - age

¿Cuál es tu edad? - How old are you?

448. movimiento - movement

Me gusta observar el movimiento de las olas - I like to watch the movement of the waves

449. visto - seen

¿Has visto esta película? - Have you seen this movie?

450. llegó - he arrived / she arrived / it arrived

¡Llegó Jazmín! - Jazmín has arrived!

451. puntos - points / dots
Debes abrir el envase por la línea de puntos - You should cut the package open along the dotted line

452. actividad - activity
Pensemos en alguna actividad para los niños - Let's think of an activity for the kids

453. bueno - good (after noun)
Tu esposo es un cocinero muy bueno - Your husband is a very good cook

454. uso - use / I use
El uso de sombreros no es común en esta región - The use of hats is not common in this region

455. niño - child / kid (masculine) / boy
Ese niño canta muy bien - That kid sings very well

456. difícil - difficult / hard
El español no es tan difícil - Spanish is not that difficult

457. joven - young
Tu madre es muy joven - Your mother is very young

458. futuro - future
En el futuro, estaremos preparados - In the future, we will be prepared

459. aquellos - those (masculine)
Aquellos árboles son cerezos - Those are cherry trees

460. mes - month
Viajaré por un mes - I will travel for a month

461. pronto - soon
Gonzalo llegará pronto - Gonzalo will get here soon

462. soy - I am
Soy Manuela Díaz, tengo una reserva - I am Manuela Díaz, I have a reservation

463. hacía - I did / he did / she did / it did
Mientras mi madre cocinaba, mi padre hacía las compras - While my mother cooked, my father did the shopping

464. nuevos - new (masculine, plural)

¡Mira mis zapatos nuevos! - Look at my new shoes!

465. nuestros - our (masculine, plural)

Creo que esos son nuestros platos - I think those are our plates

466. estaban - they were / you (ustedes) were

Mis amigas se fueron a dormir porque estaban cansadas - My friends went to sleep because they were tired

467. posibilidad - possibility

Es una posibilidad que hay que tener en cuenta - It is a possibility that must be taken into account

468. sigue - you continue (imperative) / he continues / she continues / it continues

Sigue caminando, pronto llegaremos - Continue walking, we will arrive soon

469. cerca - close / near

Estamos cerca del río - We are near the river

470. resultados - results

Llegaron los resultados de mi examen de español - The results of my Spanish test have arrived

471. educación - education

La educación es fundamental para el desarrollo - Education is essential for development

472. atención - attention

Presta atención - Pay attention

473. capacidad - capacity / ability

No tengo la capacidad de surfear - I don't have the ability to surf

474. efecto - effect

Esta ciudad tiene un efecto mágico sobre la gente - This city has a magical effect on people

475. necesario - necessary

Tu sarcasmo no es necesario - Your sarcasm is not necessary

476. valor - value

El valor de esa obra de arte es incalculable - The value of that piece of art is incalculable

476. aire - air
Amo el aire fresco en mi rostro - I love the fresh air on my face
477. investigación - research / investigation
Me dedico a la investigación - I work on research
478. siguiente - next / following
El siguiente, por favor - Next, please
479. figura - figure / shape
Jorge fue una figura paterna para mí - Jorge was a father figure to me
480. central - central
¿Dónde está la estación central? - Where is the central station?
481. comunidad - community
Esta es una comunidad muy alegre - This is a very cheerful community
482. necesidad - need / necessity
Tengo la necesidad de trabajar - I have the need to work
483. serie - series
Estoy viendo una serie muy interesante - I'm watching a very interesting series
484. organización - organization
La organización de la empresa es un desastre - The organization of the company is a disaster
485. nuevas - new (feminine, plural)
Estas son mis nuevas botas - These are my new boots
486. calidad - quality
Prefiero calidad antes que cantidad - I prefer quality over quantity
487. economía - Economy
La economía de mi país es un desastre - The economy of my country is a disaster
488. carácter - character / nature
Ana tiene un carácter muy fuerte - Ana has a very strong carácter

489. jefe - boss (masculine)
Ramiro es mi jefe - Ramiro is my boss
490. estamos - we are
No estamos cansados todavía - We are not tired yet
491. prensa - press
Deberíamos hablar con la prensa - We should talk to the press
492. control - control
Tengo el control - I'm in control
493. sociales - social / social (plural)
Oscar y Lucila son muy sociales - Oscar and Lucila are very social
494. universidad – university / college
Este es mi último año en la universidad - This is my last year in college
495. militar - military
Mi novio es militar - My boyfriend is in the military
496. al cabo de - after
Al cabo de dos días, decidimos regresar - After two days, we decided to go back
497. diez - ten
Solo tengo diez días de vacaciones - I only have ten days of vacation
498. fuerzas - strength (plural)
Ya no tengo fuerzas para seguir - I no longer have the strength to continue
499. congreso - Congress
La ley debe aprobarse en el congreso - The law must be passed in the Congress
500. hijos - children
¿Cuántos hijos tienes? - How many children do you have?
501. justicia - justice
No se puede hacer justicia por mano propia - You can't do justice on your own

502. mundial - world / worldwide

La contaminación es un problema a nivel mundial - Pollution is a worldwide problem

503. juego - game

¿Quieren jugar un juego de mesa? - Do you want to play a board game?

504. económica - economic

Hay una crisis económica en este momento - There is an economic crisis right now

505. políticos - politicians / political (plural)

No discutamos asuntos políticos - Let's not discuss political issues

506. duda - doubt

Tengo una duda - I have a doubt

507. recursos - resources

Esta universidad tiene muchos recursos - This university has many resources

508. pública - public (feminine)

Yo estudio en la universidad pública - I study in the public university

509. crisis - crisis

Dicen que hay una crisis migratoria global - They say there is a global migration crisis

510. próximo - next

¡Nos vemos el próximo jueves! - See you next Thursday!

511. tenemos - we have

No tenemos leche - We don't have any milk

512. decisión - decision

Debemos tomar una decisión - We have to make a decision

513. varias - various / several / many (feminine)

Tenemos varias opciones para la cena - We have several options for dinner

514. popular - popular

Originalmente, este guiso era una comida popular - Originally, this stew was a popular dish

515. tenido - had (participle)

¿Has tenido oportunidad de leer mi correo electrónico? - Have you had a chance to read my email?

516. apenas - barely

Apenas bajamos del avión, comenzaron nuestras aventuras - As soon as we got off the plane, our adventures began

517. época - time / epoch / age / era

Era otra época y las cosas eran distintas - It was another time and things were different

518. banco - bench / bank

Sentémonos un rato en ese banco - Let's sit on that bench for a while

518. presente - present

Debes vivir en el presente - You must live in the present

519. menor - minor / little / younger / underage

Ella es mi hermana menor, Carolina - She is my younger sister, Carolina

520. quiero - I want

Quiero pedir comida china - I want to order Chinese food

521. pasar - to pass / to go through

¿Puedo pasar? - Can I go through?

522. resultado - result / outcome

Estamos esperando el resultado de las elecciones - We are waiting for the result of the elections

523. televisión - television

Mi madre ama ver la televisión - My mother loves watching television

524. se encuentra - it's found / it's located / it is

¿Dónde se encuentra el museo de arte? - Where is the art museum?

525. gracias - thanks

Muchas gracias por tu ayuda - Thank you very much for your help

526. ministerio - ministry
Este es el Ministerio de Economía - This is the Ministry of Economy

527. conjunto - set / combination
Sucedió por un conjunto de causas - It happened for a combination of causes

528. defensa - defense
El abogado de la defensa era muy cordial - The defense lawyer was very cordial

529. alguien - someone / somebody
Alguien tocó el timbre - Someone rang the bell

530. queda - it remains / to have left / to be left
¿Cuánto tiempo nos queda? - How much time do we have left?

531. hacen - they do / you (ustedes) do
¿Qué hacen esta tarde? - What are you doing this afternoon?

532. pasa - he/she passes/goes through/ it happens / you go through (imperative)
¿Qué pasa aquí? - What's happening here?

533. resto - the rest
María y Juan salen, el resto nos quedamos - María and Juan are going out, the rest of us are staying in

534. causa - cause / reason
¿Cuál es la causa de este alboroto? - What is the cause of this uproar?

535. seguir - to follow
Te voy a seguir en Instagram - I will follow you on Instagram

536. allá - there
Mira eso, allá arriba, ¿qué es? - Look at that, up there, what is it?

537. palabra - word
No conozco esa palabra, ¿qué significa? - I don't know that word, what does it mean?

538. voy - I go
Voy al gimnasio todos los días - I go to the gym every day

539. cuya - whose (feminine)
Me está llamando mi amigo a cuya casa vamos a cenar - My friend whose house we are going to dinner is calling me

540. vamos - we go / let's go
¿Vamos a bailar esta noche? - Should we go dancing tonight?

541. mar - sea
Mira el mar, ¡está muy tranquilo! - Look at the sea, it's very calm!

542. estudios - studies
He terminado mis estudios hace un par de meses - I finished my studies a couple of months ago

543. derechos - rights / straight (plural)
Debes defender tus derechos - You must defend your rights

544. importancia - importance
Es un asunto sin importancia - It is a matter of great importance

545. cuales - which (plural)
Las reglas con las cuales jugamos son nuevas - The rules which we are using are new

546. contrario - contrary / opposite
Al contrario, creo que la comida estaba deliciosa - On the contrary, I think the food was delicious

547. fuerte - strong
Tu bebé es muy fuerte - Your baby is very strong

548. sol - sun
El sol es muy fuerte, debes usar loción - The sun is very strong, you must use lotion

549. jóvenes - young (plural)
Este lugar es muy popular entre los jóvenes - This place is very popular among young people

550. apoyo - support
Necesito todo tu apoyo - I need all your support

551. habría - there would be / it would be
Habría que pelar las papas - It would be necessary to peel the potatoes

552. *civil - civilian / civil*
Soy ingeniera civil - I am a civil engineer

553. *partidos - parties / matches / games*
Hay dos partidos políticos importantes - There are two major political parties

554. *libre - free*
No hay nada mejor que sentirse libre - There is nothing better than feeling free

555. *fuentes - sources / fountains*
¿Cuáles son tus fuentes? - What are your sources?

556. *administración - administration / management*
La administración del hotel solucionó el problema - The hotel management solved the issue

557. *común - common / normal / regular*
Es un problema común - It is a common problem

558. *dejar - to leave / to let*
Puedes dejar tu equipaje en el casillero - You can leave your luggage in the locker

559. *cine - cinema / movies*
Tengo muchas ganas de ir al cine - I really want to go to the movies

560. *salir - to go out*
Vamos a salir a escuchar flamenco - We will go out to listen to some flamenco music

561. *comunicación - communication*
Estoy estudiando Comunicación - I am studying Communication

562. *experiencia - experience*
Fue una experiencia inolvidable - It was an unforgettable experience

563. *demasiado - too much*
Creo que le puse demasiado orégano a la salsa - I think I put too much oregano in the sauce

564. *plan - plan*
¡Tengo un plan! - I have a plan!

565. respuesta - answer / response / reply

¿Cuál fue tu respuesta a su pregunta? - What was your answer to his question?

566. energía - energy

Julio tiene demasiada energía - Julio has too much energy

567. izquierda - left

Debemos doblar hacia la izquierda - We have to turn left

568. función - function

¿Cuál es la función de este botón? - What is the function of this button?

569. principal - main

Esta es la calle principal - This is the main street

570. superior - superior

El helado de esta tienda es superior a todos - The ice cream of this store is superior to all others

571. naturaleza - nature

Me gusta mucho la naturaleza - I really like nature

572. podemos - we can

¿Podemos ir al monumento después de comer? - Can we go to the monument after lunch?

573. unión - union

No fue un matrimonio, sino una unión civil - It was not a marriage, it was a civil union

574. especialmente - specially / especially

No quiero volver a casa, especialmente ahora que allí hace frío - I don't want to go home, especially now that it's cold over there

575. rey - king

Hay un rey, pero es una democracia - There is a king, but it is a democracy

576. domingo - Sunday

Nos vamos el domingo - We are leaving on Sunday

577. favor - favor

Necesito un favor - I need a favor

578. cantidad - quantity / amount

La cantidad no es tan importante como la calidad - The quantity is not as important as the quality

579. elecciones - elections

¿Cuándo son las elecciones? - When are the elections?

580. clase - class

¿A qué hora empieza la clase? - What time does the class start?

581. productos - products

En esta tienda venden productos locales - In this store they sell local products

582. españoles - Spanish (plural)

Mis primos son españoles - My cousins are Spanish

583. conocer - to know / to meet

¿Quieres conocer a mi esposa? - Would you like to meet my wife?

584. teatro - theatre

Hoy voy a ir al teatro - Today I will go to the theater

585. importantes - important (plural)

Tengo importantes planes para el próximo mes - I have important plans for next month

586. evitar - to avoid

Debemos evitar los embotellamientos - We must avoid traffic jams

587. color - color

¿Cuál es tu color preferido? - What is your favorite color?

588. actividades - activities

Hay muchas actividades de verano en la universidad - There are many summer activities at the university

589. mesa - table

La comida está en la mesa - Food is on the table

590. decía - I said / he said / she said / it said

Mi madre siempre me decía que debía ser más paciente - My mother used to tell me that I should be more patient

591. *cuyo - whose (masculine)*

Laura, cuyo novio es Miguel, no quiere venir - Laura, whose boyfriend is Miguel, doesn't want to come

592. *debido - due to*

Hay un desabastecimiento de comida debido al huracán - There is a shortage of food due to the hurricane

593. *alta - tall (feminine)*

Andrea es más alta que yo - Andrea is taller than me

594. *secretario - secretary (masculine)*

Él es Pedro, mi secretario - He is Pedro, my secretary

595. *objeto - object*

Ese es un objeto desafilado - That is a blunt object

596. *quizá - maybe / perhaps*

Quizá deberíamos volver al hotel antes de que comience la tormenta - Maybe we should go back to the hotel before the storm starts

597. *posición - position / location*

Estoy en una posición difícil - I am in a difficult position

598. *parecía - I seemed / he seemed / she seemed / it seemed*

Parecía ser una chica normal, pero resultó ser una estafadora - She seemed to be a normal girl, but she turned out to be a scammer

599. *natural - natural*

Él tiene un encanto natural - He has a natural charm

600. *elementos - elements*

¿Conoces todos los elementos de la tabla periódica? - Do you know all the elements of the periodic table?

Chapter 3 – Words 601-900

601. hubo - there was / there were
Hubo un problema con la reserva - There was a problem with the reservation

602. objetivo - goal / objective
Mi objetivo es aprender español - My goal is to learn Spanish

603. formas - shapes / ways
Hay varias formas de llegar al museo - There are several ways to get to the museum

604. única - unique / only (feminine)
Ella es la única persona en la que confío - She is the only person I trust

605. pueda - he/she/it can (subjunctive)
¿Hay alguien que pueda abrir este frasco? - Is there anyone who can open this jar?

606. origen - origin
¿Cuál es el origen de este mito? - What is the origin of this myth?

607. blanco - white (masculine)
Creo que me pondré mi sombrero blanco - I think I'll use my white hat

608. mismos - same (masculine, plural)
Siempre tenemos los mismos problemas - We always have the same problems

609. lleva - it takes / he takes / she takes

A veces, mi madre me lleva al trabajo - Sometimes my mother takes me to work

610. económico - economic (masculine)

Este es un problema económico, no político - This is an economic problem, not a political one

611. opinión - opinion

Quiero oír tu opinión - I want to hear your opinion

612. ayuda - help

Necesito ayuda para voltear la tortilla - I need help to flip the omelette

613. oficial - official

Ya es oficial: ¡nos casaremos! - It's official: we're getting married!

614. silencio - silence / quiet

Debemos permanecer en silencio - We must remain silent

615. buenos - good (masculine, plural)

Tus panqueques son muy buenos - Your pancakes are very good

616. pensar - to think / to believe

No sé qué pensar - I do not know what to think

617. república - republic

España no es una república, es una monarquía - Spain is not a republic, it's a monarchy

618. donde - where / wherever

Iré a donde yo quiera - I will go wherever I want

619. sangre - blood

Llevo la música en mi sangre - I carry music in my blood

620. encuentro - meeting / encounter

¡Qué encuentro más inesperado! - What an unexpected encounter!

621. ni siquiera - not even

No quiero comer nada, ni siquiera pastel - I don't want to eat anything, not even cake

622. autor - author

Matías es el autor del libro - Matías is the author of the book

623. reunión - meeting

Tengo una reunión de trabajo en cinco minutos - I have a work meeting in five minutes

624. haciendo - doing / making

¿Qué estás haciendo? - What are you doing?

625. suelo - soil / ground / floor

Me caí al suelo y me raspé la rodilla - I fell to the ground and scratched my knee

626. muestra - it/he/she shows / show / exhibit

Iremos a una muestra de arte - We will go to an art show

627. viejo - old (masculine)

Mi padre es muy viejo - My father is very old

628. encima - on top of / on

Dejé las llaves encima de la mesa - I left the keys on the table

629. resulta - it turns out

¡Resulta que era todo una estafa! - It turns out it was all a scam!

630. tomar - to take / to drink

Quiero tomar una foto - I want to take a picture

631. bastante - pretty / very

Estoy bastante cansado - I'm pretty tired

632. siete - seven

¡Son las siete! Debemos partir - It's seven o'clock! We must leave

633. lucha - fight / struggle

Vivir con bajos recursos es una lucha constante - Living with low incomes is a constant struggle

634. pudo - it could / he could / she could (past) / was able to

Benítez pudo ganar la pelea - Benítez was able to win the fight

635. amigos - friends (masculine)

Estos son mis amigos - These are my friends

636. línea - line

¿Puedes dibujar una línea recta? - Can you draw a straight line?

637. sur - south

Vamos a ir al sur de Argentina - We will go to the south of Argentina

638. pocos - little / few (masculine, plural)
Tengo solo unos pocos calcetines - I have only a few socks

639. medidas - measures
El gobierno tomó medidas drásticas - The government took drastic measures

640. norte - north
Hay una ciudad muy bella en el norte - There is a very beautiful city in the north

641. partes - parts
¿Sabes los nombres de las partes del cuerpo en español? - Do you know the names of body parts in Spanish?

642. iglesia - church
Hoy hemos ido a una iglesia muy bonita - Today we went to a very pretty church

643. tratamiento - treatment
Mi primo necesita tratamiento médico - My cousin needs medical treatment

644. existencia - existence
René Descartes no dudaba sobre su propia existencia - René Descartes did not doubt his own existence

645. cargo - charge / position
Tengo un cargo de mucha responsabilidad - I have a position of great responsibility

646. grande - big / large (after noun)
Tu tienda de campaña es muy grande - Your tent is very large

647. boca - mouth
Cuando caí, me golpeé la boca - When I fell, I hit my mouth

648. plaza - square / park
Nos vemos en la plaza principal a las tres de la tarde - See you at the main square at three in the afternoon

649. pie - foot
¿Tienes el pie herido? - Have you injured your foot?

650. trabajadores - workers

Los trabajadores de la zona vienen aquí durante los fines de semana - The workers in the area come here during the weekends

651. poner - to put / to place

Debes poner tu pasaporte en un lugar seguro - You must put your passport in a safe place

652. existen - they exist / there are

No existen razones para hacer algo tan disparatado - There are no reasons to do something so crazy

653. viene - he/she/it comes

El menú viene con bebida - The menu comes with a drink

654. permite - he/she/it allows

Mi trabajo me permite viajar mucho - My work allows me to travel a lot

655. análisis - analysis

Hagamos un análisis de la situación - Let's do a situation analysis

656. acto - act / event

El presidente encabezó un acto público - The president led a public event

657. hechos - facts

Debes conocer los hechos antes de opinar - You must know the facts before commenting

658. tiempos - times

Son tiempos difíciles - These are hard times

659. políticas - politics / policies

Las políticas de Estado deben mejorar la calidad de vida de los ciudadanos - State policies must improve the life quality of the citizens

660. radio - radio

Me gusta escuchar la radio - I like to listen to the radio

661. puedo - I can

Si vienes a mi ciudad, puedo alojarte en mi casa - If you come to my city, I can let you stay at my house

662. crecimiento - growth
El crecimiento de la población es muy rápido - The growth of the population is very fast

663. compañía - company
Me siento mal, necesito compañía - I feel bad, I need company

664. amigo - friend (masculine)
Tengo un amigo que vive en Barcelona - I have a friend who lives in Barcelona

665. autoridades - authorities
Llamaremos a las autoridades - We will call the authorities

666. realizar - to make
Quiero realizar un viaje por Latinoamérica - I want to make a trip through Latin America

667. acciones - actions / stocks
Tus acciones hablan más que tus palabras - Your actions speak louder than your words

668. padres - parents / fathers
¿Tus padres viven en Alemania? - Do your parents live in Germany?

669. diario - journal / newspaper / diary
Me gusta leer el diario todas las mañanas - I like reading the newspaper every morning

670. ve - he sees / she sees / it sees
Marta no ve el problema; ve la solución - Marta does not see the problem; she sees the solution

671. derecha - right
Debes girar a la derecha - You have to turn right

672. ambiente - environment / atmosphere
En este hostel hay un ambiente muy amistoso - In this hostel there is a very friendly atmosphere

673. habrá - there will be
No habrá inconvenientes - There will be no inconvenience

674. precisamente - precisely

Esto es precisamente lo que temía - This is precisely what I feared

675. enfermedad - disease / illness

El poeta tenía una enfermedad rara - The poet had a rare disease

676. especie - species

Esta es una especie en extinción - This is an endangered species

677. ejército - army

El novio de Ana trabaja en el ejército - Ana's boyfriend works in the army

678. santa - saint (feminine)

Santa Águeda es la patrona de este barrio - Saint Águeda is the patron saint of this neighborhood

679. cambios - changes

Hubo algunos cambios en nuestro itinerario - There were some changes in our itinerary

680. río - river

Ese río baja desde la montaña - That river descends from the mountain

681. sabía - I knew / he knew / she knew / it knew

Sabía que estas zapatillas viejas me iban a causar problemas - I knew that these old shoes were going to give me problems

682. seguro - safe / sure (masculine)

Este barrio es muy seguro - This neighborhood is very safe

683. espera - you wait (imperative) / he/she/it waits

¡Espera! No vayas sin mí - Wait! Don't go without me

684. momentos - moments / time

En estos momentos, nadie sabe qué sucederá - At this time, no one knows what will happen

685. viaje - trip

Nuestro viaje ha sido fantástico - Our trip has been fantastic

686. quería - I wanted / he wanted / she wanted / it wanted

Mi madre quería saber cómo te sientes - My mother wanted to know how you feel

687. ocho - *eight*
Visitaré ocho países - I will visit eight countries
688. vivir - *to live*
Me voy a vivir a España - I'm going to live in Spain
689. región - *region*
Este es el mejor queso en toda la región - This is the best cheese in the whole region
690. formación - *formation / training / education*
Gonzalo tiene mucha formación - Gonzalo has a lot of training
691. escuela - *school*
Diana y yo íbamos a la escuela juntos - Diana and I went to school together
692. cuarto - *fourth / quarter / room*
En el cuarto día de viaje, empezó a llover - On the fourth day of trip, it started raining
693. valores - *values / prices*
Si no compartes sus valores, no puedes ser su amigo - If you don't share his values, you can't be his friend
694. quedó - *it remained / turned out / it stayed*
La pintura quedó hermosa - The painting turned out beautiful
695. participación - *participation*
La participación en clase es importante - Participation in class is important
696. éxito - *success*
No hay una clave para el éxito - There is no key to success
697. baja - *short / low (feminine)*
Como la tierra es baja, hay muchas inundaciones - Since the land is low, there are many floods
698. artículo - *article*
Escribí un artículo para un blog de viajes - I wrote an article for a travel blog
699. principales - *main (plural)*
Las calles principales son estas dos - These two are the main streets

700. metros - meters
Son solo cien metros - It's only a hundred meters

701. marcha - march / demonstration
El tránsito ha sido desviado por una marcha - Traffic has been diverted due to a demonstration

702. régimen - regime
El régimen de la dictadura fue muy duro - The dictatorship regime was very tough

703. consecuencia - consequence
Esta es la consecuencia de lo que has hecho - This is the consequence of what you have done

704. conocimiento - knowledge
Tengo el conocimiento, pero no las habilidades prácticas - I have the knowledge, but not the practical skills

705. corazón - heart
El apartamento está en el corazón de la ciudad - The apartment is in the heart of the city

706. campaña - campaign
Es todo parte de una campaña publicitaria - It is all part of an advertising campaign

707. estructura - structure
Están cambiando la estructura de la empresa - They are changing the structure of the company

708. efectos - effects
Todavía siento los efectos de la medicina - I still feel the effects of the medicine

709. finalmente - finally
Finalmente, todo salió bien - Finally, everything went well

710. modelo - model
Greta trabaja como modelo - Greta works as a model

711. carta - letter
Tengo que enviar una carta de recomendación - I have to send a letter of recommendation

712. construcción - construction
Trabajo en el sector de la construcción - I work on the construction sector

713. médico - doctor
Mi hermano es médico - My brother is a doctor

714. miedo - fear
Tengo miedo de ir al bosque de noche - I'm afraid to go to the forest at night

715. mayores - older / bigger / greatest (plural)
En este viaje realicé mis mayores hazañas - On this trip I performed my greatest feats

716. entrada - entry / entrance / starter / ticket
La entrada tiene un valor de 30 euros - The ticket has a value of 30 euros

717. humanos - humans (plural)
Creo que los humanos son especiales - I believe humans are special

718. sean - they are (subjunctive)
Quiero que ellos, mis hijos, sean buenas personas - I want that they, my children, are good people

719. actitud - attitude
Tu actitud siempre es muy positiva - Your attitude is always very positive

720. deja - you leave (imperative) / he/she/it leaves
Deja eso, te lastimarás - Leave that, you'll get hurt

721. dejó - he left / she left / it left
Mi abuelo me dejó su viejo coche - My grandfather left me his old car

722. llevar - to take / to carry
¿Puedes llevar esto a la cocina? - Can you take this to the kitchen?

723. negro - black (masculine)
Quiero comprar un sombrero negro - I want to buy a black hat

724. texto - text

Me llegó un mensaje de texto - I received a text message

725. mitad - half

La mitad de la población está de vacaciones en este momento - Half of the population is on vacation right now

726. estuvo - he was / she was / it was

Mi hermana estuvo un tiempo en Madrid - My sister was in Madrid for a while

727. alrededor - around / about

Pasaré alrededor de tres días en Valencia - I will spend about three days in Valencia

728. acerca - about

Leí un libro acerca de este tema - I read a book about this subject

729. peso - weight / peso

En el aeropuerto se fijarán en el peso de tu maleta - At the airport they will notice the weight of your suitcase

730. humano - human

Todo ser humano merece los mismos derechos - Every human being deserves the same rights

731. pequeño - little / young (masculine)

Mi hijo es muy pequeño - My son is very young

732. fecha - date

La fecha de entrega de este proyecto es el miércoles - The delivery date of this project is Wednesday

733. serán - they will be

Mis hijos probablemente serán artistas - My children will probably be artists

734. doctor - doctor

Estoy estudiando para ser doctor - I'm studying to be a doctor

735. ideas - ideas

Federico tiene muy buenas ideas - Federico has very good ideas

736. vino - wine / he/she/it came

¿Te apetece una copa de vino? - Do you fancy a glass of wine?

737. materia - matter / subject

¿Cuál es tu materia preferida? - What is your favorite subject?

738. llega - he arrives / she arrives / it arrives

¿Cuándo llega la pizza? - When is the pizza arriving?

739. carrera - career / race

¡Corramos una carrera! - Let's run a race!

740. cierta - a certain (feminine)

Daniel le contó nuestro secreto a cierta persona - Daniel told our secret to a certain person

741. sola - alone (feminine)

Estoy viajando sola por el mundo - I am traveling alone around the world

742. lejos - far

Estoy muy lejos de mi hogar - I am very far away from my home

743. juez - judge

El juez decidirá tu destino - The judge will decide your destiny

744. características - characteristics

¿Cuáles son las características de esta ciudad? - What are the characteristics of this city?

745. riesgo - risk

No me gustaría correr ese riesgo - I would not like to take that risk

746. fácil - easy

Escalar es más fácil de lo que parece - Climbing is easier than it seems

747. diferencia - difference

Hay mucha diferencia entre ambas culturas - There is a lot of difference between both cultures

748. cultural - cultural

Me interesa el periodismo cultural - I am interested in cultural journalism

749. libros - books

He traído muchos libros - I brought many books

750. práctica - *practice*
Es cuestión de práctica - It's a matter of practice
751. mayo - *May*
El primero de mayo haremos una fiesta - On May the 1st we will have a party
752. nuestras - *our (feminine, plural)*
Nuestras maletas se han perdido - Our bags are lost
753. programas - *programs*
Me gustan solo dos programas de televisión - I like only two TV programs
754. memoria - *memory*
Tengo una memoria pésima - I have a terrible memory
755. llegado - *arrived*
¡Ha llegado mi guitarra! - My guitar has arrived!
756. plazo - *term / deadline*
El plazo para pedir la beca ha terminado - The deadline to apply for the scholarship is over
757. expresión - *expression*
Es una expresión local - It is a local expression
758. diciembre - *December*
Me quedaré hasta diciembre - I will stay until December
759. mantener - *to maintain / to keep*
Debemos mantener la calma - We must keep calm
760. enero - *January*
Enero es el mes más caluroso aquí - January is the hottest month over here
761. volver - *to go back / to return*
¿Quieres volver al hotel? - Do you want to return to the hotel?
762. cuadro - *painting / picture*
Mi amiga me regaló un cuadro - My friend gave me a painting
763. producto - *product*
Este es un producto local - This is a local product
764. produce - *he produces / she produces / it produces*
Mi familia produce lácteos - My family produces dairy

765. *europea - European*
Tengo la ciudadanía europea - I have the European citizenship
766. *conciencia - conscience*
Mi conciencia está tranquila - My conscience is clear
767. *tenían - they had / used to have*
Mis abuelos tenían una tienda de golosinas - My grandparents used to have a candy store
768. *atrás - behind / back*
Laura se escondió atrás de la puerta - Laura hid behind the door
769. *creación - creation*
La creación artística es un trabajo muy difícil - Artistic creation is very difficult work
770. *precio - price*
¿Cuál es el precio de esta mermelada? - What is the price of this jam?
771. *película - movie*
¿Te apetece ver una película? - Do you feel like watching a movie?
772. *puerto - port*
En el puerto, hay varios restaurantes de mariscos - In the port, there are many seafood restaurants
773. *fuego - fire*
Es una bella fogata, pero deben recordar apagar el fuego antes de ir a dormir - It's a beautiful campfire, but you must remember to put out the fire before going to sleep
774. *cuestión - matter*
Es todo una cuestión de tiempo - It's all a matter of time
775. *pasó - it happened*
¿Cuándo pasó esto? - When did this happen?
776. *costa - coast / shore*
Alquilamos una casa en la costa - We rented a house on the coast

777. supuesto - supposed / assumption

Es solo un supuesto, no estoy segura - It's just an assumption, I'm not sure

778. local - local

Quiero conocer la cultura local - I want to know the local culture

779. habla - he/she/it speaks (present) / you speak (imperative)

Mi padre habla español porque es peruano - My father speaks Spanish because he is Peruvian

780. aspectos - aspects

Había algunos aspectos del asunto que no conocíamos - There were some aspects of the matter that we did not know

781. sala - room / living room

Te espero en la sala - I'll wait for you in the living room

782. cámara - camera

¿Has traído la cámara? - Did you bring the camera?

783. vuelta - turn / return

Date la vuelta mientras me visto - Turn around while I get dressed

784. vía - through / way / railroad / train track

Esta es la vieja vía del tren - This is the old train track

785. mirada - look / eyes

Puedo ver en tu mirada que estás feliz - I can see in your eyes that you are happy

786. mejores - best (plural)

Son las mejores vacaciones de mi vida - These are the best holidays of my life

787. informe - report

¿Está listo el informe? - Is the report ready?

788. unidad - unity / unit

Un hormiguero se comporta como una unidad - An anthill behaves like a unit

789. distintos - different (plural)

Tenemos planes distintos hoy - We have different plans today

790. suerte - luck
Tienes mucha suerte - You are very lucky
791. tales - such (plural)
Tales asuntos me exceden - Such matters exceed me
792. mira - he/she/it looks (present) / you look (imperative)
¡Mira! ¡Una llama! - Look! A llama!
793. llamada - call
Recibí una llamada de trabajo - I received a job call
794. técnica - technique
Preparan las arepas con una técnica especial - They prepare the arepas with a special technique
795. título - title / header
¿Cómo es el título del libro que estás leyendo? - What is the title of the book you are reading?
796. principios - beginnings / beginning
A principios del siglo pasado, hubo un gran terremoto - At the beginning of the last century, there was a great earthquake
797. octubre - October
Nos conocimos en octubre - We met in October
798. volvió - he/she/it came back
Mi hermana volvió después de viajar por un año - My sister returned after traveling for a year
799. período - period
Estudio Literatura del período medieval - I study Literature of the medieval period
800. encontrar - to find
¡Tenemos que encontrar un baño! - We have to find a toilet!
801. democracia - democracy
Esto es una democracia, debemos votar - This is a democracy, we must vote
802. aumento - raise / increase
Le pedí un aumento a mi jefa - I asked my boss for a raise
803. fútbol - football / soccer
Vamos a jugar un partido de fútbol - Let's play a soccer match

804. prueba - test / he/she/it tries / you try (imperative)
Prueba esta sopa, ¡está riquísima! - Try this soup, it's delicious!
805. consumo - consumption
Ha aumentado el consumo de productos dietéticos - The consumption of dietary products has increased
806. pese a - although / despite
Pese al clima, pasamos días maravillosos - Despite the weather, we had wonderful days
807. ocasiones - occasions
Solo uso este vestido en ocasiones especiales - I only wear this dress on special occasions
808. exterior - exterior / abroad
Quiero vivir en el exterior - I want to live abroad
809. solución - solution
Encontré una solución a nuestro problema - I found a solution to our problem
810. u - or (before o)
Podemos comer un sándwich u otra cosa - We can eat a sandwich or something else
811. hija - daughter
Esta es mi hija, Julia - This is my daughter, Julia
812. sueño - dream / sleepy
¡Tengo mucho sueño! - I'm very sleepy!
813. capaz - capable
No serías capaz de hacer algo así - You wouldn't be capable of doing something like that
814. ocasión - ocasion
En esta ocasión, las cosas serán distintas - On this occasion, things will be different
815. industria - industry
En esta ciudad, la industria es central - In this city, industry is central
816. adelante - front / in front of / ahead / forward
Quiero sentarme adelante - I want to sit in the front

817. salida - exit
¿Dónde está la salida? - Where is the exit?

818. ciencia - science
La ciencia crece todos los días - Science grows everyday

819. asunto - matter / issue
Este es un asunto muy delicado - This is a very delicate matter

820. asociación - association
Esta asociación protege los derechos de los inmigrantes - This association protects the rights of immigrants

821. puso - he put / she put / it put (past)
Mi madre puso el vaso sobre la mesa – My mother put the glass on the table

822. intereses - interests
Nuestros intereses son muy distintos - Our interests are very different

823. oro - gold
¿Ese anillo es de oro? - Is that ring made of gold?

824. podrá - he/she/it will be able to (can)
Algún día podrá cumplir sus sueños - Someday she will be able to fulfill her dreams

825. pregunta - question
Tengo una pregunta, profesor - I have a question, professor

826. oposición - opposition
Pedro es del partido de la oposición - Pedro is from the opposition party

827. entrar - to enter / to go in
¿Vas a entrar a la casa? - Are you going to go inside the house?

828. señora - madam / Mrs. / Ms.
Señora, se le ha caído algo - Madam, you dropped something

829. señaló - he/she/it pointed out / pointed
El bebé señaló el cielo - The baby pointed to the sky

830. dolor - pain / ache
Tengo mucho dolor de cabeza - I have a bad headache

831. zonas - zones / areas
Hay varias zonas de la isla que debes visitar - There are several areas of the island that you must visit

832. comercio - commerce / trade / store
El comercio se vio afectado por el temporal - Trade was affected by the storm

833. operación - operation / surgery
La operación fue un éxito - The surgery was a success

834. tribunal - tribunal / court
Un tribunal decidirá su castigo - A court will decide his punishment

835. instituciones - institutions
Las mejores instituciones educativas son públicas - The best educational institutions are public

836. temas - subjects / themes / issues
Me gustan los temas felices - I like happy subjects

837. junio - June
¿Ya estamos en junio? ¡El tiempo pasa volando! - Are we in June already? Time flies!

838. marco - frame
Me gusta más el marco que la pintura - I like the frame more than the painting

839. sectores - sectors
Hay sectores de la sociedad que son muy vulnerables - There are sectors of society that are very vulnerable

840. hacerlo - to do it
Hay que comprar pan, ¿puedes hacerlo tú? - We need to buy bread, can you do it?

841. aspecto - aspect / look
Siempre tiene un aspecto muy desprolijo - He always looks very sloppy

842. razones - reasons
Tienes muchas razones para viajar - You have many reasons to travel

843. contenido - content

Me gusta la portada del libro, pero no el contenido - I like the cover of the book, but not the content

844. juicio - judgment / trial / lawsuit

Héctor ganó el juicio - Héctor won the lawsuit

845. electoral - electoral

Este será año electoral - This will be an election year

846. considera - he/she/it considers / you consider (imperative)

Olga considera que es su derecho - Olga considers it her right

847. tendrá - he/she/it will have

Julieta tendrá su bebé el mes que viene - Juliet will have her baby next month

848. mucha - a lot of (feminine)

Hay mucha gente, vamos a otro lado - There are too many people, let's go elsewhere

849. voluntad - will / willpower

Kevin no tiene la voluntad de trabajar - Kevin doesn't have the will to work

850. dicen - they say

Dicen que esa estatua da buena suerte - They say that statue brings good luck

851. recuerdo - memory / I remember

Recuerdo cuando venía aquí de pequeño - I remember when I came here as a child

852. área - area / region

Vivo en un área rural - I live in a rural area

853. aparece - he/she/it appears / shows up

De tanto en tanto aparece una ardilla en el jardín - From time to time a squirrel shows up in the garden

854. vio - he/she/it saw

Mi hermano vio lo que me enviaste - My brother saw what you sent me

855. cama - bed

¿Esta es nuestra cama? - Is this our bed?

856. aun - even

Siempre duermo con calcetines, aun en verano - I always sleep with socks on, even in the summer

857. presenta - *he presents / she presents / it presents*

Hoy Jorge presenta su tesis - Today Jorge presents his thesis

858. revolución - *revolution*

La revolución cubana fue hace mucho tiempo - The Cuban revolution happened a long time ago

859. busca - *he/she/it searches / looks for*

Mi esposa busca empleo - My wife is looking for a job

860. abril - *April*

Debes venir en abril, es la época más linda - You must come in April, it's the most beautiful time

861. violencia - *violence*

Estamos en contra de todo tipo de violencia - We are against all types of violence

862. primeras - *first (feminine, plural)*

Son las primeras flores en florecer - These are the first flowers to bloom

863. pequeña - *little (feminine)*

Quiero una pizza pequeña, por favor - I want a small pizza, please

864. armas - *guns / arms / weapons*

Portar armas no es legal aquí - Bearing arms is not legal here

865. debía - *I/he/she/it owed / had to*

Ayer debía ir al dentista, pero lo olvidé - Yesterday I had to go to the dentist, but I forgot

866. esfuerzo - *effort*

Debes hacer un esfuerzo - You must make an effort

867. humana - *human (feminine)*

La actividad humana afecta el medioambiente - Human activity affects the environment

868. posibilidades - possibilities
Tenemos varias posibilidades para esta noche - We have several possibilities for tonight

869. centros - centers
Hay tres centros de salud en el barrio - There are three health centers in the neighborhood

870. profesional - professional
Soy traductora profesional - I am a professional translator

871. asimismo - likewise / also
Pablo dijo, asimismo, que quería regresar - Pablo said, likewise, that he wanted to return

872. grado - degree / grade
Si sube la temperatura un grado más, me derretiré - If the temperature rises one more degree, I will melt

873. has - you have (auxiliary)
¿Ya has ido a la biblioteca? - Have you already been to the library?

874. toma - take / he/she/it takes (present) / you take (imperative)
Toma este libro, te gustará - Take this book, you'll like it

875. distintas - different (feminine, plural)
Hay distintas formas de viajar - There are different ways to travel

876. material - material
Tengo material como para escribir un libro - I have enough material to write a book

877. carne - meat / flesh
No como carne - I don't eat meat

878. llama - he/she/it calls / llama
Mi hija se llama Sara - My daughter's name is Sara

879. particular - particular
Tengo un problema muy particular - I have a very particular problem

880. trabajar - to work
Mañana debo trabajar por la mañana - Tomorrow I have to work in the morning

881. propuesta - proposition / proposal

Tengo una propuesta de trabajo para ti - I have a job proposal for you

882. muerto - dead (masculine)

El pez está muerto - The fish is dead

883. precios - prices

¿Dónde puedo ver precios de las bebidas? - Where can I see the prices of the drinks?

884. reforma - reform / renovation

Deberíamos hacer una reforma en la casa - We should do a house renovation

885. hermano - brother

Mi hermano es abogado - My brother is a lawyer

886. corte - cut / court

Quiero probar un nuevo corte de cabello - I want to try a new haircut

887. comenzó - he/she/it began / started

Todo comenzó hace diez años - It all started ten years ago

888. etapa - phase / stage

Estoy en una etapa muy confusa
 - I am going through a very confusing phase

889. no obstante - however

Tengo sueño; no obstante, quiero ver la película hasta el final - I'm sleepy; however, I want to watch the movie until the end

890. pone - he puts / she puts / it puts

Mi padre siempre pone a sus hijos como una prioridad - My father always puts his children as a priority

891. diversos - diverse (masculine, plural)

Los alumnos son muy diversos - The students are very diverse

892. visita - visit / he/she/it visits

Deberíamos hacer una visita a tus primos - We should pay a visit to your cousins

893. concepto - concept

No entiendo el concepto - I do not understand the concept

894. pacientes - patients

Tengo demasiados pacientes esta semana - I have too many patients this week

895. semanas - weeks

Viajaremos por cuatro semanas - We will travel for four weeks

896. tipos - types / kinds

¿Cuántos tipos de calabaza hay? - How many types of pumpkin are there?

897. solamente - only / just

Hoy solamente quiero descansar - Today I just want to rest

898. deseo - desire / wish / I wish / I want

Deseo viajar por siempre - I want to travel forever

899. sistemas - systems

Ella es experta en sistemas informáticos - She is an expert in computer systems

900. encuentran - they find

Mis amigos siempre encuentran la forma de divertirse - My friends always find a way to have fun

Chapter 4 – Words 901-1200

901. siguientes - next / following (plural)

¿Tienes un plan para los siguientes días? - Do you have a plan for the following days?

902. suficiente - sufficient / enough

No tengo tiempo suficiente para hacer todo - I don't have enough time to do everything

903. marzo - March

En marzo comienzan las clases - Classes begin in March

904. propios - own / of one's own (masculine, plural)

No tengo esquíes propios - I don't have skis of my own

905. jamás - never

Jamás comí en un restaurante tan caro - I never ate in such an expensive restaurant

906. dan - they give

Mis padres me dan muchos ánimos - My parents give me lots of encouragement

907. club - club

Soy miembro de un club de cine - I am a member of a movie club

908. instituto - institute

Trabajo en un instituto de idiomas - I work in a language institute

909. constitución - constitution

Es un derecho protegido por la Constitución - It is a right protected by the Constitution

910. curso - course / class
Quiero tomar un curso de cocina - I want to take a cooking course

911. lenguaje - language
Los lingüistas estudian el lenguaje - Linguists study language

912. estilo - style
Me gusta su estilo - I like her style

913. rosa - pink / rose
¿Dónde está mi cuaderno rosa? - Where is my pink notebook?

914. imposible - impossible
Esta es una misión imposible - This is an impossible mission

915. buscar - to look for / to search for
Vamos a buscar un sitio para comer - We are going to look for a place to eat

914. peor - worse / worst
Lo peor del viaje fue cuando perdimos el equipaje - The worst part of the trip was when we lost our luggage

915. piel - skin
Tengo la piel quemada por el sol - My skin is sunburnt

916. arriba - up
Su habitación está en el piso de arriba - Your room is upstairs

917. generales - general (plural)
Hay algunas cuestiones generales en el proyecto que hay que corregir - There are some general issues in the project that must be corrected

918. septiembre - September
Estoy viviendo aquí desde septiembre - I have been living here since September

919. blanca - white (feminine)
Esa flor blanca es preciosa - That white flower is beautiful

920. aquellas - those (feminine)
Aquellas montañas son más altas de lo que parecen - Those mountains are taller than they seem

921. teoría - theory
Tengo una teoría al respecto - I have a theory about it

922. animales - animals
Hay muchos animales autóctonos - There are many native animals

923. hicieron - they did
Mis primos hicieron una fiesta - My cousins threw a party

924. larga - long (feminine)
Hay una fila muy larga, vamos a otro lado - There is a very long line, let's go elsewhere

925. perdido - lost (masculine)
Creo que estoy perdido - I think I'm lost

926. imágenes - images / pictures
Quiero un libro con imágenes - I want a book with pictures

927. paciente - pacient
Soy paciente del doctor Gutiérrez - I am a patient of Doctor Gutiérrez

928. conseguir - to get / to achieve
Deberíamos conseguir una mesa - We should get a table

929. máximo - maximum
¿Cuál es el máximo que quieres gastar hoy? - What is the maximum you want to spend today?

930. noviembre - November
En los primeros días de noviembre habrá un festival - In the first days of November there will be a festival

931. líder - leader
Gabriela es la líder de la expedición - Gabriela is the expedition leader

932. hospital - hospital
¿Quieres que vayamos al hospital? - Do you want us to go to the hospital?

933. diversas - diverse (feminine)
Hay diversas formas de llegar al aeropuerto - There are several ways to get to the airport

934. vuelve - he/she/it comes back/returns / you return/come back (imperative)

¡Vuelve! Has olvidado tu cartera - Come back! You have forgotten your wallet

935. destino - fate / destiny

Era nuestro destino venir aquí - It was our fate to come here

936. en torno a - around

La temperatura se encuentra en torno a los veinte grados - The temperature is around twenty degrees

937. proyectos - projects

Estoy trabajando en dos proyectos simultáneos - I am working on two simultaneous projects

938. flores - flowers

¿Te gustan las flores? - Do you like flowers?

939. niveles - levels

Los niveles de humedad son muy altos - The humidity levels are very high

940. afirmó - he/she/it affirmed / asserted / said / claimed

El acusado afirmó que era inocente - The defendant claimed he was innocent

941. explicó - he/she/it explained

La dentista le explicó que debía quitarle la muela - The dentist explained that she had to remove the tooth

942. somos - we are

Somos alemanes - We are German

943. términos - terms

¿Puedes explicarlo en términos más sencillos? - Can you explain it in simpler terms?

944. premio - prize

La escritora ganó un premio literario - The writer won a literary prize

945. tercera - third (feminine)

Es la tercera vez que vengo a Chile - It's the third time I've come to Chile

946. simple - simple

El problema es complejo, pero la solución es simple - The problem is complex, but the solution is simple

947. trabajos - works / jobs

Tengo dos trabajos - I have two jobs

948. factores - factors

¿Has considerado todos los factores? - Have you considered all the factors?

949. fuente - source / fountain

Tira una moneda en la fuente - Throw a coin into the fountain

950. cielo - sky / heaven

El cielo está nublado - The sky is cloudy

951. ambas - both

Esas son mis hermanas. Ambas son abogadas - Those are my sisters. Both of them are lawyers

952. mismas - same (feminine, plural)

¡Tenemos las mismas zapatillas! - We have the same running shoes!

953. actualmente - currently

Actualmente, es más fácil trabajar desde casa - Currently, it is easier to work from home

954. conocido - known / acquaintance (masculine)

Tengo un conocido que tomó un café con Frank Sinatra - I have an acquaintance who had a coffee with Frank Sinatra

955. condición - condition

La condición del edificio es deplorable - The condition of the building is deplorable

956. ejercicio - exercise / workout

Voy a salir un rato a hacer ejercicio - I'm going out for a while to exercise

957. cree - he/she/it believes / thinks

Mi madre cree que no iré por Navidad; será una sorpresa - My mother thinks I won't go for Christmas; it will be a surprise

958. par - couple / pair / two
Tengo un par de preguntas - I have a couple of questions
959. ocurre - it happens
¿Qué ocurre aquí? - What's going on here?
960. ti - you (after preposition)
Tengo algo para ti - I have something for you
961. espíritu - spirit
Ellos creen que todo en la naturaleza tiene un espíritu - They believe that everything in nature has a spirit
962. lengua - tongue / language
¿Cuál es tu lengua materna? - What is your mother tongue?
963. responsabilidad - responsibility
Tengo una responsabilidad muy grande - I have a very big responsibility
964. digo - I say
Cuando digo lo que pienso, me meto en problemas - When I say what I think, I get in trouble
965. distancia - distance
¿Cuánta distancia hay desde aquí hasta Cabo Polonio? – What is the distance from here to Cabo Polonio?
966. organismo - organism
Los humanos somos organismos pluricelulares - Humans are multicellular organisms
967. cruz - cross
Esa cruz fue diseñada por un famoso arquitecto - That cross was designed by a famous architect
968. evolución - evolution
Darwin desarrolló la teoría de la evolución - Darwin developed the theory of evolution
969. realmente - really
Es realmente difícil comprender su acento - It's really hard to understand his accent
970. francés - French (masculine)
Yo soy francés - I am French

971. novela - novel

Quiero escribir una novela - I want to write a novel

972. alma - soul

La música está en el alma de esta cultura - Music is at the soul of this culture

973. doble - double

Podríamos salir en una cita doble - We could go out on a double date

974. anteriores - previous (plural)

Mis gafas anteriores eran rojas - My previous glasses were red

975. obtener - to obtain / to get

¿Qué quieres obtener con este viaje? - What do you want to get by doing this trip?

976. dije - I said

Le dije a Carlos que debería ser más independiente - I said to Carlos he should be more independent

977. selección - selection

He hecho una selección de películas de terror para esta noche - I've made a selection of horror movies for tonight

978. podido - been able to / can (past participle)

¿Has podido dormir? - Have you been able to sleep?

979. nación - nation

Los intereses de la nación y los del individuo rara vez coinciden - The interests of the nation and those of the individual rarely coincide

980. ido - gone (past participle)

¿Has ido al Museo de San Telmo? - Have you gone to the San Telmo Museum?

981. crear - to create

Podríamos crear una historia - We could create a story

982. motivo - reason / motif

¿Por qué motivo renunciaste? - What's the reason for your resignation?

983. tercer - third (masculine)
Estamos en el tercer mes del año - We are in the third month of the year

984. detrás - behind
Creo que hay un enchufe detrás de la puerta - I think there is a plug behind the door

985. significa - it means
¿Qué significa esto? - What does this mean?

986. empleo - job / work / employment
Estoy buscando un nuevo empleo - I am looking for a new job

987. escrito - written
¿Has escrito un libro? - Have they written a book?

988. departamento - apartment / department
Heredé un departamento de mis abuelos - I inherited an apartment from my grandparents

989. contacto - contact
¿Me pasas la información de contacto de Sandra? - Can you send me Sandra's contact information?

990. casas - houses
Esas casas están a la venta - Those houses are for sale

991. red - network / net
Pescan con una red - They fish using a net

992. rostro - face
Mi rostro está quemado por el sol - My face is sunburnt

993. oportunidad - opportunity
Florencia me comentó sobre una oportunidad de inversión - Florencia told me about an investment opportunity

994. procesos - processes
Los procesos de producción son largos - The production processes are long

995. terreno - land / terrain
Este terreno es de mi madre - This land belongs to my mother

996. daba - he/she/it gave / used to give

Mi abuela siempre me daba un dulce cuando la veía - My grandmother used to give me a sweet every time I saw her

997. calles - streets

No andes por las calles después de la medianoche - Don't walk the streets after midnight

998. lista - list / ready (feminine)

¿Estás lista para salir? - Are you ready to go out?

999. nacionales - national (plural) / nationals

Los platos nacionales son la empanada y el asado - The national dishes are the empanada and the asado

1000. funciones - functions

¿Cuáles son tus funciones en tu nuevo puesto? - What are your functions in your new position?

1001. leyes - laws

Conozco las leyes locales - I know the local laws

1002. acceso - access

No tengo acceso a internet - I do not have internet access

1003. técnico - technical (masculine)

Hay que solucionar un problema técnico - We must solve a technical problem

1004. visión - vision

Mi visión no es muy buena - My vision is not very good

1005. preguntó - he/she/it asked

Gabriel me preguntó si me gustaría salir con él - Gabriel asked me if I would like to go out with him

1006. grave - grave / serious

Tiene una enfermedad grave - He has a serious illness

1007. tenga - that he/she/it has / turns (subjunctive) / you have (imperative)

Cuando Lucía tenga cinco años, nos iremos de viaje - When Lucia turns five, we will go on a trip

1008. lunes - Monday

¿Hoy es lunes? - Is it Monday today?

1009. aplicación - app / application
He enviado una aplicación a la universidad - I have sent an application to the university

1010. junta - board / he/she/it picks up
Gloria es miembro de la junta de directores - Gloria is a member of the board of directors

1011. lugares - places
Hay muchos lugares que quiero ver en este país - There are many places that I want to see in this country

1012. verano - Summer
¡Nos vemos en el verano! - See you in the summer!

1013. capítulo - chapter
¿Por qué capítulo vas? - What chapter are you on?

1014. pensamiento - thought / thinking
El pensamiento occidental está cambiando - Western thinking is changing

1015. frecuencia - frequency
Viajo con frecuencia - I travel with frequency

1016. gestión - management
Diego está a cargo de la gestión del hotel - Diego is in charge of the hotel management

1017. viernes - Friday
El viernes vamos a cocinar tacos - On Friday we will cook tacos

1018. sitio - site / place
Amo este sitio - I love this place

1019. agosto - August
Las clases comienzan en agosto - Classes begin in August

1020. propiedad - property
No puedes tomar eso, es de mi propiedad - You can't take that, it's my property

1021. profesionales - professionals / professional (plural)
Ellos son cocineros profesionales - They are professional cooks

1022. *últimas - last (feminine, plural)*

¿Dónde quieres pasar las últimas horas de nuestro viaje? - Where do you want to spend the last hours of our trip?

1023. *gusta - he/she/it likes*

A Pedrito no le gusta el tomate - Pedrito doesn't like tomato

1024. *objetivos - goals / objectives*

¿Cuáles son tus objetivos profesionales? - Which are your career goals?

1025. *movimientos - movements*

Hay muchos movimientos sociales que apoyan esta ley - There are many social movements that support this law

1026. *alcalde - mayor (masculine)*

El alcalde es muy querido por todos - The mayor is very dear to everyone

1027. *ejecutivo - executive*

El poder ejecutivo no hace la ley - The executive branch does not make the law

1028. *ciudadanos - citizens*

Los ciudadanos europeos pueden viajar libremente por la Unión Europea - European citizens can freely travel through the European Union

1029. *necesidades - needs*

Debes pensar en las necesidades de los que menos tienen - You must think about the needs of those who have less

1030. *exposición - exposition / exhibition / show*

Estamos organizando una exposición de fotografía - We are organizing a photography exhibition

1031. *término - term / end / word*

Ese es un término nuevo, no lo conozco - That's a new word, I don't know it

1032. *veinte - twenty*

Mi vuelo parte en veinte horas - My flight leaves in twenty hours

1033. cuál - which / what (within a question)

¿Cuál de estos es tu automóvil? - Which one of these is your car?

1034. clara - clear (feminine)

Tengo una idea clara de lo que quiero hacer - I have a clear idea of what I want to do

1035. altura - height

La montaña tiene una altura de mil quinientos metros - The mountain has a height of fifteen hundred meters

1036. pequeños - little / small / young (masculine) / little ones

Los cachorros son muy pequeños - The puppies are very little

1037. presión - pressure

La presión atmosférica es muy baja - The atmospheric pressure is very low

1038. moral - moral

Es un dilema moral - It is a moral dilemma

1039. lograr - to achieve

¡Lo vamos a lograr! - We are going to achieve it!

1040. comité - committee

Soy parte del comité de organización - I am part of the organizing committee

1041. teléfono - phone

¿Puedo usar su teléfono? - Can I use your phone?

1042. asuntos - matters / issues

Hay asuntos urgentes sobre los que debemos trabajar - There are urgent matters on which we must work

1043. peligro - danger

¿Estamos en peligro? - Are we in danger?

1044. escena - scene

Esta es mi escena preferida - This is my favorite scene

1045. gusto - taste / flavor

Mi gusto de helado preferido es el chocolate - My favorite ice cream flavor is chocolate

1046. palacio - palace
Vamos a visitar un palacio abandonado - We are going to visit an abandoned palace
1047. hotel - hotel
Nos conocimos en el hotel - We met at the hotel
1048. aseguró - he/she/it made sure / ensured / assured
Hugo me aseguró que no iba a ser un problema - Hugo assured me that it was not going to be a problem
1049. isla - island
Hay vuelos directos a la isla cada media hora - There are direct flights to the island every half hour
1050. guardia - guard / watch
La guardia civil está investigando el asunto - The civil guard is investigating the issue
1051. confianza - confidence
Tengo confianza absoluta en mis amigos - I have absolute confidence in my friends
1052. ciudades - cities
Visitamos cinco ciudades en veinte días - We visited five cities in twenty days
1053. esperar - to wait
Debemos esperar el taxi en la puerta - We must wait for the taxi at the door
1054. café - coffee
¿Quieres un café con leche? - Do you want a coffee with milk?
1055. demanda - lawsuit
Mi padre le hizo una demanda a la empresa donde trabajaba - My father made a lawsuit to the company where he used to work
1056. personajes - characters
Me gustan los personajes realistas - I like realistic characters
1057. directamente - directly
Desde el aeropuerto, iremos directamente a la cama - From the airport, we will go directly to bed

1058. *salió - he/she/it came out / went out*
¿Ya salió la nueva canción de Ricky Martin? - Did Ricky Martin's new song come out yet?

1059. *discurso - speech*
El presidente de la empresa dio un discurso - The president of the company gave a speech

1060. *representantes - representatives*
Somos representantes de nuestro país - We are representatives of our country

1061. *normal - normal*
¿Qué es una persona normal, después de todo? - What is a normal person, after all?

1062. *pena - shame / pity*
Es una pena que no hayamos podido ir al museo - It's a shame we couldn't go to the museum

1063. *jugadores - players*
Los jugadores de este equipo son los mejores - The players of this team are the best

1064. *supone - he/she/it supposes*
Se supone que no lloverá en toda la semana - It is not supposed to rain all week

1065. *industrial - industrial*
Este solía ser un barrio industrial - This used to be an industrial neighborhood

1066. *referencia - reference*
Necesito una carta de referencia para solicitar un trabajo - I need a reference letter to apply for a job

1067. *febrero - February*
En febrero, fuimos a un festival de música - In February, we went to a music festival

1068. *entender - to understand*
Entender otro idioma es más fácil que hablarlo - Understanding another language is easier than speaking it

1069. esté - he/she/it is (subjunctive)

¿Tienes alguna cerveza que esté bien fría? - Do you have any beer that is very cold?

1070. física - physical (feminine) / physics

Nunca me ha gustado la actividad física - I have never liked physical activity

1071. dejado - left (participle)

Alguien te ha dejado un paquete - Someone left you a package

1072. alimentos - food / nourishment

Los alimentos que uno consume afectan la salud - The food you eat affects your health

1073. pies - feet

Tengo los pies helados - My feet are freezing

1074. protección - protection

La protección de la piel es importante para prevenir el cáncer - Skin protection is important to prevent cancer

1075. autores - authors

No conozco autores catalanes - I do not know any Catalan authors

1076. marido - husband

Mi marido es arquitecto - My husband is an architect

1077. podrían - they could

Tus palabras podrían traerte problemas - Your words could bring you problems

1078. llamada - call

Necesito hacer una llamada - I need to make a call

1079. brazos - arms

Mis brazos están cansados - My arms are tired

1080. intervención - intervention

Tuvo que pasar por una intervención quirúrgica - He had to go through a surgical intervention

1081. sal - salt / you get out (imperative)

Sal de aquí y tráeme la sal - Get out of here and bring me the salt

1082. páginas - pages
¿Cuántas páginas tiene el libro? - How many pages does the book have?

1083. nueve - nine
¡Obtuve un nueve en el examen de español! - I got a nine on the Spanish exam!

1084. pueblos - people
Para los pueblos originarios, este lugar era sagrado - For the native people, this place was sacred

1085. temporada - season
Estoy viendo la segunda temporada de la serie que me recomendaste - I'm watching the second season of the series that you recommended

1086. tus - your (plural)
Tus hermanos son geniales - Your brothers are great

1087. abajo - down / underneath
¿Buscaste abajo del sofá? - Did you look under the sofa?

1088. aquello - that
Aquello que se ve en el cielo es una tormenta - That in the sky is a storm

1089. maestro - master / teacher
Juan fue mi maestro en la primaria - Juan was my primary school teacher

1090. internacionales - international (plural)
Soy estudiante de Relaciones Internacionales - I am an International Relations student

1091. técnicas - techniques / technical (feminine, plural)
Hay muchas técnicas para prender una fogata - There are many techniques to light a fire

1092. estás - you are
¿Estás ocupada? - Are you busy?

1093. esposa - wife
Mi esposa está de viaje por España - My wife is traveling around Spain

1094. crítica - critique / critical (feminine)
El libro es una crítica al neoliberalismo - The book is a critique to neoliberalism

1095. totalmente - totally
Estoy totalmente agotada - I'm totally exhausted

1096. perder - to lose
No debemos perder el rumbo - We must not lose our way

1097. venta - sale
Voy a hacer una venta de jardín - I will host a garden sale

1098. finales - endings / final (plural)
Amo los finales felices - I love happy endings

1099. contar - to tell
¿Te puedo contar un secreto? - Can I tell you a secret?

1100. diferencias - differences
No hay diferencias entre tu opinión y la mía - There are no differences between your opinion and mine

1101. familiar - familiar / relative
Tu rostro se me hace familiar - Your face looks familiar

1102. kilómetros - kilometers
¿Cuántos kilómetros hemos recorrido ya? - How many kilometers have we traveled so far?

1103. mala - bad / evil (feminine)
Tuve una mala experiencia con la agencia de viajes - I had a bad experience with the travel agency

1104. fundamental - fundamental
Es fundamental que trabajemos en equipo - It is fundamental that we work as a team

1105. enorme – enormous / huge
¡Tengo un problema enorme! - I have a huge problem!

1106. puedan - they can (subjunctive)
¿Tienes amigos que puedan trabajar con nosotros? - Do you have friends who can work with us?

1107. líneas - lines
En la mitad de la obra, olvidé mis líneas - In the middle of the play, I forgot my lines

1108. ofrece - he/she/it offers
Mi nuevo jefe me ofrece su ayuda constantemente - My new boss is constantly offering me his help

1109. comercial - commercial
Trabajo en el área comercial - I work in the commercial area

1110. pan - bread
Me olvidé de comprar el pan - I forgot to buy bread

1111. aires - air / airs / look
El gato saltó por los aires - The cat jumped through the air

1112. profesor - professor / teacher
Trabajo como profesor en la universidad - I work as a professor at the university

1113. inversión - investment
Es una inversión muy segura - It is a very safe investment

1114. municipal - municipal
El gobierno municipal es muy eficiente - The municipal government is very efficient

1115. declaraciones - declarations / statements
El hombre hizo varias declaraciones contradictorias ante la justicia - The man made several contradictory statements to the justice

1116. funcionarios - officials
Los funcionarios de gobierno pueden entrar por la otra puerta - Government officials can enter through the other door

1117. aguas - waters
Las aguas del río bajan desde la montaña - The waters of the river descend from the mountain

1118. responsable - responsible
Soy responsable por el bienestar de mis hijos - I am responsible for the welfare of my children

1119. sábado - *Saturday*
Te esperamos el sábado - We will be waiting for you on Saturday

1120. alguno - *some*
¿Alguno de ustedes tiene un chicle? - Do any of you have chewing gum?

1121. federal - *federal*
Este país tiene un gobierno federal - This country has a federal government

1122. señala - *he/she/it points out*
El bebé señala lo que desea comer - The baby points out what he wants to eat

1123. conflicto - *conflict*
Hay un conflicto armado en Medio Oriente - There is an armed conflict in the Middle East

1124. dicha - *joy / said*
Mi dicha es infinita - My joy is infinite

1125. dirigentes - *leaders*
Los dirigentes sindicales son todos hombres - The union leaders are all men

1126. cambiar - *to change*
Esto debe cambiar - This must change

1127. superficie - *surface / area*
¿Sabes cómo calcular la superficie de un triángulo? - Do you know how to calculate the surface of a triangle?

1128. necesita - *he/she/it needs*
Mi planta necesita agua - My plant needs water

1129. estudiantes - *students*
Conocí un grupo de estudiantes alemanes - I met a group of German students

1130. tantos - *so many (masculine)*
Ya visitamos tantos países que estoy desorientada - We already visited so many countries that I am disoriented

1131. golpe - punch / blow
Su muerte fue un duro golpe para el barrio - Her death was a severe blow to the neighborhood

1132. públicos - public (masculine, plural)
Los asuntos públicos deben ser transparentes - Public affairs must be transparent

1133. públicas - public (feminine, plural)
Las políticas públicas no son sencillas - Public policies are not simple

1134. equipos - teams / equipments
Hay dos equipos listos para jugar - Two teams are ready to play

1135. literatura - literature
Me gusta la literatura latinoamericana - I like Latin American literature

1136. pruebas - tests
Debo hacer varias pruebas antes de que me contraten - I have to do several tests before I get hired

1137. circunstancias - circumstances
Hay circunstancias que nos obligaron a viajar después - There are circumstances that forced us to travel later

1138. tienes - you have
¿Tienes algo de beber? - Do you have something to drink?

1139. documento - document / file
Estoy esperando un documento importante - I am waiting for an important document

1140. fiesta - party
Me invitaron a una fiesta - I was invited to a party

1141. simplemente - simply / just
Simplemente obedece a tu madre - Just obey your mother

1142. aceite - oil
Necesitamos aceite de oliva - We need olive oil

1143. establecer - to establish / set
Hay que establecer reglas en esta casa - We have to set rules in this house

1144. médicos - doctors

Mi tía no confía en los médicos - My aunt does not trust doctors

1145. eres - you are

Eres muy rápida, ¡espérame! - You are very fast, wait for me!

1146. locales - local (plural)

Los problemas locales también afectan al resto del país - Local problems also affect the rest of the country

1147. empezó - he/she/it started / began

¡Ella empezó! - She started it!

1148. pobre - poor

Mi abuelo era muy pobre - My grandfather was very poor

1149. debería - I/he/she/it should

¿Crees que debería llevar un vino a la fiesta? - Do you think I should bring a bottle of wine to the party?

1150. llevó - he/she/it took

Mi esposo llevó a nuestro hijo a la escuela - My husband took our son to school

1151. parlamento - parliament

El Parlamento Europeo es muy poderoso - The European Parliament is very powerful

1152. territorio - territory

No hay dos lugares iguales en todo el territorio - No two places are the same throughout the territory

1153. sale - he/she/it goes out / comes out

¿Cuándo sale tu libro? - When is your book coming out?

1154. treinta - thirty

Tengo treinta años - I am thirty years old

1155. coche - car

Vine en coche - I came by car

1156. clases - classes

Doy clases de guitarra - I teach guitar

1157. afirma - he/she/it claims

Diana afirma que la estafaron - Diana claims that she was cheated

1158. oficiales - officers

Pidamos indicaciones a esos oficiales de policía - Let's ask those police officers for directions

1159. diálogo - dialogue

Debes tener diálogo con tus colegas - You must have dialogue with your colleagues

1160. respeto - respect

Tengo mucho respeto por tu trabajo - I have a lot of respect for your work

1161. tratado - treaty / tried (participle)

He tratado de llamarte por horas - I've tried calling you for hours

1162. llevaba - he/she/it took / used to take (imperfect past)

Mi madre me llevaba a la escuela en bicicleta - My mother used to take me to school by bicycle

1163. revista - magazine

Escribí un artículo para una revista - I wrote an article for a magazine

1164. copa - wine glass

¿Quieres una copa de vino? - Do you want a glass of wine?

1165. pintura - painting / paint

Quiero comprar una pintura para mi sala de estar - I want to buy a painting for my living room

1166. nombres - names

¿Qué nombres tienen pensados para su bebé? - What names are you considering for your baby?

1167. propósito - purpose

¿Cuál es el propósito de tu visita? - What is the purpose of your visit?

1168. leche - milk

Pon un poco de leche en mi café, por favor - Put some milk in my coffee, please

1169. actualidad - present

En la actualidad, eso no es un problema - In the present, that is not a problem

1170. constituye - it constitutes

Divulgar información personal constituye una violación a nuestro acuerdo - Disclosing personal information constitutes a violation of our agreement

1171. tarea - task / homework

Tengo una tarea muy importante para ti - I have a very important task for you

1172. alcanzar - to reach

¿Puedes alcanzar ese frasco? - Can you reach that jar?

1173. competencia - competition / competence

Hugo participó en una competencia de ajedrez - Hugo participated in a chess competition

1174. normas - norms

Lee las normas de la piscina - Read the pool norms

1175. plata - silver / money

¿Esos aretes son de plata? - Are those earrings made of silver?

1176. vecinos - neighbours

Mis vecinos son muy amables - My neighbors are very kind

1177. fenómeno - phenomenon

Es un fenómeno inusual - It is an unusual phenomenon

1178. intención - intention

Tengo la intención de quedarme a vivir - I have the intention to stay to live

1179. dando - giving

Esta computadora me está dando problemas - This computer is giving me problems

1180. diputados - deputies

Los diputados son electos cada cuatro años - Deputies are elected every four years

1181. judicial - judicial

Hay un conflicto judicial - There is a judicial conflict

1182. cualquiera - any / anyone

Cualquiera de nosotros puede hacerlo - Any of us can do it

1183. fe - faith
Tengo fe en la ciencia - I have faith in science
1184. jornada - day
Ha sido una jornada larga - It has been a long day
1185. ganar - to win
Juego para ganar, no para divertirme - I play to win, not to have fun
1186. candidato - candidate
Él es el candidato más popular - He is the most popular candidate
1187. calor - heat / hot
Tengo mucho calor - I am very hot
1188. esperanza - hope
Aún hay esperanza - There is still hope
1189. recién - just now / recently
Recién escuché las noticias - I just heard the news
1190. suele - he/she/it normally... / often... / usually... (verb)
María suele comportarse bien - Maria usually behaves well
1191. miles - thousands
Todavía nos quedan miles de kilómetros por recorrer - We still have thousands of kilometers to go
1192. ritmo - rhythm
No pierdas el ritmo - Don't lose the rhythm
1193. vive - he/she/it lives
Mi abuela vive aquí cerca - My grandmother lives nearby
1194. quizás - maybe / perhaps
Quizás deberíamos pedir indicaciones - Maybe we should ask for directions
1195. pasos - steps
¿Ya has aprendido los pasos de baile? - Have you already learned the dance steps?
1196. sensación - sensation
Tengo la sensación de que nos aguarda una sorpresa - I have a sensation that a surprise awaits us

1197. representación - representation

Este libro es una fiel representación de la realidad - This book is a faithful representation of reality

1198. presidencia - presidency

Hay varios candidatos para la presidencia - There are several candidates for the presidency

1199. triunfo - triumph

El partido terminó en un triunfo... del equipo contrario - The match ended in a triumph... of the opposing team

1200. ayuntamiento - town hall

Ese es el viejo ayuntamiento de la ciudad - That is the old town hall

Chapter 5 – Words 1201-1500

1201. plantas - plants
¿Puedes regar mis plantas mientras estoy de viaje? - Can you water my plants while I'm away?

1202. niña - girl
Raquel es solo una niña - Raquel is just a girl

1203. frío - cold
¡Tengo mucho frío! - I feel very cold!

1204. tono - tone / shade
Me gusta ese tono de azul - I like that shade of blue

1205. compañeros – companions / classmates / workmates
Estos son mis compañeros de la universidad - These are my university classmates

1206. quieren - they want
Mis padres quieren que vayamos a cenar - My parents want us to go to dinner

1207. pesos - pesos
El precio de un kilo de tomate es ciento veinte pesos - The price of one kilo of tomato is one hundred and twenty pesos

1208. delante - in front of
Delante del edificio hay una biblioteca - In front of the building there is a library

1209. propias - own / of one's own (feminine, plural)
A veces no comprendo mis propias palabras - Sometimes I don't understand my own words

1210. plano - plan / flat

Me gustaría ver el plano de la casa - I would like to see the plan of the house

1211. enfermedades - diseases

Las vacunas protegen a la gente de las enfermedades - Vaccines protect people from diseases

1212. institución - institution

Esta institución tiene reglas muy estrictas - This institution has very strict rules

1213. edificio - building

El edificio es muy antiguo - The building is very old

1214. nota - note / he/she/it notes / you note (imperative)

Toma nota de todo lo que diga el profesor en clase - Take note of everything the teacher says in class

1215. jugar - to play

¿Quieres jugar al fútbol? - Do you want to play football?

1216. representa - he/she/it represents

Supuestamente, el político representa los intereses del pueblo - Supposedly, the politician represents the interests of the people

1217. gesto - gesture

¿Qué significa ese gesto? - What does that gesture mean?

1218. mensaje - message

Tengo un mensaje para ti - I have a message for you

1219. vasco - Basque (masculine)

Mi apellido es vasco, pero yo soy de Argentina - My last name is Basque, but I'm from Argentina

1220. pudiera - could

Si pudiera, iría - If I could, I would go

1221. influencia - influence

Enrique tiene mucha influencia en la oficina - Enrique has a lot of influence in the office

1222. pocas - little / few (feminine, plural)

Tengo pocas amigas - I have just a few friends

1223. realizado - done / carried out (participle)

El operativo realizado por la policía fue un éxito - The operation carried out by the police was a success

1224. conducta - behaviour

Tu conducta es inapropiada - Your behavior is inappropriate

1225. objetos - objects

¡Cuántos objetos extraños hay en esta tienda! - There are so many strange objects in this store!

1226. tamaño - size

¡Mira el tamaño de esas manzanas! - Look at the size of those apples!

1227. provincia - province

Esta provincia es la más pequeña del país - This province is the smallest in the country

1228. europeo - European

El edificio tiene un estilo muy europeo - The building has a very European style

1229. verde - green

¿Tienes una pluma verde? - Do you have a green pen?

1230. informó - he/she/it informed

El médico me informó los resultados del estudio - The doctor informed me of the study results

1231. escribir - to write

Le voy a escribir un correo a mi familia - I will write an email to my family

1232. materiales - materials

Necesito comprar materiales para la clase de arte - I need to buy materials for the art class

1233. cumplir - to comply / to fulfill

Voy a cumplir con todo lo que prometí - I will fulfill everything I promised

1234. pidió - he/she/it asked / ordered

Alex me pidió matrimonio - Alex asked me to marry him

1235. alumnos - students
Tengo cinco alumnos, por el momento - I have five students, at the moment

1236. ámbito - ambit / scope / field
Ella es muy respetada en el ámbito de la ciencia - She is highly respected in the field of science

1237. muertos - dead (plural)
Cuando regresé a casa, mis cactus estaban muertos - When I came home my cacti were dead

1238. explica - he/she/it explains
La maestra les explica a los alumnos la teoría de la evolución - The teacher explains to the students the theory of evolution

1239. consecuencias - consequences
Toda acción tiene consecuencias - Every action has consequences

1240. refiere - he/she/it refers / means
¿A qué se refiere con eso? - What does he mean by that?

1241. comer - to eat
¿Qué quieres comer esta noche? - What do you want to eat tonight?

1242. fines - purposes / end / endings
La pintora nació a fines del siglo pasado - The painter was born at the end of the last century

1243. versión - version
Prefiero la versión original de la película - I prefer the original version of the movie

1244. abierto - open
El restaurante ya está abierto, ¿vamos? - The restaurant is open already, shall we go?

1245. debate - debate
Un debate interesante comenzó en el hostel - An interesting debate started at the hostel

1246. barrio - neighborhood
En mi barrio hay un lindo cine - In my neighborhood there is a nice cinema

1247. labor - work / labour
La labor doméstica es trabajo - Domestic labour is work

1248. fondos - funds / backgrounds
Los fondos de la empresa son insuficientes para este proyecto - The company funds are insufficient for this project

1249. justo - just / fair
¡No es justo! - It's not fair!

1250. tradición - tradition
Este festival es parte de la tradición del país - This festival is part of the country's tradition

1251. diferente - different
Me gustas porque eres diferente del resto - I like you because you are different from the rest

1252. piensa - he/she/it thinks
¿Qué piensa tu hermana sobre esto? - What does your sister think about this?

1253. tecnología - technology
Trabajo en el desarrollo de tecnología informática - I work in the development of computer technology

1254. mantiene - he/she/it maintains / supports
Mi madre mantiene a toda la familia - My mother supports the whole family

1255. situaciones - situations
Viví situaciones muy difíciles durante el último año - I lived through very difficult situations in the last year

1256. fase - phase
Mi hijo está pasando por una fase de rebeldía - My son is going through a rebel phase

1257. histórico - historic / historical (masculine)
Este es un edificio histórico - This is a historical building

1258. agentes - agents / officers
Esos agentes de policía pueden ayudarnos - Those police officers can help us

1259. planta - plant
Marcos me regaló una planta por mi cumpleaños - Marcos gave me a plant for my birthday

1260. actuación - acting / performance
La actuación de Sara fue impresionante - Sara's performance was impressive

1261. iban - they went / used to go
Mis abuelos iban a caminar al parque todas las mañanas - My grandparents used to go to the park every morning

1262. actos - acts / ceremonies
Tras los actos inaugurales, comenzó la celebración - After the opening ceremonies, the celebration began

1263. posibles - possible (plural)
Mis objetivos son desafiantes, pero posibles - My goals are challenging, but possible

1264. león - lion
En el zoológico había un león - In the zoo there was a lion

1265. mamá - mom
Mi mamá es ingeniera informática - My mom is a computer engineer

1266. velocidad - speed
El taxi iba a toda velocidad - The taxi was going full speed

1267. familiares - relatives / familiar (plural)
Tengo familiares en Sudamérica - I have relatives in South America

1268. especies - species (plural)
¿Cuántas especies de flamencos hay en la isla? - How many species of flamingos are there on the island?

1269. cabe - it fits
Ese sombrero no cabe en la maleta - That hat does not fit in the suitcase

1270. asamblea - assembly
No se decidió nada en la asamblea - Nothing was decided at the assembly
1271. comunidades - communities
Todas las comunidades de la zona se oponen a la represa - All the communities in the area oppose the dam
1272. museo - museum
El museo cierra los lunes - The museum closes on Mondays
1273. conferencia - conference
Viajé a Bogotá por una conferencia - I traveled to Bogotá to go to a conference
1274. prácticamente - practically
Recorrimos prácticamente todo el país - We toured practically the entire country
1275. autoridad - authority
¿Quién es la máxima autoridad de este lugar? - Who is the highest authority in this place?
1276. sujeto - subject / guy
Gaspar es un sujeto tranquilo y agradable - Gaspar is a calm and pleasant guy
1277. tratar - to try
Voy a tratar de estudiar más duro - I will try to study harder
1278. hacerse - to do it to oneself / to get something done
Marta debe hacerse un análisis de sangre - Marta has to get a blood test done
1279. pérdida - loss / leak
Hay una pérdida de gas - There is a gas leak
1280. dificultades - difficulties
Olivia tuvo dificultades para llegar - Olivia had difficulties getting here
1281. rato - time / while
Nos vemos en un rato - See you in a while

1282. pagar - to pay

Deberíamos pagar nuestra cuenta y pedir un Uber - We should pay our bill and get an Uber

1283. colegio - school / college

Mis hijos están en el colegio - My children are at school

1284. sabes - you know

¿Sabes cómo llegar al concierto? - Do you know how to get to the concert?

1285. personaje - character

Homero es mi personaje preferido - Homer is my favorite character

1286. áreas - areas

Hay varias áreas en conflicto dentro de la región - There are several areas of conflict within the region

1287. audiencia - audience / public

La audiencia es muy exigente - The audience is very demanding

1288. doce - twelve

Una docena tiene doce huevos - A dozen has twelve eggs

1289. haga - that I make / that /he/she/it makes (subjunctive)

¿Quieres que haga una tarta? - Do you want me to make a cake?

1290. periódico - newspaper / journal

¿Has leído el periódico de esta mañana? - Did you read the newspaper this morning?

1291. distribución - distribución

Emiliano trabaja en una empresa de distribución - Emiliano works in a distribution company

1292. ausencia - absence

No soporto tu ausencia - I can't stand your absence

1293. entrevista - interview

El periodista hizo una entrevista a un músico famoso - The journalist did an interview with a famous musician

1294. recibió - he/she/it received

Mi hermana recibió una beca doctoral - My sister received a doctoral scholarship

1295. añadió - he/she/it added
El profesor añadió una pregunta al examen - The teacher added a question to the exam

1296. cocina - kitchen
Ven a la cocina un momento - Come to the kitchen for a moment

1297. edición - editing / edition
Lanzarán una edición especial por el aniversario del álbum - They will release a special edition for the anniversary of the album

1298. económicos - economic (masculine, plural)
Los problemas económicos del país son muy complejos - The country's economic problems are very complex

1299. naturales - natural (plural)
Las reservas naturales del país son enormes - The country's natural reserves are huge

1300. al parecer - apparently
Al parecer, se ha cancelado el evento - Apparently, the event has been canceled

1301. santo - saint (masculine)
Esta pintura representa a Santo Tomás - This painting represents Saint Thomas

1302. vieja - old (feminine)
Esta vieja mochila ha viajado conmigo por muchos años - This old backpack has traveled with me for many years

1303. corresponde - it corresponds
Lo que sucedió no se corresponde con lo que los economistas previeron - What happened does not correspond to what economists predicted

1304. decidió - he/she/it decided
Mi jefe decidió darme un ascenso - My boss decided to give me a promotion

1305. llegada - arrival
Estoy esperando la llegada del autobús - I'm waiting for the arrival of the bus

1306. comienza - he/she/it begins / starts

¿A qué hora comienza la película? - What time does the movie start?

1307. organizaciones - organizations

Tengo experiencia en organizaciones sin fines de lucro - I have experience in non-profit organizations

1308. tendencia - tendency

La población tiene tendencia a crecer - Population has the tendency to grow

1309. escenario - stage

Extraño estar en el escenario - I miss being on stage

1310. en definitiva - definitely / in short

En definitiva, todo terminó bien - In short, everything ended well

1311. deberá - he/she/it will have to

Señor, deberá presentar su documento - Sir, you will have to show your ID card

1212. indicó - he/she/it indicated / showed

Un amable señor me indicó cómo llegar - A kind gentleman showed me how to get here

1313. noticia - news (singular)

¡Tengo una noticia! - I have some news!

1314. inglés - English

No quiero hablar en inglés - I do not want to speak in English

1315. reina - queen

La reina de Inglaterra tiene 93 años - The Queen of England is 93 years old

1316. ustedes - you (plural, formal in Spain, informal and formal in Latin America)

¿Ustedes son hermanos? - Are you siblings?

1317. madera - wood

Fabriqué una silla de madera - I made a wooden chair

1318. alemán - German

Yo soy alemán, pero vivo en Francia - I am German, but I live in France

1319. habitantes - inhabitants / people
Los habitantes del pueblo son muy amables - The villagers are very friendly

1320. recibir - to receive
Voy a recibir un bono navideño - I will receive a Christmas bonus

1321. salvo - except
Todos iremos, salvo Jorge - We will all go, except for Jorge

1322. familias - families
En este edificio viven unas quince familias - About fifteen families live in this building

1323. miembro - member (masculine)
Soy miembro del club de polo - I am a member of the polo club

1324. escritor - writer (masculine)
Mi hermano es escritor - My brother is a writer

1325. conoce - he/she/it knows
Mi esposa conoce a tu esposo - My wife knows your husband

1326. cuidado - care
¡Ten mucho cuidado con eso! - Be very careful with that!

1327. identidad - identity
¿Tienes tu documento de identidad? - Do you have your identity card?

1328. quiso - he/she/it wanted to
Laura no quiso venir - Laura did not want to come

1329. pareja - couple
Marcos y Ariel son una pareja muy simpática - Marcos and Ariel are a very nice couple

1330. evidente - evident
Es evidente que el problema es grave - It is evident that the problem is serious

1331. ciertos - certain (masculine, plural)
Tengo ciertos asuntos que resolver - I have certain issues to solve

1332. siguen - they continue / they follow

Esos perros me siguen a todos lados - Those dogs follow me everywhere

1333. declaración - statement

Tomás hizo una declaración ante el juez - Tomás made a statement before the judge

1334. cadena - chain

Necesito una cadena para atar mi bicicleta - I need a chain to lock my bike

1335. acaba - he/she/it ends / finishes / has just

Susana acaba de llegar - Susana has just arrived

1336. consiste - it consists

¿En qué consiste la prueba? - What does the test consist of?

1337. presentación - presentation

Mañana tengo que hacer una presentación importante - I have to make an important presentation tomorrow

1338. cuentas - accounts / mathematical operations

Soy encargado de tres cuentas de clientes - I am in charge of three customer accounts

1339. azul - blue

¿Dónde está mi gorra azul? - Where's my blue cap?

1340. década - decade

¡Es el evento de la década! - It's the event of the decade!

1341. puertas - doors

Cierra todas las puertas con llave - Lock all doors

1342. comida - food

Quiero probar la comida local - I want to try the local food

1343. de inmediato - immediately / right away

¿Quiere otro café? ¡De inmediato! - Would you like another coffee? Right away!

1344. marca - brand / mark

No me importa la marca, me importa la calidad - I don't care about the brand, I care about the quality

1345. antiguo – antique / old
Este bosque es muy antiguo - This forest is very old

1346. rojo - red (masculine)
¿Me prestas tu lápiz labial rojo? - Can I borrow your red lipstick?

1347. debemos - we must
Debemos apresurarnos - We must hurry

1348. instante - instant
¡Ven en este instante! - Come here this instant!

1349. operaciones - operations / surgeries
El banco realiza miles de operaciones financieras cada hora - The bank carries out thousands of financial operations every hour

1350. iniciativa - initiative
Por iniciativa del presidente, se hará un acto público - At the initiative of the President, there will be a public act

1351. caer - to fall
Ese árbol va a caer en cualquier momento - That tree is going to fall at any moment

1352. luna - moon
Esta noche hay luna llena - Tonight there is a full moon

1353. veía - he/she/it saw / used to see / used to watch (imperfect past)
Cuando era pequeña, veía televisión todo el tiempo - When I was little, I used to watch television all the time

1354. verdadero - true
El testimonio fue verdadero, pero insuficiente - The testimony was true, but insufficient

1355. habitación - room
Quiero reservar una habitación doble, por favor - I want to book a double room, please

1356. manifestó - he/she/it manifested / expressed
El vecino manifestó su descontento - The neighbor expressed his discontent

1357. tío - uncle

Mi tío es enfermero - My uncle is a nurse

1358. quedado - stayed / remained (participle)

Me he quedado toda la tarde en la habitación, leyendo - I stayed in the room all afternoon, reading

1359. martes - Tuesday

Todos los martes tomo clases de español - Every Tuesday I take Spanish lessons

1360. pleno - full / complete / mid (masculine)

El avión está en pleno vuelo - The plane is in mid-flight

1361. declaró - he/she/it declared / testified

El testigo declaró ante el juez - The witness testified before the judge

1362. juegos - games

¿Jugamos a un juego de mesa? - Shall we play a board game?

1363. mínimo - minimum

¿Cuál el salario mínimo en el país? - What is the minimum wage in the country?

1364. aparición – apparition / appearance

Denunciaron la aparición de ratas en el edificio - They denounced the appearance of rats in the building

1365. estará - he/she/it will be

El artista estará presente en la inauguración de la exposición - The artist will be present at the opening of the exhibition

1366. transporte - transport / transportation

Debemos contratar transporte para ir mañana al aeropuerto - We must hire transportation to go to the airport tomorrow

1367. ven - they see

Los gatos ven en la oscuridad - Cats can see in the dark

1368. pretende - he/she/it pretends / intends / expects

Mi jefe pretende que trabaje el sábado - My boss expects me to work on Saturday

1369. tantas - so many (feminine)

El edificio tiene tantas oficinas que siempre me pierdo - The building has so many offices that I always get lost

1370. sede - headquarters

Hay una sede de mi universidad en Buenos Aires - There is a headquarters of my university in Buenos Aires

1371. comportamiento - behaviour

El comportamiento de Santiago fue inapropiado - Santiago's behavior was inappropriate

1372. periodistas - journalists

Los periodistas trabajan para encontrar la verdad - Journalists work to find the truth

1373. animal - animal

El elefante es mi animal preferido - The elephant is my favorite animal

1374. convertido - turned into / become (masculine)

Te has convertido en un gran amigo - You have become a great friend

1375. brazo - arm

Me duele el brazo derecho - My right arm hurts

1376. hermanos - brothers / siblings

Nosotros somos hermanos - We are brothers

1377. rico - rich / tasty / delicious (masculine)

¡Tu pastel está muy rico! - Your cake is delicious!

1378. anunció - he/she/it announced

El presidente anunció medidas de urgencia - The president announced emergency measures

1379. presupuesto - budget

¿Cuál es nuestro presupuesto? - What's our budget?

1380. estrategia - strategy

Nuestra estrategia es esperar - Our strategy is to wait

1381. naciones - nations

Las naciones van más allá de los límites geográficos - Nations go beyond geographical frontiers

1382. utilizar - to use

¿Puedo utilizar tu cargador? - Can I use your charger?

1383. buenas - good (feminine, plural)

Bautista tiene buenas intenciones - Bautista has good intentions

1384. compromiso - compromise / engagement

¿Oíste del compromiso de Iara y Juan? - Did you hear about Iara and Juan's engagement?

1385. acaso - perhaps / maybe / by any chance

¿Acaso dije algo malo? - Perhaps I said something wrong?

1386. completo - complete / entire (masculine)

Lisa leyó el libro completo en una tarde - Lisa read the entire book in one afternoon

1387. pelo - hair

Quiero cortarme el pelo - I want to get a haircut

1388. piedra - stone / rock

El niño lanzó una piedra al agua - The boy threw a stone into the water

1389. medicina - medicine

Abuelo, debes tomar tu medicina todos los días - Grandpa, you must take your medicine every day

1390. campos - fields

Mi bisabuelo era dueño de muchos campos - My great-grandfather owned many fields

1391. liga - league

La liga de fútbol española es muy popular - The Spanish soccer league is very popular

1392. vaya - that I go / that he/she/it goes (subjunctive) / you go (formal, imperative)

Laura me pidió que vaya a su casa - Laura asked me to go to her house

1393. disposición - disposition / arrangement

Debemos planear la disposición de los asientos - We have to plan the sitting arrangement

1394. permanente - permanent

Me ofrecieron un puesto permanente - I was offered a permanent position

1395. método - method

Desarrollé un método para que todo quepa en la maleta - I developed a method so that everything fits in the suitcase

1396. sentía - I/he/she/it felt / was feeling

Hugo no se sentía muy bien - Hugo was not feeling very well

1397. próxima - next (feminine)

La próxima vez, llegaremos más temprano - Next time, we will arrive earlier

1398. tierras - lands

Estas tierras pertenecen al Estado - These lands belong to the State

1399. error - mistake / error

Mi error fue confiar demasiado - My mistake was trusting too much

1400. incremento - increase

Hubo un incremento en las ventas - There was an increase in sales

1401. piso - floor / ground

Creo que su chupete está en el piso - I think her pacifier is on the floor

1402. similar - similar

Tu camiseta es similar a la mía - Your shirt is similar to mine

1403. viento - wind

¡Hay demasiado viento! Vamos adentro - It's too windy! Let's go inside

1404. salvador - savior

Daniel fue el salvador de la fiesta - Daniel was the savior of the party

1405. seres - beings

Los seres humanos pueden ser egoístas - Human beings can be selfish

1406. posteriormente - later / subsequently

Posteriormente, el problema se solucionó - Later on, the problem was solved

1405. dispuesto - willing (masculine)

¿Estás dispuesto a levantarte temprano? - Are you willing to get up early?

1406. poeta - poet

Neruda era un poeta chileno - Neruda was a Chilean poet

1407. económicas - economic (feminine, plural)

Nuestras dificultades económicas son pasajeras - Our economic difficulties are temporary

1408. secreto - secret

Facundo me contó un secreto - Facundo told me a secret

1409. funcionamiento - functioning

El técnico verificó el funcionamiento de la máquina - The technician checked the functioning of the machine

1410. debajo - under / underneath

Hay un calcetín debajo de la cama - There is a sock under the bed

1411. recordar - to remember

Debes recordar lo que te voy a decir - You must remember what I am going to tell you

1412. presentó - he/she/it presented / introduced

Cecilia me presentó a su familia - Cecilia introduced me to her family

1413. jueves - Thursday

El jueves haremos una excursión a Toledo - On Thursday we will go on a tour to Toledo

1414. corriente - current / normal / ordinary

Soy una persona común y corriente - I am an ordinary person

1415. ingresos - income

Debes administrar mejor tus ingresos - You must better manage your income

1416. intento – try / attempt
Hubo un intento de fuga en la prisión - There was an attempt to escape in prison

1417. tuvieron - they had
Gaby y Freda tuvieron un hijo - Gaby and Freda had a son

1418. colores - colors
Prefiero los colores oscuros - I prefer dark colors

1419. altos - tall (masculine, plural)
Esos árboles son muy altos - Those trees are very tall

1420. hojas - leaves / papers / sheets
Las hojas de los árboles se caen en otoño - Tree leaves fall in autumn

1421. probablemente - probably
Todo saldrá bien... probablemente - Everything will work out... probably

1422. búsqueda - search
Mi búsqueda laboral fue un fracaso - My job search was a failure

1423. pequeñas - little
Las manos del bebé son muy pequeñas y delicadas - The baby's hands are very small and delicate

1424. oferta - offer
Hicimos una oferta por la casa - We made an offer on the house

1425. oficina - office
Nos vemos mañana en la oficina - See you tomorrow at the office

1426. produjo - he/she/it produced
El artista produjo muchas obras nuevas - The artist produced many new works

1427. pasada - past / passed (feminine)
Su vida pasada es un misterio - His past life is a mystery

1428. volumen - volume
¿Podrías bajar el volumen? - Could you turn down the volume?

1429. parecen - they seem

Tus padres parecen muy agradables - Your parents seem very nice

1430. causas - causes

Necesitamos identificar las causas del problema - We need to identify the causes of the problem

1431. dieron - they gave

Mis alumnos me dieron un regalo por Navidad - My students gave me a Christmas present

1432. división - division

La división de bienes se llevó adelante tras el divorcio - The division of property was carried out after the divorce

1433. darle - to give him/her/it

Deberíamos darle algo de comer a la tortuga - We should give the turtle something to eat

1434. clave - key / password

¿Cuál es la clave del wifi? - What is the wifi password?

1435. reciente - recent

Una publicación reciente arrojó luz sobre el asunto - A recent publication shed light on the matter

1436. votos - votes

Necesitamos más votos positivos - We need more positive votes

1437. logró - he/she/it accomplished

Raúl logró lo que se había propuesto - Raúl accomplished what he had set out to do

1438. piernas - legs

Mis piernas están muy doloridas, porque ayer fui al gimnasio - My legs are sore, because yesterday I went to the gym

1439. sirve - he/she/it serves

El sumiller sirve el vino - The sommelier serves the wine

1440. deuda - debt

Tengo una pequeña deuda con mi hermana - I have a small debt to my sister

1441. noticias - news (plural)
Andrea tiene noticias importantes - Andrea has important news

1442. menores - minor / smaller (plural) / minors
En este bar no pueden entrar menores de edad - Minors cannot enter this bar

1443. querido - dear (masculine)
Querido Oscar, espero que estés bien - Dear Oscar, I hope you are well

1444. pago - payment
Ya he realizado el pago - I have already made the payment

1445. fig - higo
¿Quieres un poco de dulce de higo? - Do you want some fig jam?

1446. recuerda - you remember (imperative) / he/she/it remembers
Recuerda lo que te aconsejó tu madre - Remember what your mother advised you

1447. podrán - they will be able to (can, future)
Tus amigos podrán dormir en la habitación de huéspedes - Your friends can sleep in the guest room

1448. independencia - independence
La independencia argentina se logró en 1816 - Argentine independence was achieved in 1816

1449. ataque - attack
Después de ver la película, teme que haya un ataque extraterrestre - After watching the movie, he's afraid that there will be an alien attack

1450. igualmente - equally / likewise / still
Estoy cansada, pero igualmente debo ir a trabajar - I'm tired, but I still have to go to work

1451. necesaria - necessary
¿Es necesaria tanta sal en la comida? - Is so much salt in the food necessary?

1452. quedan - they remain / to have left

¿Cuántas manzanas nos quedan? - How many apples do we have left?

1453. regional - regional

Es un problema regional, no nacional - It is a regional problem, not a national one

1454. decisiones - decisions

Tengo que tomar decisiones difíciles - I have to make difficult decisions

1455. concepción - conception

Las ideas cambian mucho desde su concepción hasta su concreción - Ideas change a lot from their conception to their fulfilment

1456. llegaron - they arrived

Mis amigos llegaron anoche - My friends arrived last night

1457. siente - he/she/it feels

Mi padre no se siente muy bien - My father is not feeling very well

1458. juntos - together (masculine, plural)

¿Estáis viajando juntos? - Are you traveling together?

1459. sabemos - we know

No sabemos cómo llegar al puerto - We don't know how to get to the port

1460. ropa - clothes

No tengo ropa limpia - I do not have clean clothes

1461. parque - park

¿Hay un parque por aquí? - Is there a park around here?

1462. empresarios - businessmen (masculine)

Mañana recibiremos a un grupo de empresarios españoles - Tomorrow we will welcome a group of Spanish businessmen

1463. conmigo - with me

¿Vienes conmigo a hacer las compras? - Are you coming with me to do the shopping?

1464. procedimiento - procedure
Debemos seguir el procedimiento legal - We must follow the legal procedure

1465. suma - sum / addition
La suma de las compras es de 55 euros - The shopping adds up to 55 euros

1466. elección - election / choice
Es tu elección - It's your choice

1467. leer - to read
¡Quiero leer un libro de aventuras! - I want to read an adventure book!

1468. feliz - happy
Estoy muy feliz por mi nuevo empleo - I am very happy for my new job

1469. ninguno - no / none / no one
Ninguno de mis amigos quiere ir al cine - None of my friends want to go to the cinema

1470. continuación - continuation / next
A continuación, debes batir la crema - Next, you must whip the cream

1471. ministros - ministers
Los ministros y ministras organizaron una reunión de urgencia - The ministers organized an emergency meeting

1472. verdadera - true (feminine)
Mi verdadera pasión es la música - My true passion is music

1473. reacción - reaction
¿Cuál fue su reacción ante la noticia? - What was his reaction to the news?

1474. podían - they could
En el pasado, las mujeres no podían votar - In the past, women couldn't vote

1475. tanta – so / so much (feminine)
¡Tengo tanta hambre! - I am so hungry!

1476. tomó - he/she/it took
Greta tomó la servilleta y la arrojó a la basura - Greta took the napkin and threw it in the bin

1477. mente - mind
La mente es muy compleja - The mind is very complex

1478. tradicional - traditional
Este es un baile tradicional de la región - This is a traditional dance of the region

1479. abierta - open (feminine)
La farmacia está abierta - The pharmacy is open

1480. breve - brief / short
El comunicado del presidente fue breve pero importante - The president's statement was brief but important

1481. aparecen - they appear / show up
De noche, aparecen luciérnagas en el jardín - At night, fireflies appear in the garden

1482. trataba - he/she/it tried
Rita trataba de hacer las cosas bien, pero todo le salía mal - Rita tried to do things right, but everything went wrong

1483. recibido - received (participle)
¿Has recibido el paquete? - Have you received the package?

1484. mejorar - to improve
Debes mejorar tu conducta - You must improve your behavior

1485. ciertas - certain (feminine, plural)
Hay ciertas cosas que no puedo contarte aún - There are certain things that I can't tell you yet

1486. aparte - besides / on the side
Sí, quiero salsa, pero la quiero aparte - Yes, I want gravy, but I want it on the side

1487. cárcel - jail / prison
El mafioso vivió el resto de su vida en la cárcel - The mobster lived the rest of his life in prison

1488. entidad - entity
Trabajo para una entidad gubernamental - I work for a government entity

1489. investigaciones - investigations / researches
Hay investigaciones cruciales en proceso - Crucial investigations are underway

1490. temperatura - temperature
La temperatura de la sopa está perfecta - The soup temperature is perfect

1491. siento - I feel
Siento un ligero dolor de cabeza - I feel a slight headache

1492. directa - direct (feminine)
Estamos en comunicación directa con el Ministro de Economía - We are in direct communication with the Minister of Economy

1493. portavoz - spokesperson
Lorena es la portavoz de la empresa - Lorena is the company's spokesperson

1494. responsables - responsible (plural)
Hugo y Jorge son padres responsables - Hugo and Jorge are responsible parents

1495. ventana - window
Cierra la ventana, por favor - Close the window please

1496. contrato - contract / agreement
Debes cumplir con el contrato - You must comply with the agreement

1497. elemento - element
Tuve que estudiar el nombre de cada elemento de la tabla periódica - I had to study the name of each element on the periodic table

1498. privada - private (feminine)
Esta es una fiesta privada - This is a private party

1499. quince - fifteen
Mi sobrina cumplió quince años - My niece turned fifteen years old

1500. veo - I see
No veo bien sin mis gafas - I can't see well without my glasses

Chapter 6 – Words 1501-1800

1501. os - you (plural, Spain)
   Os diré un secreto - I will tell you a secret
1502. firma - signature / company
   Necesito tu firma en este documento - I need your signature on this document
1503. incluye - he/she/it includes
   El libro incluye varias recetas - The book includes several recipes
1504. pobres - poor (plural)
   Las personas más pobres necesitan protección durante el invierno - The poorest people need protection during the winter
1505. vas - you go
   ¿A dónde vas? - Where are you going?
1506. abogado - lawyer (masculine)
   Este es Tomás, mi abogado - This is Tomás, my lawyer
1507. presentar - to present / to introduce
   Te quiero presentar a mi familia - I want to introduce you to my family
1508. gobernador - governor
   No me gusta el gobernador actual - I don't like the current governor
1509. próximos - next (masculine, plural)
   Tenemos muchos planes para los próximos días - We have many plans for the next days

1510. hablando - talking
Estoy hablando por teléfono con mi abuela - I'm talking on the phone with my grandmother

1511. canal - channel
Cambia el canal - Change the channel

1512. tráfico - traffic
¡El tráfico está terrible! - The traffic is terrible!

1513. capitán - capitain
Mi abuelo era capitán de un barco - My grandfather was the captain of a ship

1514. personalidad - personality
Me gusta la personalidad de Flavia - I like Flavia's personality

1515. género - gender / genre
Me gusta escribir en género de terror - I like to write in horror genre

1516. generación - generation
Mi generación no se preocupa por esas cosas - My generation doesn't care about those things

1517. documentos - documents
Estoy esperando documentos muy importantes - I am waiting for very important documents

1518. espectáculo - show
Nos invitaron a un espectáculo de comedia - They invited us to a comedy show

1519. vivo - alive / live
El filósofo sigue vivo, ¡tiene más de cien años! - The philosopher is still alive, he is over a hundred years old!

1520. tendría - he/she/it would have
Hoy tendría que ir a la biblioteca - Today I would have to go to the library

1521. preguntas - questions
Tengo algunas preguntas que hacerte - I have some questions to ask you

1.522. inmediatamente - immediately
Ven inmediatamente - Come immediately
1.523. cien - a hundred / one hundred
Pedro gana cien pesos por hora - Pedro earns one hundred pesos per hour
1.524. colaboración - collaboration
Escribí el libro en colaboración con mi esposo - I wrote the book in collaboration with my husband
1.525. hermana - sister
Mi hermana es diseñadora - My sister is a designer
1.526. mío - mine
¡Ese libro es mío! - That book is mine!
1.527. cincuenta - fifty
Tengo cincuenta correos sin leer - I have fifty unread emails
1.528. sorpresa - surprise
Le haremos una fiesta sorpresa a Ramona - We will throw a surprise party for Ramona
1.529. regiones - regions
Visité varias regiones de Italia - I visited several regions of Italy
1.530. carga - load / freight / burden
No quiero ser una carga para mis padres - I don't want to be a burden to my parents
1.531. bienes - goods
Los bienes materiales no son importantes - Material goods are not important
1.532. masa - mass / dough
Estoy preparando una masa para hacer pizzas - I am preparing a dough to make pizzas
1.533. cartas - letters
Mi abuelo enviaba cartas de amor a mi abuela - My grandfather used to send love letters to my grandmother
1.534. reyes - kings
Los reyes asistieron al evento - The king and queen attended the event

1535. principalmente - mainly

El problema se debe, principalmente, a la contaminación - The problem is mainly due to contamination

1536. puestos - positions

Tenemos varios puestos que cubrir en la empresa - We have several positions to fill in the company

1537. sombra - shadow / shade

Vamos a la sombra de aquel árbol - Let's go under the shade of that tree

1538. criterios - criteria

Sus son distintos de los míos - Her criteria are different from mine

1539. abrir - to open

¿Me ayudas a abrir este frasco? - Can you help me open this jar?

1540. cuyos - whose

Mi profesor, cuyos exámenes reprobé, me odia - My teacher whose exams I failed hates me

1541. filosofía - philosophy

La filosofía oriental influyó a Occidente - Eastern philosophy influenced the West

1542. miró - he/she/it looked / watched

Yaiza me miró - Yaiza looked at me

1543. negra - black (feminine)

¿Dónde está mi sudadera negra? - Where's my black sweatshirt?

1544. margen - margin

No tenemos mucho margen de error - We don't have much margin for error

1545. artista - artist

Daniela es artista visual - Daniela is a visual artist

1546. constante - constant

Hay tráfico constante en esta calle - There is constant traffic on this street

1547. encontraba - he/she/it found / used to find (imperfect past)
Llegamos tarde porque no encontraba mis calcetines - We were late because I couldn't find my socks

1548. gastos - expenses
Mis padres pagan el alquiler, pero yo pago los gastos - My parents pay the rent, but I pay for the expenses

1549. morir - to die
Mis plantas van a morir si mi padre se olvida de regarlas - My plants will die if my father forgets to water them

1550. espacios - spaces
Hay varios espacios de trabajo en el edificio - There are several workspaces in the building

1551. figuras - figures
Es una de las figuras más importantes del mundo de la moda - He is one of the most important figures in the fashion world

1552. miércoles - Wednesday
Los miércoles no trabajo - I don't work on Wednesdays

1553. venido - come (participle)
¿Habías venido a mi casa alguna vez? - Have you come to my house before?

1554. indica - he/she/it indicates / tells
El profesor le indica al alumno cómo resolver el ejercicio - The teacher tells the student how to solve the exercise

1555. comienzo - beginning / start
El comienzo del libro es muy atrapante - The beginning of the book is very engaging

1556. diseño - design
Me interesa el diseño industrial - I am interested in industrial design

1557. cuarenta - forty
Tengo un contrato por cuarenta días - I have a forty-day contract

1558. encontró - he/she/it found
Rosa encontró un anillo en el suelo - Rosa found a ring on the ground

1559. poesía - poetry

Marcos me compró un libro de poesía - Marcos bought me a book of poetry

1560. planes - plans

¿Tienes planes para esta noche? - Do you have plans for tonight?

1561. negocios - businesses

Andrea es una mujer de negocios - Andrea is a businesswoman

1562. integración - integration

La integración cultural es fundamental - Cultural integration is essential

1563. caída - fall

La caída del imperio romano fue en el año 476 - The fall of the Roman Empire was in the year 476

1564. entrega - delivery

La entrega se realizará entre las 8 y las 10 am - The delivery will be made between 8 and 10 am

1565. acuerdos - agreements

Los acuerdos de confidencialidad tienen valor legal - Confidentiality agreements have legal value

1566. preciso - precise (masculine)

El trabajo de Gastón es muy preciso - Gastón's work is very precise

1567. cuello - neck

Me duele el cuello - My neck hurts

1568. banda - band

La banda que tocó en la boda era genial - The band that played at the wedding was great

1569. suyo - yours (formal) / his / hers

El libro no es mío, es suyo - The book is not mine, it's his

1570. realiza - he/she/it makes / performs

Walter realiza reparaciones - Walter makes repairs

1571. frase - phrase / sentence
Hoy oí una frase que me gustó - Today I heard a phrase that I liked

1572. bases – basis / foundations
Libertad, igualdad y fraternidad son las bases de la civilización occidental - Liberty, equality and fraternity are the foundations of western civilization

1573. siglos - centuries
Este problema existe hace varios siglos - This problem has existed for several centuries

1574. decidido - decided (masculine)
He decidido mudarme a España - I have decided to move to Spain

1575. sentir - to feel
Es normal sentir ansiedad antes de un cambio tan grande - It is normal to feel anxiety before such a big change

1576. artistas - artists
Los artistas trabajan muchas horas al día - Artists work many hours a day

1577. asegura - he/she/it assures / affirms / claims
Mi madre asegura que vio un duende en el jardín - My mother claims she saw a goblin in the garden

1578. culpable - guilty
Me siento culpable por haber mentido - I feel guilty for lying

1579. original - original
Este cuento es muy original - This story is very original

1580. únicamente - only
La oficina de correos abre únicamente de lunes a viernes - The post office is only open Monday through Friday

1581. unidades - unities
¿Cuántas unidades hay en una docena? - How many units are there in a dozen?

1582. ocurrió - it happened
El accidente ocurrió a la medianoche - The accident happened at midnight

1583. sexo - sex
En esta película hay escenas de sexo - In this movie there are sex scenes

1584. entra - he/she/it enters
El perro entra en la casa - The dog enters the house

1585. hayan - that they have (auxiliary)
¿Tienes amigos que hayan ido a Costa Rica? - Do you have friends who have gone to Costa Rica?

1586. resolver - to solve
Tenemos que resolver este asunto - We have to solve this issue

1587. misión - mission
Tenemos una misión - We have a mission

1588. caja - box / register
¿Qué hay en esa caja? - What's in that box?

1589. considerar - to consider
Debemos considerar los deseos de todos los involucrados - We must consider the wishes of everyone involved

1590. extranjeros - foreigners
En este barrio hay muchos extranjeros - There are many foreigners in this neighborhood

1591. extremo - extreme (masculine)
Este es un caso extremo - This is an extreme case

1592. periodista - journalist
Soy periodista independiente - I'm a freelance journalist

1593. reducción - reduction
Hubo una reducción de personal en la empresa - There was a reduction of staff in the company

1594. matrimonio - marriage
Mi matrimonio es muy feliz - My marriage is very happy

1595. quieres - you want
¿Quieres ir a caminar? - Do you want to go for a walk?

1596. películas - films / movies
¿Has visto películas interesantes últimamente? - Have you seen interesting movies lately?

1597. fui - I went / I was
Ayer fui al supermercado - Yesterday I went to the supermarket

1598. laboral - work / working
Tengo un problema laboral - I have a work problem

1599. importa - it matters
No importa qué digan, tú eres talentoso - No matter what they say, you are talented

1600. seguía - he/she/it continued / followed (imperfect)
Aún en sus últimos días, Oscar Wilde seguía siendo muy gracioso - Even in his last days, Oscar Wilde continued to be very funny

1601. negocio - business
El negocio del turismo se vio muy afectado por el huracán - The tourism business was severely affected by the hurricane

1602. sexual - sexual
La reproducción de algunas plantas es sexual, mientras que la de otras es asexual - The reproduction of some plants is sexual, while that of others is asexual

1603. enseñanza - teaching
Mi abuela me dejó una gran enseñanza - My grandmother left me a great teaching

1604. agregó - he/she/it added
El profesor agregó una tarea adicional al final del semestre - The teacher added an additional assignment at the end of the semester

1605. labios - lips
Celeste se pintó los labios frente al espejo - Celeste put on lipstick on her lips in front of the mirror

1606. resolución - resolution
¿Tienes alguna resolución de año nuevo? - Do you have a New Year's resolution?

1607. fundación - foundation

Trabajo en una fundación caritativa en Medellín - I work at a charitable foundation in Medellín

1608. hará - he/she/it will do / will make

Nadie sabe qué hará Milena mañana - No one knows what Milena will do tomorrow

1609. depende - he/she/it depends

Inés depende de su familia - Inés depends on her family

1610. actor - actor

Mi padre es actor - My father is an actor

1611. técnicos - technical (plural) / technicians

Tenemos algunos problemas técnicos - We have some technical problems

1612. belleza - beauty

Mira ese paisaje, ¡qué belleza! - Look at that landscape, so much beauty!

1613. titular - headline

El titular del periódico era sensacionalista - The newspaper headline was sensationalist

1614. logrado - accomplished

He logrado lo que me proponía - I have accomplished what I set out to do

1615. víctimas - victims

¡Fuimos víctimas de un robo! - We were victims of a robbery!

1616. detalles - details

Te contaré los detalles más tarde - I'll tell you the details later

1617. europeos - European (masculine, plural)

Mis abuelos eran europeos - My grandparents were European

1618. caballo - horse

Hay un caballo en el campo - There is a horse in the field

1619. huelga - strike

Los empleados hicieron una huelga - The employees went on strike

1620. carretera - road
Debes mirar siempre la carretera - You should always keep your eyes on the road

1621. norteamericano - North American
México es un país norteamericano - Mexico is a North American country

1622. producir - to produce
El país debe producir más que nunca - The country must produce more than ever

1623. antigua - old / antique (feminine)
Esta mansión es muy antigua - This mansion is very old

1624. alianza - alliance
El gobierno hizo una alianza con los empresarios - The government made an alliance with the business sector

1625. físico - physical (masculine)
Tengo un problema físico - I have a physical problem

1626. sacar - to take out
¿Puedes sacar la basura? - Can you take out the trash?

1627. publicidad - advertisement / advertising
Matías trabaja en publicidad - Matías works in advertising

1628. previsto - provided / foreseen
El gobierno ha previsto este problema - The government has foreseen this problem

1629. entorno - surrounding / environment
Hay una mala influencia en su entorno - There is a bad influence on his environment

1630. preocupación - concern
La preocupación de Ana no es infundada - Ana's concern is not unfounded

1631. resistencia - resistance
La resistencia de todo artefacto tiene un límite - The resistance of every artifact has a limit

1632. murió - he/she/it died

Cuando mi perro murió, me puse muy triste - When my dog died, I was very sad

1633. saben - they know

Mis padres saben que no quiero ser médico - My parents know that I don't want to be a doctor

1634. generalmente - generally

Generalmente, me acuesto a las once - I generally go to bed at eleven

1635. dormir - to sleep

Me gusta dormir con la radio encendida - I like to sleep with the radio on

1636. individuo - individual

Eres un individuo, pero también eres parte de una sociedad - You are an individual, but you are also part of a society

1637. cuerpos - bodies

Los cuerpos reales no suelen ser como los de la publicidad - Real bodies are usually not like those you see in advertising

1638. corto - short

Hace calor, me pondré un pantalón corto - It's hot, I'll put on some shorts

1639. organismos - organisms

Los organismos de derechos humanos estuvieron de acuerdo - Human rights organisms agreed

1640. especiales - special (plural)

Hay que tomar medidas especiales - Special measures must be taken

1641. internet - internet

¿Cómo es el nombre de la red de internet? - What is the name of the internet network?

1642. bancos - benches / banks

Hay dos bancos Santander en el pueblo - There are two Santander banks in town

1643. jugador - *player*
Di María es mi jugador de fútbol preferido - Di María is my favorite football player

1644. esfuerzos - *efforts*
Debemos unir nuestros esfuerzos para que el proyecto tenga éxito - We must join our efforts so that the project succeeds

1645. beneficios - *benefits*
¿Cuáles son los beneficios de tu nuevo empleo? - What are the benefits of your new job?

1646. terminar - *to finish*
Tengo que terminar este ensayo - I have to finish this essay

1647. equilibrio - *balance*
Debes encontrar el equilibrio entre trabajo y familia - You must find the balance between work and family

1648. oído - *hearing / heard / ear*
¿Has oído las novedades? - Have you heard the news?

1649. lectura - *lecture / reading*
Es un libro sencillo, de lectura ligera - It is a simple, light reading book

1650. piezas - *pieces*
El rompecabezas tiene mil piezas - The puzzle has a thousand pieces

1651. límites - *limits / boundaries / bounds*
Su curiosidad no tiene límites - Your curiosity knows no bounds

1652. aproximadamente - *approximately / about*
Estoy aquí hace aproximadamente cinco días - I have been here for about five days

1653. abre - *it opens*
La tienda abre a las tres - The store opens at three

1654. llevado - *taken (masculine)*
He llevado un regalo a mi abuelo - I've taken a gift to my grandfather

1655. privado - *private (masculine)*
Me llegó un mensaje privado - I received a private message

1656. salón - hall / living room / room
Quiero redecorar el salón - I want to redecorate the living room
1657. actuales - current
Los eventos actuales llevaron al cierre del festival - Current events led to the closure of the festival
1658. graves - grave / serious (plural)
El gobierno tiene graves problemas - The government has serious problems
1659. sonrisa - smile
Me gusta mucho tu sonrisa - I really like your smile
1660. foto - picture / photo
Tomemos una foto - Let's take a picture
1661. perspectiva - perspective
Mira el problema en perspectiva - Look at the problem in perspective
1662. cifra - cipher / number / figure
La cifra de infectados con sarampión aumentó - The number of measles infections increased
1663. crédito - credit
¿Aceptan tarjeta de crédito? - Do you take credit cards?
1664. interesante - interesting
Estoy leyendo un artículo muy interesante - I'm reading a very interesting article
1665. constitucional - constitutional
Lo que está haciendo el presidente no es constitucional - What the president is doing is not constitutional
1666. aceptar - to accept
Voy a aceptar la oferta de trabajo - I will accept the job offer
1667. producido - produced (masculine)
He producido dos películas - I have produced two movies
1668. bolsa - bag
¿Dónde dejé mi bolsa? - Where did I leave my bag?
1669. factor - factor
El tabaco es un factor de riesgo - Tobacco is a risk factor

1670. *noches - nights*
Hemos reservado tres noches en este hotel - We have booked three nights at this hotel

1671. *reconocimiento - acknowledgement / recognition*
La profesora obtuvo el máximo reconocimiento de la universidad - The professor obtained the highest recognition from the university

1672. *juventud - youth*
En mi juventud, yo era un atleta - In my youth, I was an athlete

1673. *habitual - usual / regular*
Soy un cliente habitual de esta cafetería - I am a regular customer of this coffee shop

1674. *categoría - category*
Esta aplicación recomienda el número de raciones de cada categoría de alimento - This app recommends the number of servings from each food category

1675. *requiere - he/she/it requires*
El señor Ramírez requiere tu presencia en su oficina - Mr. Ramírez requires your presence in his office

1676. *fuese - that he/she/it were*
Desearía que todo fuese distinto - I wish everything were different

1677. *impresión - impression*
Tengo la impresión de que Amalia es una buena chica - I have the impression that Amalia is a good girl

1678. *llamar - to call*
Tengo que llamar a mi madre - I have to call my mother

1679. *duro - hard (masculine)*
Este turrón está demasiado duro - This nougat is too hard

1680. *universal - universal*
La muerte es una preocupación universal - Death is a universal concern

1681. explicar - to explain
¿Me puedes explicar qué ha sucedido? - Can you explain what has happened?

1682. presentan - they present
Los anfitriones del programa presentan las noticias - The hosts of the TV show present the news

1683. realización - realization / completion
El proyecto está en la etapa de realización - The project is in the completion stage

1684. rápido - quick / fast
¡Ven rápido! - Come quickly!

1685. científicos - scientists (masculine)
Los científicos hicieron un gran descubrimiento - Scientists made a great discovery

1686. serio - serious (masculine)
Este es un asunto muy serio - This is a very serious matter

1687. científico - scientist (masculine)
Jaime quiere ser científico - Jaime wants to be a scientist

1688. comprender - to understand
Debes comprender sus sentimientos - You must understand her feelings

1689. reino - kingdom
España es un reino, no una república - Spain is a kingdom, not a republic

1690. preparación - preparation
¿Cómo va la preparación para la excursión? - How is the preparation for the excursion going?

1691. síntomas - symptoms
¿Cuáles son tus síntomas? - What are your symptoms?

1692. recuperación - recovery
La recuperación será lenta - Recovery will be slow

1693. utilización - use
Se prohíbe la utilización de fuegos artificiales - The use of fireworks is prohibited

1694. fuertes - strong (plural)
Mis brazos no son muy fuertes - My arms are not very strong
1695. sonido - sound
¿Qué es ese sonido? - What is that sound?
1696. inteligencia - intelligence
Tu inteligencia te ha salvado - Your intelligence has saved you
1697. conversación - conversation
Estoy en medio de una conversación - I'm in the middle of a conversation
1698. establece - to establish
¿Qué establece la ley al respecto? - What does the law establish in this regard?
1699. hubiese - if I/he/she/it had (auxiliary)
Habría sido perfecto si no hubiese llovido - It would have been perfect if it hadn't rained
1700. plena – plain / full (feminine)
Tengo confianza plena en Marta - I have full confidence in Marta
1701. venía - I/he/she/it came (imperfect past)
Yo venía del norte y ella venía del sur - I came from the north and she came from the south
1702. realizó - he/she/it made / performed
El chamán realizó el ritual - The shaman performed the ritual
1703. francesa - French (feminine)
Clotilde es francesa - Clotilde is French
1704. legal - legal
Creo que habrá un inconveniente legal - I think there will be a legal inconvenience
1705. abrió - he/she/it opened
Gabriel abrió la puerta - Gabriel opened the door
1.506. alegría - joy
Leticia los recibió con alegría - Leticia received them with joy
1.507. ojo - eye
Me duele un ojo - My eye hurts

1708. ocurrido - *happened*

¿Qué ha ocurrido? - What has happened?

1709. vuelto – *come back / returned (participle)*

¿Has vuelto a tu trabajo? - Have you returned to your work?

1708. diputado - *deputy*

El diputado era un hombre muy elegante - The deputy was a very elegant man

1709. correspondiente - *corresponding*

Debes dirigirte a la oficina correspondiente - You must go to the corresponding office

1710. interna - *internal (feminine)*

Estamos teniendo una discusión interna - We are having an internal discussion

1711. musical - *musical*

Me gustaría ir al teatro a ver un musical - I would like to go to the theater to see a musical play

1712. segundos - *seconds*

El nuevo año comenzará en unos segundos - The new year will begin in a few seconds

1713. recientemente - *recently*

Ana me visitó recientemente - Ana visited me recently

1714. empieza - *he/she/it begins / starts*

El carnaval empieza mañana - The carnival begins tomorrow

1715. decreto - *decree*

El decreto presidencial cambió las cosas - The presidential decree changed things

1716. pareció - *he/she/it seemed*

Me pareció extraño verla allí – It seemed strange to see her there

1717. células - *cells*

El ADN está dentro de nuestras células - DNA is inside our cells

1718. suelen - *they normally... / they usually... (verb)*

Mis padres suelen viajar en el verano - My parents usually travel in the summer

1719. perfectamente - perfectly
Soy perfectamente consciente de los riesgos - I am fully aware of the risks

1720. azúcar - sugar
¿Quiere azúcar o edulcorante? - Do you want sugar or sweetener?

1721. inversiones - investments
He hecho inversiones muy lucrativas - I have made very lucrative investments

1722. concentración - concentration
Prefiero evitar la concentración de personas - I prefer to avoid the concentration of people

1723. espalda - back
Me duele mucho la espalda - My back hurts a lot

1724. producen - they produce
Mis padres producen vinos - My parents produce wine

1725. democrática - democratic (feminine)
Esta es una sociedad democrática - This is a democratic society

1726. respondió - he/she/it responded / answered
Laura jamás respondió mi mensaje - Laura never answered my message

1727. sucede - it happens
¿Qué sucede? – What happens?

1728. contexto - context
En este contexto, debemos permanecer tranquilos - In this context, we must remain calm

1729. claramente - clearly
Claramente, el problema no se solucionará solo - Clearly, the problem will not solve itself

1730. paredes - walls
Quiero pintar las paredes de verde - I want to paint the walls green

1731. motivos - reasons / motives

¿Cuáles son los motivos por los que quieres renunciar? - What are the reasons why you want to resign?

1732. ciencias - sciences

La historia está dentro de las ciencias sociales - History is within the social sciences

1733. tuve - I had

Nunca tuve un amigo tan confiable como Adrián - I never had a friend as trustworthy as Adrián

1734. argentino - Argentinian / Argentine

Federico es argentino, pero vive en Madrid - Federico is Argentinian, but he lives in Madrid

1735. inicio - start / beginning

El inicio de las clases es el 13 de marzo - The start of classes is on March 13

1736. mercados - markets

Los mercados se vieron afectados por la pandemia - Markets were affected by the pandemic

1737. métodos - methods

Miriam usa sus propios métodos - Miriam uses her own methods

1738. estudiar - to study

¿Qué vas a estudiar cuando seas mayor? - What are you going to study when you're older?

1739. interpretación - interpretation

Su interpretación de la ley es tendenciosa - His interpretation of the law is biased

1740. culturales - cultural (plural)

¿Habrá actividades culturales esta noche? - Will there be any cultural activities tonight?

1741. prisión - prison

El maleante fue a prisión - The thug went to prison

1742. llevan - they take

Ellos llevan a su hijo a la playa - They take their child to the beach

1743. amplio - large/wide
Hubo un amplio corte de luz - There was a wide power outage

1744. queremos - we want
Queremos llegar a la cima mañana por la tarde - We want to reach the summit by tomorrow afternoon

1745. apertura - opening
El horario de apertura es a las cinco de la tarde - The opening time is at five in the afternoon

1746. dedos - fingers / toes
El cenicero cayó sobre los dedos de mis pies - The ashtray fell on my toes

1747. vale la pena - it is worth
¿Vale la pena visitar esa ciudad? - Is that city worth visiting?

1748. creer - to believe
Quiero creer en sus palabras, pero es difícil - I want to believe his words, but it's hard

1749. voto - vote
Mi voto es negativo - My vote is negative

1750. participar - to participate
Es importante participar en la asamblea - It is important to participate in the assembly

1751. corrupción - corruption
Dicen que hay mucha corrupción en este gobierno - They say there is a lot of corruption in this government

1752. histórica - historical / historic
Hicieron una reconstrucción histórica de la batalla - They made a historical reconstruction of the battle

1753. papá - dad
Papá, ¿viste las llaves de mi auto? - Dad, did you see my car keys?

1754. voces - voices
Debemos oír las voces de los menos afortunados - We must hear the voices of the less fortunate

1755. pienso - I think / I believe
Pienso que deberíamos comprar más provisiones - I think we should buy more supplies

1756. ángel - angel
¡Eres un ángel! - You're an angel!

1757. inicial - initial
Mi hija está en el nivel inicial - My daughter is at the initial level

1758. escala - scale
El terremoto marcó un seis en la escala de Richter - The earthquake measured 6 on the Richter scale

1759. estrellas - stars
En el campo, podemos ver más estrellas - In the countryside, we can see more stars

1760. página - page
Voy por la página cuarenta - I'm on page forty

1761. temor - fear
Mi mayor temor es que cancelen el vuelo - My biggest fear is that they cancel the flight

1762. encontrado - found (participle)
¿Has encontrado tu cargador? - Have you found your charger?

1763. compra - purchase
Ayer hicimos una gran compra en línea - Yesterday we made a big purchase online

1764. pensó - he/she/it thought
Mi madre pensó que yo mentía - My mother thought I was lying

1765. dudas - doubts
Tengo dudas sobre este asunto - I have doubts about this matter

1766. reconocer - to recognize
¿Puedes reconocer a tu madre en esta fotografía? - Can you recognize your mother in this photograph?

1767. máxima - maximum
La velocidad máxima permitida son 120 kilómetros por hora - The maximum speed allowed is 120 kilometers per hour

1768. actuar - to act
Debemos actuar rápido - We must act fast
1769. reales - real / royal (plural)
Jazmín no tiene problemas reales - Jasmine has no real problems
1770. universo - universe
El universo se komplotó a nuestro favor - The universe plotted in our favor
1771. directo - direct
Hay un tren directo a las nueve de la mañana - There is a direct train at nine in the morning
1772. negociaciones - negotiations
Las negociaciones fueron un éxito - The negotiations were successful
1773. instalaciones - installations / premises / facilities
Hugo se encarga de las instalaciones sanitarias - Hugo is in charge of the sanitary facilities
1774. artículos - articles
Escribí varios artículos esta semana - I wrote several articles this week
1775. aparato - apparatus / gadget / appliance
Este aparato sirve para hacer pastas caseras - This appliance is used to make homemade pasta
1776. lleno - full (masculine)
Mi automóvil está lleno - My car is full
1777. intelectual - intellectual
Martín es un intelectual - Martín is an intellectual
1778. cifras - ciphers / digits
Cien es un número de tres cifras - One hundred is a three-digit number
1779. jardín - garden
Hay una ardilla en el jardín - There is a squirrel in the garden
1780. vacío - empty
El apartamento está vacío - The apartment is empty

1781. ciclo - cycle
El ciclo lectivo termina en diciembre - The school cycle ends in December

1782. valle - valley
En este valle se produce vino - In this valley wine is produced

1783. pensaba - I/he/she/it thought / used to think / was thinking (imperfect past)
¿Qué pensaba mi padre cuando dijo eso? - What was my father thinking when he said that?

1784. forman - they form
Esos tres puntos forman un triángulo - Those three points form a triangle

1785. dirigente - leader
El dirigente sindical dio un discurso - The union leader gave a speech

1786. pide - he/she/it asks for
Mi abuela siempre me pide que le compre chocolates - My grandmother always asks me to buy her chocolates

1787. vehículos - vehicles
Necesitamos tres vehículos para llevar a todo el mundo - We need three vehicles to take everyone

1788. cuestiones - matters
Hay cuestiones que tenemos que resolver - There are matters that we have to solve

1789. puesta - set / setting
La puesta del sol será en diez minutos - The sunset will be in ten minutes

1790. llamó - he/she/it called
Llamó tu hermana - Your sister called

1791. mostró - he/she/it showed
El guía nos mostró las ruinas - The guide showed us the ruins

1792. pecho - chest
Siento un dolor en el pecho - I feel a pain in my chest

1793. honor - honor

El caballero peleó por su honor - The knight fought for his honor

1794. pedir - to ask for

Te tengo que pedir un favor - I have to ask you a favor

1795. formar - to form

Deberíamos formar un equipo de fútbol - We should form a football team

1796. numerosos - numerous / several

Tengo numerosos amigos en México - I have numerous friends in Mexico

1797. seguramente - surely

Seguramente te vea mañana en la playa - I will surely see you tomorrow on the beach

1798. extraño - strange (masculine) / I miss

Extraño a mis padres - I miss my parents

1799. recurso - resource

El bosque es el recurso natural principal de esta región - The forest is the main natural resource in this region

1800. independiente - independent / freelance

Soy un periodista independiente - I am a freelance journalist

Chapter 7 – Words 1801-2100

1801. posiciones - positions
Hay varias posiciones abiertas en mi empresa - There are several open positions in my company

1802. sociedades - societies
La llegada de los españoles fue un choque entre dos sociedades - The arrival of the Spaniards was a clash between two societies

1803. exteriores - exteriors / foreign
Las relaciones exteriores del país han mejorado - The foreign relations of the country have improved

1804. cita - date / appointment
Esta noche tengo una cita con Ana - I have a date with Ana tonight

1805. período - period
Durante un largo período, fuimos muy felices - For a long period, we were very happy

1806. propuestas - propositions / offers / proposals
Tuve dos propuestas laborales - I had two job offers

1807. empleados - employees
Mi empresa tiene solo cinco empleados - My company has only five employees

1808. teniendo - having / owning
Comenzó teniendo una hectárea, y ahora es dueño de casi toda la región - He started by owning a hectare, and now he owns almost the entire region

1809. agencia - agency
Juan trabaja en una agencia de publicidad - Juan works in an advertising agency

1810. cuadros - paintings / pictures
Pinté cinco cuadros durante el verano - I painted five pictures over the summer

1811. partida - departure
No quiero que llegue el momento de tu partida - I don't want the time for your departure to arrive

1812. tensión - tension
Hay mucha tensión entre vosotros - There is a lot of tension between you two

1813. mirar - to look / to watch
No quiero mirar más fotos de tu gato - I don't want to look at more photos of your cat

1814. rica - rich / tasty / delicious (feminine)
¡Tu polenta está muy rica! - Your polenta is delicious!

1815. mexicano - Mexican
Me gusta el hip hop mexicano - I like Mexican hip hop

1816. modelos - models
Tengo varios modelos de vestido para que te pruebes - I have several dress models for you to try on

1817. regreso - comeback
A tu regreso, hablaremos con tranquilidad - Upon your return, we will talk calmly

1818. gobiernos - Governments
Los gobiernos cambian cada cuatro años - Governments change every four years

1819. constituyen - they constitute / they are
Tus gritos constituyen una molestia para el resto de nosotros - Your screams are a nuisance to the rest of us

1820. absoluta - absolute
Tengo absoluta confianza en Rosa - I have absolute confidence in Rosa

1821. clima - weather

El clima es muy extraño por aquí - The weather is very weird around here

1822. criterio - criterion / criteria

Tenemos un criterio similar para elegir ropa - We have a similar criterion for choosing clothes

1823. latina - Latina

Yo soy latina, pero mi padre es español - I am Latina, but my father is Spanish

1824. continúa - he/she/it continues

La banda continúa tocando - The band continues to play

1825. punta - point / tip

Esto es solo la punta del iceberg - This is just the tip of the iceberg

1826. amplia - wide / spacious

Tu cocina es muy amplia - Your kitchen is very spacious

1827. registro - registry / I register / I record

En mi diario, registro todo lo que me ocurre durante el día - In my journal, I record everything that happens to me during the day

1828. sesión - session

La sesión ha concluido - The session has ended

1829. patria - homeland

Esta es mi patria, no quiero marcharme - This is my homeland, I don't want to leave

1830. posee - he/she/it has

La empresa posee muchos recursos - The company has many resources

1831. entró - he/she/it entered / went into

Julieta entró en el bar - Juliet entered the bar

1832. servir - to serve

¿Quieres servir el helado? - Do you want to serve the ice cream?

1833. lluvia - rain

La lluvia arruinó nuestros planes - The rain ruined our plans

1834. ganado - won (participle)
¡Olga ha ganado un premio! - Olga has won an award!

1835. pasando - passing through / showing
Están pasando una película muy buena por la tele - They are showing a very good movie on TV

1836. construir - to build
Quiero construir mi propia casa - I want to build my own house

1837. completa - complete / full (feminine)
Tengo la colección completa - I have the complete collection

1838. personales - personal (plural)
Tengo problemas personales - I have personal problems

1839. reducir - to reduce
Hay que reducir el impacto ambiental - The environmental impact must be reduced

1840. desarrollar - to develop
Deberíamos desarrollar una app - We should develop an app

1841. alcance - reach / scope
¿Cuál es el alcance de tu proyecto? - What is the scope of your project?

1842. deporte - sport
¿Cuál es tu deporte preferido? - What's your favorite sport?

1843. pacto - pact
Hagamos un pacto - Let's make a pact

1844. elaboración - elaboration
El ministro está trabajando en la elaboración de un plan de emergencia - The minister is working on the elaboration of an emergency plan

1845. quedaba - it remained / it was left
¿No quedaba ningún tomate en la despensa? - Was there no tomato left in the pantry?

1846. vicepresidente - vice president
El vicepresidente hizo un anuncio - The vice president made an announcement

1847. alcohol - alcohol
No me gusta el alcohol - I do not like alcohol
1848. fórmula - formula
No hay una fórmula mágica para ser exitoso - There is no magic formula to be successful
1849. inferior - inferior / bottom
El libro está en el estante inferior - The book is on the bottom shelf
1850. tasa - rate
La tasa de nacimientos ha aumentado - The birth rate has increased
1851. expertos - experts
Deja que los expertos opinen sobre el tema - Let the experts comment on the issue
1852. extranjero - foreigner
Él es extranjero, pero no es refugiado - He is a foreigner, but he is not a refugee
1853. diciendo - saying
¿Qué estás diciendo? - What are you saying?
1854. olvidar - to forget
No debemos olvidar el agua - We must not forget the water
1855. presentes - present (plural)
En la boda, solo estaban presentes los novios y los dos testigos - At the wedding, only the bride, the groom and the two witnesses were present
1856. pensando - thinking
¿En qué estás pensando? - What are you thinking?
1857. esperaba - he/she/it waited
¿Qué esperaba Lucía que sucediera? - What did Lucia expect to happen?
1858. código - code
El código de la caja fuerte es 1234 - The safe code is 1234

1859. cooperación - cooperation
La cooperación internacional es fundamental - International cooperation is essential

1860. fotografía - photography / picture
¡Toma una fotografía de ese paisaje! - Take a picture of that landscape!

1861. batalla - battle
Fue una verdadera batalla legal - It was a real legal battle

1862. alternativa - alternative
¿Hay alguna alternativa? - Is there any alternative?

1863. nacido - born (masculine)
¡El hijo de Laura ha nacido ayer! - Laura's son was born yesterday!

1864. árboles - trees
El perro corrió hacia los árboles - The dog ran towards the trees

1865. penal – penal / criminal
Soy abogado penal - I am a criminal lawyer

1866. llena - full (feminine)
Esta noche habrá luna llena - Tonight there will be a full moon

1867. siguió - he/she/it continued / followed
El joven siguió el río por varios kilómetros - The young man followed the river for several kilometers

1868. hablaba - I/he/she/it spoke / was talking (imperfect past)
Belén hablaba con sus amigas por teléfono - Belén was talking to her friends on the phone

1869. turismo - tourism
En este momento del año hay mucho turismo - At this time of the year there is a lot of tourism

1870. papeles - papers
Perdí unos papeles importantes - I lost some important papers

1871. a menudo - often
Mi prima me visita a menudo - My cousin visits me often

1872. papa - potato

La tortilla se hace con papa y huevo - The Spanish omelette is made with potatoes and eggs

1873. populares - popular (plural)

Lucas y Marina son muy populares en la escuela - Lucas and Marina are very popular at school

1874. estación - station

¿Cómo puedo llegar a la estación de tren? - How can I get to the train station?

1875. rápidamente - quickly

Ven rápidamente, tengo algo que mostrarte - Come quickly, I have something to show you

1876. sección - section

Quiero leer la sección de deportes del periódico - I want to read the sports section of the newspaper

1877. determinado - determined (masculine)

En un momento determinado, oirás mi señal - At a determined moment, you will hear my signal

1878. convertirse - to transform into / to become / to turn into

Esto no va a convertirse en un inconveniente - This is not going to become an inconvenience

1879. global - global

La empresa hizo una campaña global - The company ran a global campaign

1880. negociación - negotiation

Estamos en medio de una negociación - We are in the middle of a negotiation

1881. instrumento - instrument

¿Tocas algún instrumento? - Do you play any instrument?

1882. dura - it lasts

¿Cuánto dura la película? - How long does the movie last?

1883. significado - meaning

¿Cuál es el significado de esta palabra? - What is the meaning of this word?

1884. intensidad - intensity

La intensidad de la luz puede regularse - The light intensity can be regulated

1885. posterior - posterior / subsequent

En una reunión posterior, el empresario reformuló su oferta - In a subsequent meeting, the businessman reformulated his offer

1886. múltiples - multiple (plural)

Hay múltiples modelos de móviles entre los que puedes elegir - There are multiple mobile models from which you can choose

1887. gas - gas

Había una fuga de gas - There was a gas leak

1888. nuevamente - again

Te veré nuevamente en unos días - I will see you again in a few days

1889. hierro - iron

Las lentejas tienen mucho hierro - Lentils have a lot of iron

1890. seguido - following / followed (masculine)

Te he seguido en Instagram - I have followed you on Instagram

1891. once - eleven

Mi sobrina Maia tiene once años - My niece Maia is eleven years old

1892. conseguido - achieved / obtained (masculine)

He conseguido lo que estaba buscando - I obtained what I was looking for

1893. di - you say (imperative)

Di lo que piensas - Say what you think

1894. soledad - loneliness / solitude

La anciana vive en soledad - The old woman lives in solitude

1895. mirando - looking / watching

Raúl está mirando la televisión - Raúl is watching television

1896. presentado - introduced / presented

Uriel me ha presentado a su familia - Uriel has introduced me to his family

1897. instrumentos - instruments
Frida toca varios instrumentos - Frida plays several instruments
1898. supo - he/she/it knew
Mi madre nunca supo cocinar - My mother never knew how to cook
1899. disco - record / disc / album
El cantante lanzó su nuevo disco - The singer released his new album
1900. festival - festival
Ha comenzado el festival de la ciudad - The town festival has begun
1901. llegan - they arrive
Mis hijos llegan de la escuela a las tres - My children arrive from school at three
1902. mezcla - mix / he/she/it mixes/shuffles / you mix/shuffle (imperative)
Mezcla las cartas, por favor - Shuffle the cards, please
1903. medicinas - medicines
El médico te recetará las medicinas adecuadas para tu problema - The doctor will prescribe the appropriate medicines for your problem
1904. vivienda - household / house
Compartimos una vivienda entre tres amigos - We share a house among three friends
1905. escuchar - to listen
Debes escuchar lo que dice la profesora - You must listen to what the teacher says
1906. completamente - completely
Estoy completamente agotada - I am completely exhausted
1907. ideal - ideal
Eres el compañero de viajes ideal - You are the ideal travel companion

1908. cáncer - cancer

Los científicos hicieron avances en la lucha contra el cáncer - Scientists made strides in the fight against cancer

1909. textos - texts

Tengo que leer tres textos para la universidad - I have to read three texts for university

1910. hambriento - hungry

Estoy muy hambriento - I am very hungry

1911. solidaridad - solidarity

Debemos confiar en la solidaridad de nuestros vecinos - We must have trust in the solidarity of our neighbors

1912. continuar - to continue

¿Podemos continuar con la reunión? - Can we continue with the meeting?

1913. porcentaje - percentage

¿Cuál es el porcentaje de mujeres en la compañía? - What is the percentage of women in the company?

1914. artes - arts

Me gustan las artes visuales - I like visual arts

1915. vienen - they come

¿Cuándo vienen tus amigos? - When are your friends coming?

1916. hacían - they did (imperfect past)

¿Qué hacían tus padres en Tailandia? - What were your parents doing in Thailand?

1917. lector - reader

El lector cerró el libro - The reader closed the book

1918. estructuras - structures

Las estructuras más sólidas son las de hormigón - The strongest structures are those made of concrete

1919. venir - to come

¿Vas a venir esta noche? - Are you coming tonight?

1920. castillo - castle

En España, visité un castillo - In Spain, I visited a castle

1921. opción - option / choice
No tengo opción - I do not have a choice

1922. comentó - he/she/it commented
El periodista comentó que le parecía un asunto muy complejo - The journalist commented that it seemed to him a very complex matter

1923. ganó - he/she/it won
Mi vecino ganó la lotería - My neighbor won the lottery

1924. amenaza - threat
El gato es una amenaza para las ratas - The cat is a threat to rats

1925. representante - representative
Soy representante de la embajada - I am representative of the embassy

1926. comerciales - commercials / commercial (plural)
Las relaciones comerciales entre los dos países son fuertes - Commercial relations between the two countries are strong

1927. puedes - you can
¿Puedes venir? - Can you come?

1929. planeta - planet
Todo el planeta está en riesgo por el calentamiento global - The entire planet is at risk from global warming

1930. perdió - he/she/it lost
Mi hijo perdió su zapato - My son lost his shoe

1931. beneficio - benefit / profit
Obtengo un pequeño beneficio por cada venta - I get a small profit for each sale

1932. buscando - searching / looking for
Estoy buscando mi adaptador - I'm looking for my adapter

1933. sentimientos - feelings
Tengo sentimientos por Carmen - I have feelings for Carmen

1934. comprar - to buy
¿Puedes comprar algo de comer? - Can you buy something to eat?

1935. quedar - to remain / to stay
Hoy me quiero quedar durmiendo hasta tarde - Today I want to stay up late

1936. accidente - accident
Hubo un accidente - There was an accident

1937. ventaja - advantage
Tienes ventaja sobre el resto porque has jugado antes - You have an advantage over the rest because you have played before

1938. impuesto - tax
Han creado un nuevo impuesto - They have created a new tax

1939. dejando - leaving / stopping / quitting
Estoy dejando de fumar - I am quitting smoking

1940. distinto - different (masculine)
Te ves distinto - You look different

1941. tía - aunt
Mi tía es dueña de una tienda de flores - My aunt owns a flower shop

1942. semejante - similar
¿Has visto antes algo semejante? - Have you ever seen something similar to this?

1943. españolas - Spanish (feminine, plural)
Gloria y Amanda son españolas - Gloria and Amanda are Spanish

1944. occidental - western
La cultura occidental es una combinación de muchas culturas - Western culture is a combination of many cultures

1945. capaces - capable (plural)
Mis padres son capaces de todo por mí - My parents are capable of everything for me

1946. científica - scientist (feminine)
La comunidad científica se puso de acuerdo - The scientific community agreed

1947. tengan - they have / you have (subjunctive)
¡No tengan miedo! - Do not have fear!

1948. ruido - noise

¿Qué fue ese ruido? - What was that noise?

1949. individuos - individuals

La policía busca a tres individuos sospechosos - Police are looking for three suspected individuals

1950. víctima - victim

Úrsula ha sido la víctima de un fraude - Úrsula has been the victim of a fraud

1951. vestido - dress

¡Qué lindo vestido! - What a nice dress!

1952. moda - fashion

Vogue es una revista de moda - Vogue is a fashion magazine

1953. títulos - titles

Dime los títulos de los libros que necesitas - Tell me the titles of the books you need

1954. diagnóstico - diagnosis

El diagnóstico fue positivo, ¡estoy sana! - The diagnosis was positive, I am healthy!

1955. experiencias - experiences

Contadme vuestras experiencias - Tell me your experiences

1956. espejo - mirror

Necesitamos un espejo en la habitación - We need a mirror in the room

1957. puente - bridge

Ahora, debemos cruzar ese puente y luego doblar a la derecha - Now we have to cross that bridge and then turn right

1958. ingreso - entry / income / entrance

El ingreso a la tienda se hace por la puerta de la esquina - The entrance to the store is through the corner door

1959. sueños - dreams

Es el trabajo de mis sueños - It is the job of my dreams

1960. vehículo - vehicle

Necesitamos un vehículo para recorrer la zona - We need a vehicle to tour the area

1961. convierte - he/she/it turns intro
La bruja convierte a los niños en ratones - The witch turns the children into mice

1962. viejos - old (masculine, plural)
Estos zapatos son muy viejos - These shoes are very old

1963. empezar - to begin / to start
Las clases van a empezar la semana que viene - School is going to start next week

1964. profesores - teachers / professors
Mis profesores de la secundaria eran excelentes - My high school teachers were excellent

1965. pasión - passion
Diana siente pasión por lo que hace - Diana has passion for what she does

1966. basta - enough / stop
¡Basta! ¡A dormir! - Enough! Go to sleep!

1967. democrático - democratic (masculine)
El sistema democrático no es infalible - The democratic system is not infallible

1968. sintió - he/she/it felt
Tiago sintió que alguien se acercaba - Tiago felt someone approaching

1969. dijeron - they said
Mis vecinos me dijeron que quieren vender su casa - My neighbors said they want to sell their house

1970. comunes - common (plural)
Las patatas y las batatas son ingredientes comunes en la región - Potatoes and sweet potatoes are common ingredients in the region

1971. sentimiento - feeling
Julián no soportaba su sentimiento de culpa - Julian couldn't stand his feeling of guilt

1972. sentencia - sentence
La sentencia del juez fue muy dura - The judge's sentence was very harsh

1973. *estatal* - *statal / state*
Esta es una escuela estatal - This is a state school
1974. *amanecer* - *dawn*
Bailamos hasta el amanecer - We danced until dawn
1975. *moderna* - *modern (feminine)*
Tu casa es muy moderna - Your house is very modern
1976. *impacto* - *impact*
Estas medidas económicas tendrán un impacto positivo - These economic measures will have a positive impact
1977. *complejo* - *complex (masculine)*
Es un problema demasiado complejo - It is too complex a problem
1978. *denuncia* - *complaint*
Héctor puso una denuncia al municipio - Héctor filed a complaint with the municipality
1979. *toro* - *bull*
El toro atacó al torero - The bull attacked the bullfighter
1980. *tabla* - *board*
¿Tienes una tabla para picar la cebolla? - Do you have a board to chop the onion?
1981. *delito* - *crime*
Tirar basura en la reserva natural es un delito - Littering in the nature reserve is a crime
1982. *ventas* - *sales*
Las ventas bajaron durante marzo - Sales fell during March
1983. *dominio* - *domain*
La información estatal es dominio público - State information is in the public domain
1984. *entidades* - *entities*
Las entidades gubernamentales deben aplicar las nuevas normas de inmediato - Government entities must apply the new rules immediately

1985. superiores - superiors

¿Qué te han dicho tus superiores? - What have your superiors told you?

1986. candidatos - candidates

Los candidatos participaron en un debate - The candidates participated in a debate

1987. gloria - glory

El artista pasó de la gloria al fracaso en pocos años - The artist went from glory to failure in a few years

1988. índice - index

En el índice aparecen los títulos de todos los capítulos - The titles of all the chapters appear in the index

1989. raíz - root

La raíz del árbol rompió el piso - The root of the tree cracked the floor

1990. recordó - he/she/it remembered

Mónica recordó dónde había dejado la llave - Monica remembered where she had left the key

1991. absoluto - absolute (masculine)

Los estudiantes manifestaron su rechazo absoluto a la guerra – The students expressed their absolute rejection of war

1992. agricultura - agriculture

La agricultura es la actividad principal de la región - Agriculture is the main activity of the region

1993. composición - composition

José se dedica a la composición musical - José works in musical composition

1994. cuando - when

Te veré cuando regreses - I will see you when you come back

1995. terminó - he/she/it finished / ended

Inés terminó de entrenar a las cinco de la tarde - Inés finished training at five in the afternoon

1996. fueran - they were (subjunctive)

Me gustaría que mis padres fueran más comprensivos - I would like my parents were more understanding

1997. asistencia - assistance

El paciente requiere la asistencia de la enfermera - The patient requires the assistance of the nurse

1998. explicación - explanation

¡Merezco una explicación! - I deserve an explanation!

1999. torres - towers

Si bien la catedral es medieval, las torres fueron construidas hace pocos años - Although the cathedral is medieval, the towers were built a few years ago

2000. lógica - logic

Según su lógica, debería devolverle el dinero con intereses - According to his logic, I should return the money with interests

2001. triste - sad

Estoy triste por tu partida - I am sad for your departure

2002. avión - plane

Es mi primera vez en un avión - It's my first time on a plane

2003. enfermo - ill / sick (masculine)

Leonardo está enfermo - Leonardo is ill

2004. cuyas - whose (feminine)

Asturias es la comunidad española cuyas empresas cuentan con más mujeres - Asturias is the Spanish community whose companies have more women

2005. excepción - exception

Tú eres la excepción a la regla - You are the exception to the rule

2006. habló - he/she/it spoke / talked

Liliana habló con Diego sobre los resultados de la encuesta - Liliana spoke with Diego about the results of the survey

2007. placer - pleasure

Siento mucho placer cuando como chocolate - I feel a lot of pleasure when I eat chocolate

2008. humor - mood
Tengo muchos cambios de humor desde que estoy embarazada - I'm having many mood swings since I'm pregnant

2009. mecanismos - mechanisms
Debemos mejorar los mecanismos de seguridad - We must improve the security mechanisms

2010. cerebro - brain
Mi cerebro está agotado después de ocho horas de clases - My brain is exhausted after eight hours of classes

2011. caliente - hot
El café está muy caliente - The coffee is very hot

2012. excelente - excellent
El concierto fue excelente - The concert was excellent

2013. darse cuenta - to realize
Los turistas deben darse cuenta de que esta playa no es un basurero - Tourists must realize that this beach is not a dump

2014. conocimientos - knowledge
El filósofo comparte sus conocimientos con los alumnos - The philosopher shares his knowledge with the students

2015. príncipe - prince
Él era el príncipe de un reino muy lejano - He was the prince of a distant kingdom

2016. religión - religion
No discriminamos a los candidatos por su religión - We do not discriminate against applicants because of their religion

2017. ganas - the will / the desire
Tengo ganas de comer algo picante - I feel the desire of eating something spicy

2018. críticas - criticism
Carlos no es bueno aceptando críticas - Carlos is not good at accepting criticism

2019. profunda - deep / profound (feminine)
¡Cuidado! La piscina es muy profunda - Watch out! The pool is very deep

2020. manifestaciones - demonstrations
Hay manifestaciones todos los días - There are demonstrations every day

2021. dosis - dose
¿Qué dosis te indicó el médico? - What dose did the doctor prescribe?

2022. baño - bathroom / toilet
¿Hay alguien en el baño? - Is there someone in the bathroom?

2023. paro - unemployment
Mi hermano está en paro hace tres meses - My brother has been unemployed for three months

2024. profundo - deep / profound (masculine)
Sentí un dolor muy profundo cuando ella me dejó - I felt a very deep pain when she left me

2025. conceptos - concepts
Entiendo los conceptos, pero no sé explicarlos - I understand the concepts, but I don't know how to explain them

2026. depresión - depression
La depresión es una enfermedad grave - Depression is a serious illness

2027. altas - tall / high (feminine, plural)
Estas son las montañas más altas del continente - These are the highest mountains on the continent

2028. pared - wall
Isabel colgó el cuadro en la pared - Isabel hung the painting on the wall

2029. liberación – liberation / release
La liberación de los rehenes fue un éxito - The release of the hostages was a success

2030. estrella - star
¡Mira esa estrella fugaz! - Look at that shooting star!

2031. duración - duration
La obra de teatro tiene una duración de dos horas - The duration of the play is two hours

2032. perro - dog
Tengo un perro y dos gatos - I have a dog and two cats
2033. intentar - to try
Deberías intentar hablar en español para aprender más rápido - You should try to speak Spanish to learn faster
2034. aumentar - to increase
El supermercado va a aumentar los precios - The supermarket will increase the prices
2035. asesinato - murder
El asesinato ocurrió a las tres de la mañana - The murder occurred at three in the morning
2036. órdenes - orders
Debes seguir las órdenes del oficial - You must follow the officer's orders
2037. roja - red (feminine)
La camioneta roja es de mi novio - The red truck belongs to my boyfriend
2038. permiten - they allow
Mis responsabilidades no me permiten tomarme vacaciones - My responsibilities do not allow me to take time off
2039. añade - he/she/it adds / you add (imperative)
Añade un poco más de azúcar - Add a little more sugar
2040. poca - little (feminine)
Lucía tiene poca paciencia - Lucía has little patience
2041. recibe - he/she/it receives
Julia recibe una sorpresa de sus amigas - Julia receives a surprise from her friends
2042. muchacho - boy / guy
Daniel es un muchacho muy curioso - Daniel is a very curious boy
2043. considerado – considered / considerate
¡Qué considerado eres! - How considerate are you!

2044. conversaciones - conversations

He tenido varias conversaciones sobre el asunto con Florencia - I have had several conversations on the matter with Florencia

2045. tendrán - they will have

Juana y Roberto tendrán que esperar - Juana and Roberto will have to wait

2046. definición - definition

¿Cuál es la definición de "vicisitud"? - What is the definition of "vicissitude"?

2047. viven - they live

Mis primas viven en Lima, la capital de Perú - My cousins live in Lima, the capital of Peru

2048. consideran - they consider

Los directivos consideran que es necesario recortar el presupuesto - The board members consider that it is necessary to cut the budget

2049. restos - remains

Estos son los restos de una civilización antigua - These are the remains of an ancient civilization

2050. tomado - taken

¿Has tomado algo para el dolor de cabeza? - Have you taken something for your headache?

2051. estadio - stadium

El estadio está lleno - The stadium is full

2052. actores - actors

Los actores de la película son muy famosos - The actors in the film are very famous

2053. debió - he/she/it should have / owed / must have

Josefina debió de ir a la biblioteca - Josefina must have gone to the library

2054. conviene - it is convenient

¿Me conviene pedir un préstamo ahora? - Is it convenient for me to apply for a loan now?

2055. errores - mistakes

Has cometido algunos errores de ortografía - You have made some spelling mistakes

2056. negros - black (plural)

¿Me prestas tus guantes negros? - Can I borrow your black gloves?

2057. humanidad - humankind / humanity

La humanidad no está perdida - Humanity is not lost

2058. individual - individual

La tarea es individual, no podemos hacerla juntos - Homework is individual, we cannot do it together

2059. hogar - home

Estoy yendo a mi hogar - I'm going home

2060. conocida - known (feminine)

Ella era una cantante muy conocida hace muchos años - She was a well-known singer many years ago

2061. acontecimientos - events

Los acontecimientos nos obligaron a cancelar el espectáculo - The events forced us to cancel the show

2062. minuto - minute

¡Espera un minuto! - Wait a minute!

2063. millón - million

Ese fósil tiene más de un millón de años - That fossil is over a million years old

2064. pantalla - screen

El bebé mira la pantalla - The baby looks at the screen

2065. estadounidense - American (from the US)

Yo soy estadounidense, ¿tú de dónde eres? - I'm from the US, where are you from?

2066 progreso - progress

Hemos hecho un enorme progreso en la clase de hoy - We have made tremendous progress in today's class

2067. inició - he/she/it began / started / initiated

El problema inició en junio - The problem started in June

2068. pieza - piece
Falta la última pieza del rompecabezas - The last piece of the puzzle is missing

2069. firme - firm
Era un rey firme y severo - He was a firm and severe king

2070. fundamentales - fundamental / essential
Los impuestos son fundamentales para el país - Taxes are essential for the country

2071. olor - scent / smell
¡Siente el olor de estas flores! – Feel the smell of these flowers!

2072. graciosos – funny (masculine, plural)
Encuentro sus chistes muy graciosos - I find his jokes very funny

2073. autonomía - autonomy
La provincia tiene autonomía limitada - The province has limited autonomy

2074. esencial - essential
Lo esencial es invisible a los ojos - The essential is invisible to the eyes

2075. exige - he/she/it demands
Irene exige que todo sea perfecto - Irene demands that everything is perfect

2076. viva - alive / living (feminine)
La langosta está viva al momento de cocinarla - The lobster is alive at the time of cooking

2077. norteamericana - North American (feminine)
La región norteamericana cuenta con un tratado de libre comercio - The North American region has a free trade agreement

2078. nacimiento - birth
Estoy esperando con ansiedad el nacimiento de mi hija - I am anxiously awaiting the birth of my daughter

2079. polvo - dust
Hay polvo sobre los estantes - There's dust on the shelves

2080. *fundamentalmente - fundamentally*
Mariana me pidió, fundamentalmente, que no diga nada - Mariana asked me, fundamentally, not to say anything

2081. *impuestos - taxes*
¿Tus impuestos están en orden? - Are your taxes in order?

2082. *implica - it implies*
Aceptar este trabajo implica un compromiso de tiempo completo - Accepting this job implies a full time commitment

2083. *utiliza - he/she/it uses*
El mecánico utiliza sus herramientas para reparar el coche - The mechanic uses his tools to repair the car

2084. *totalidad - whole / entirely / totally*
El río está contaminado en su totalidad - The river is totally polluted

2085. *discusión - discussion*
La discusión terminó bruscamente - The discussion ended abruptly

2086. *italiano - Italian*
Soy argentina pero también tengo el pasaporte italiano - I am an Argentinian but I also have the Italian passport

2087. *postura - posture*
Debes mejorar tu postura - You must improve your posture

2088. *clientes - clients*
Tengo varios clientes en Inglaterra - I have several clients in England

2089. *luces - lights*
Enciende las luces, por favor - Turn on the lights please

2090. *encontramos - we find / we found*
Encontramos un café realmente acogedor - We found a really cozy cafe

2091. *liberal - liberal*
Mi padre es liberal y mi madre es conservadora - My father is a liberal and my mother is a conservative

2092. interno - internal

El motor tiene un problema interno - The engine has an internal problem

2093. dientes - teeth

Me rompí dos dientes - I broke two teeth

2094. sesenta - sixty

Mi madre hará una fiesta por su cumpleaños de sesenta - My mother will throw a party for her sixtieth birthday

2095. exactamente - exactly

Hace exactamente cien años comenzó la Ley Seca en Estados Unidos - Exactly one hundred years ago the Dry Law began in the United States

2096. compañero - companion / mate (masculine)

Mi compañero de clase es un pesado - My classmate is annoying

2097. cuento - short story / tale

¿Quieres que te lea un cuento? - Do you want me to read you a story?

2098. virus - virus

El virus se propagó por todos los ordenadores - The virus spread through all the computers

2099. tareas - tasks / chores

Debes cumplir con tus tareas hogareñas - You must do your house chores

2100. evaluación - evaluation

El inspector realizará una evaluación completa - The inspector will perform a full evaluation

Chapter 8 – Words 2101-2400

2101. máquina - machine
Compré una máquina que hace capuchino - I bought a cappuccino machine

2102. funcionario - official
Ricardo es funcionario del Estado - Ricardo is a state official

2103. señalar - to point out
No debes señalar a la gente - You shouldn't point people

2104. residencia - residency
En la residencia viven treinta ancianos - Thirty elderly live in the residence

2105. absolutamente - absolutely
Estoy absolutamente convencido de que Agustín miente - I am absolutely convinced that Agustín is lying

2106. dolor - pain
Tengo dolor en las articulaciones - I have joint pain

2107. nació - he/she/it was born
Mi sobrina nació ayer - My niece was born yesterday

2108. ánimo - encouragement / cheer up
¡Ánimo! Todo estará bien - Cheer up! Everything will be fine

2109. caminos - roads
El intendente ordenó la reparación de los caminos - The mayor ordered the repairment of the roads

2110. torneo - tournament
Nos he inscrito en un torneo de baile - I've signed us up for a dance tournament

2111. acabar - to finish / to end
Debes acabar tus vegetales - You must finish your vegetables

2112. fracaso - failure
El plan fue un fracaso - The plan was a failure

2113. recorrido - journey / route
Tenemos el recorrido planeado - Our route is planned

2114. contiene - it contains
La botella contiene jugo de naranja - The bottle contains orange juice

2115. eficacia - efficiency
Me preocupa tanto la eficacia como la eficiencia - I am concerned with both effectiveness and efficiency

2116. policías – cops / policemen
Los policías llegaron de inmediato - The policemen arrived immediately

2117. concreto - concrete / specific
Debes proponer un plan concreto - You must propose a specific plan

2118. determinar - to determine
El médico intentó determinar la causa del síntoma - The doctor tried to determine the cause of the symptom

2119. haberse - to have (auxiliary)
¿Por qué podría haberse retrasado? - Why could he have been delayed?

2120. reglas - rules
¿Conoces las reglas de este juego? - Do you know the rules of this game?

2121. ríos - rivers
Los dos ríos se unen antes de desembocar en el mar - The two rivers meet before emptying into the sea

2122. redacción - *writing / newsroom*
Debo mejorar mi redacción - I must improve my writing

2123. localidad - *location / town*
Gonnet es una localidad muy pequeña - Gonnet is a very small town

2124. escuelas - *schools*
Las escuelas cerrarán por la inundación - Schools will close due to the flood

2125. distinta - *different (feminine)*
Esta situación es distinta - This situation is different

2126. seguida - *followed (feminine)*
Pasó caminando una pata, seguida por tres patitos - One duck walked past, followed by three ducklings

2127. paisaje - *landscape*
Toma una foto a ese paisaje increíble - Take a picture of that incredible landscape

2128. comprobar - *to check*
Debemos comprobar todos los hechos narrados por el testigo - We must check all the facts narrated by the witness

2129. numerosas - *numerous (feminine, plural)*
Hemos recibido numerosas consultas respecto al nuevo servicio - We have received numerous inquiries regarding the new service

2130. creciente - *growing*
Hay una población creciente de zarigüeyas - There is a growing population of opossums

2131. serían - *they would be*
Serían, en total, diez euros con cincuenta céntimos, por favor - It would be, in total, ten euros and fifty cents, please

2132. crimen - *crime*
El crimen jamás se resolvió - The crime was never solved

2133. conocía - *he/she/it knew*
Yo conocía a tu padre, era un gran hombre - I knew your father, he was a great man

2134. pintor - painter (masculine)
El pintor terminó su pintura - The painter finished his painting
2135. suya - hers/his/its
Esa taza no es mía, es suya - That mug is not mine, it's hers
2136. definitivamente - definitely
Definitivamente volveré a esta ciudad - I will definitely return to this city
2137. propiedades - properties
El señor González es dueño de varias propiedades en Madrid - Mr. González owns several properties in Madrid
2138. cierre - closure
El cierre de la fábrica fue un duro golpe para la comunidad - The closure of the factory was a severe blow to the community
2139. jueces - judges
Los jueces deben ser completamente imparciales - Judges must be completely impartial
2140. ofrecer - to offer
Debes ofrecer algo de beber a los invitados - You must offer the guests something to drink
2141. estaría - he/she/it would be
Si no se hubiera cancelado el vuelo, ahora estaría en Barcelona - If the flight had not been canceled, I would now be in Barcelona
2142. frontera - frontier / border
Debemos cruzar la frontera - We must cross the border
2143. virgen - virgin
Con estos olivos se produce aceite de oliva extra virgen - These olive trees produce extra virgin olive oil
2144. clasificación - classification
La clasificación del equipo depende de este partido - The team classification depends on this match
2145. municipales - municipal
Hay varios eventos municipales durante este mes - There are several municipal events during this month

2146. marina - navy
Hugo trabaja en la marina - Hugo works in the Navy

2147. abuela - grandmother
La abuela de Raquel nos hizo galletas - Raquel's grandmother made cookies for us

2148. componentes - components
El orden de los componentes no altera el producto - The order of the components does not alter the product

2149. adecuada - right / adequate (feminine)
Debes usar la loción adecuada para tu piel - You should use the right lotion for your skin

2150. resultó - he/she/it turned out
La serie resultó mucho más interesante de lo que esperaba - The series turned out to be much more interesting than I expected

2151. esperando - waiting
Estamos esperando un milagro - We are waiting for a miracle

2152. oscuro - dark (masculine)
El cielo está muy oscuro, ¿crees que lloverá? - The sky is very dark, do you think it will rain?

2153. parecido - similar (masculine)
Tu maletín es parecido al mío - Your briefcase is similar to mine

2154. detenido - detained / stopped / arrested (masculine)
Han detenido al sospechoso - The suspect has been arrested

2155. gasto - expense
La extracción de tu muela fue un gasto inesperado - The removal of your tooth was an unexpected expense

2156. malo - bad (masculine)
Ese video es muy malo - That video is very bad

2157. pura - pure (feminine)
Bebe agua pura del río - Drink pure water from the river

2158. investigadores - researchers
Los investigadores están confundidos - The researchers are confused

2159. cargos - charges

Presentaron cargos contra el ladrón - They filed charges against the thief

2160. cayó - he/she/it fell

El globo cayó al suelo - The balloon fell to the ground

2161. pasaba - I/he/she/it passed / happened

¿Qué pasaba ayer cuando te llamé? - What was happening yesterday when I called you?

2162. abandonar - to abandon

Solo un monstruo puede abandonar un perro - Only a monster can abandon a dog

2163. sierra - mountain range / saw

Cortamos el tronco con una sierra - We cut the log using a saw

2164. lima - lime

Quiero una rodaja de lima - I want a slice of lime

2165. apareció - he/she/it appeared / showed up

El gato finalmente apareció - The cat finally showed up

2166. secretaria - secretary (feminine)

Esta es Belén, mi secretaria - This is Belén, my secretary

2167. pausa - pause

Pon el juego en pausa por un minuto - Pause the game for a minute

2168. prácticas - practices / internship

Hice mis prácticas en un hospital importante - I did my internship in a major hospital

2169. cortés - polite

Luis es muy cortés - Luis is very polite

2170. siguiendo - following

Te estoy siguiendo en Instagram - I'm following you on Instagram

2171. conclusión - conclusion

Llegué a la conclusión de que quiero renunciar - I reached the conclusion that I want to resign

2172. convirtió - he/she/it turned into / became
El sapo se convirtió en un príncipe - The toad became a prince
2173. hipótesis - hypothesis
Tengo una hipótesis - I have a hypothesis
2174. editorial - editorial
Estoy trabajando en un proyecto editorial - I am working on an editorial project
2175. petróleo - oil
El petróleo domina la economía - Oil dominates the economy
2176. estén - they are (subjunctive)
Espero que mis padres estén listos para la noticia - I hope my parents are ready for the news
2177. playa - beach
Vamos a la playa - Let's go to the beach
2178. invierno - winter
El invierno no es muy frío por aquí - Winter is not very cold around here
2179. convenio - agreement
El director firmó un convenio - The director signed an agreement
2180. infantil - childish / for children
Lisa es un poco infantil - Lisa is a little childish
2181. extensión - extension
Pedí una extensión de mi beca - I asked for an extension on my scholarship
2182. horno - oven
¿Apagaste el horno? - Did you turn off the oven?
2183. límite - limit
Haz cruzado el límite - You have crossed the limit
2184. elegido - chosen (masculine)
He elegido un lindo hotel - I have chosen a nice hotel
2185. concurso - contest
Participé en un concurso de fotografía - I participated in a photography contest

2186. probable - probable / likely
Es probable que llueva esta noche - It's likely to rain tonight
2187. observar - to observe
Me gusta observar la naturaleza - I like to observe nature
2188. déficit - deficit
El país está en déficit - The country is in a deficit
2189. reconoce - he/she/it recognizes / acknowledges
Blanca reconoce que tiene un problema - Blanca acknowledges that she has a problem
2190. anual - annual
La asociación hace una celebración anual - The association holds an annual celebration
2191. trabajando - working
Estoy trabajando - I am working
2192. responde - he/she/it responds / replies / answers
Le envié un mensaje, pero no responde - I sent him a message, but he's not replying
2193. tren - train
El tren tiene un vagón comedor - The train has a dining car
2194. presidencial - presidential
Esta es la suite presidencial - This is the presidential suite
2195. vías - train tracks
El muchacho caminaba por las vías - The boy was walking along the train tracks
2196. interesado – interested (masculine, singular)
No estoy interesado en tu opinión - I am not interested in your opinion
2197. supremo - supreme (masculine)
El caso llegó al tribunal supremo de justicia - The case reached the supreme court of justice
2198. enemigo - enemy
Mi perro tiene un enemigo - My dog has an enemy

2199. respectivamente - respectively

Gonzalo y Martín dormirán en las camas 105 y 106, respectivamente - Gonzalo and Martín will sleep in beds 105 and 106, respectively

2200. dificultad - difficulty

El hombre tiene dificultad para respirar - The man has difficulty breathing

2201. similares - similar (plural)

Nuestras camisas son similares - Our shirts are similar

2202. entiende - he/she/it understands

El bebé entiende lo que decimos - The baby understands what we say

2203. morales - moral (plural)

Hay que considerar los impedimentos morales - Moral impediments must be considered

2204. alimentación - nutrition / nourishment / diet

Quiero mejorar mi alimentación - I want to improve my diet

2205. norma - norm / rule

La norma más importante es que no hay normas - The most important rule is that there are no rules

2206. mental - mental

Debo cuidar mi salud mental - I must take care of my mental health

2207. soluciones - solutions

Necesito soluciones, no más problemas - I need solutions, not more problems

2208. adecuado - adequate / suitable

Compra un champú adecuado para tu cabello - Buy a shampoo that is suitable for your hair

2209. cuánto - how much

¿Cuánto caminamos hoy? - How much did we walk today?

2210. santos - saints

Esta ciudad tiene varios santos patronos - This city has several patron saints

2211. amistad - friendship
Tu amistad es muy importante para mí - Your friendship is very important to me
2212. derrota - defeat
El partido terminó en una derrota - The match ended in defeat
2213. consiguió - he/she/it achieved / got
Christian consiguió una beca - Christian got a scholarship
2214. positivo - positive (masculine)
Las medidas tuvieron un impacto positivo - The measures had a positive impact
2215. compañías - companies
Rebecca fundó dos compañías exitosas - Rebecca founded two successful companies
2216. ejecución - execution
La ejecución de las obras públicas está en proceso - The execution of public works is in process
2217. expresó - he/she/it expressed
El abogado expresó sus preocupaciones - The lawyer expressed his concerns
2218. embajador - ambassador
El embajador vendrá a cena - The ambassador will come to dinner
2219. dulce - sweet
Quiero comer algo dulce - I want to eat something sweet
2220. promedio - average
En promedio, caminamos diez kilómetros por día - On average, we walked ten kilometers a day
2221. letras - letters
¿Sabes todas letras del abecedario? - Do you know all the letters of the alphabet?
2222. academia - academy
Estoy estudiando español en una academia de idiomas - I am studying Spanish in a language academy

2223. mando - charge / command

Sara está al mando - Sara is in charge

2224. costumbre - custom

La costumbre aquí es saludarse con un beso - The custom here is to greet each other with a kiss

2225. colectivo - collective

Estoy participando en un proyecto de arte colectivo - I am participating in a collective art project

2226. piedras - stones / rocks

Mi madre colecciona piedras de todo el mundo - My mother collects stones from all over the world

2227. rasgos - features

La actriz tiene rasgos hermosos - The actress has beautiful features

2228. industriales - industrial (plural)

En el norte hay muchas ciudades industriales - In the north there are many industrial cities

2229. mía - mine (feminine)

Esa mochila es mía - That backpack is mine

2230. protesta - demonstration / strike / protest

Hay una protesta en el centro - There is a protest in the city center

2231. viajes - trips / travels

El año pasado hice dos viajes a Brasil - Last year I made two trips to Brazil

2232. chica - girl / young woman

Conocí una chica en Argentina - I met a girl in Argentina

2233. periódicos - newspapers

Los periódicos no siempre dicen la verdad - Newspapers don't always tell the truth

2234. moneda - currency / coin

Tengo que cambiar euros por la moneda local - I have to exchange euros for the local currency

2235. órganos - organs

El ozono es un químico que daña a los pulmones y a otros órganos - Ozone is a chemical that damages lungs and other organs

2236. comunicado - statement

El gobierno emitió un comunicado - The government issued a statement

2237. mantenimiento - maintenance

Tomás se encarga del mantenimiento del sitio web - Tomás is in charge of the maintenance of the website

2238. geografía - geography

Estudio Geografía en la universidad - I study Geography at university

2239. manejo - driving / handling

Necesito clases de manejo - I need driving classes

2240. fría - cold (feminine)

Quiero una cerveza fría - I want a cold beer

2241. patrimonio - heritage

Este edificio es patrimonio de la humanidad - This building is a World Heritage Site

2242. exclusivamente - exclusively

Este salón es exclusivamente para miembros del club - This room is exclusively for club members

2243. antiguos - old (plural)

Encontraron unos libros antiguos en la biblioteca - They found some old books in the library

2244. universidades - universities

Las mejores universidades están en esta zona - The best universities are in this area

2245. frecuente - frequent

Es frecuente que llueva por unos minutos – It is frequent that it rains for a few minutes

2246. oficio - job / occupation

¿Cómo va tu nuevo oficio? - How is your new job going?

2247. ayudar - to help

Quiero ayudar a los otros - I want to help others

2248. pedido - request / order

Hice un pedido hace una semana - I made an order a week ago

2249. superar - to overcome

Tenemos que superar nuestros problemas - We have to overcome our problems

2250. auto - car

¿Dónde dejamos el auto? - Where did we leave the car?

2251. relato - story

Te contaré un relato - I will tell you a story

2252. unido - united / close (masculine)

Jorge está muy unido a su madre - Jorge is very close to his mother

2253. sentado - sitting (masculine)

Estoy sentado en un banco, en el parque - I'm sitting on a bench in the park

2254. quisiera - I wish / he/she/it wishes / would like to

Quisiera ver el vestido que usarás en la boda - I would like to see the dress that you will wear at the wedding

2255. detalle - detail

Cada detalle de la película fue creado por los guionistas - Every detail of the film was created by the writers

2256. quedaron - they remained

Las preocupaciones quedaron atrás - The concerns remained behind

2257. obligado - mandatory / forced / required (masculine)

Estoy obligado a asistir al bautismo - I am required to attend the baptism

2258. libres - free (plural)

Al fin somos libres - We are finally free

2259. acabó - it ended / it's over / it finished

¡Todo se acabó! - It's all over!

2260. aeropuerto - airport
¿Podrías llevarme al aeropuerto? - Could you take me to the airport?

2261. pobreza - poverty
La mitad de la población vive en la pobreza - Half of the population lives in poverty

2262. reflexión - meditation / thinking / consideration
Después de mucha reflexión, decidimos despedirlo - After much consideration, we decided to fire him

2263. cumbre - summit / top / peak
Natalia está en la cumbre de su carrera - Natalia is at the peak of her career

2264. imaginación - imagination
Dante tiene mucha imaginación - Dante has a lot of imagination

2265. cubano - Cuban (masculine)
Dago es cubano - Dago is Cuban

2266. solar - solar / sun
No olvides la loción solar - Don't forget the sun lotion

2267. costo - cost
¿Cuál es el costo de despedir a un empleado? - What is the cost of firing an employee?

2268. hubieran - they would have / had
Si hubieran hecho lo que dije, no estarían en este embrollo - If they had done what I said, they wouldn't be in this mess

2269. tesis - thesis
Estoy trabajando en mi tesis doctoral - I am working on my doctoral thesis

2270. catalán - Catalan
Yaiza prefiere hablar en catalán - Yaiza prefers to speak Catalan

2271. hice - I did / I made
Hice todo lo que me pediste - I did everything you asked me to

2272. oír - to hear
¿Puedes oír eso? - Can you hear that?

2273. estabilidad - stability
La estabilidad económica depende de muchos factores - Economic stability depends on many factors

2274. vaso - glass
Quiero un vaso de agua, por favor - I want a glass of water, please

2275. mecanismo - mechanism
El mecanismo del reloj es sencillo - The clock mechanism is simple

2276. escribe - he/she/it writes
Mi abuela escribe poemas de amor - My grandmother writes love poems

2277. aprender - to learn
Quiero aprender a hacer bombones - I want to learn how to make chocolates

2278. cambiado - changed (masculine)
¿Has cambiado de peinado? - Have you changed your hair?

2279. naturalmente - naturally
La fermentación sucede naturalmente - Fermentation happens naturally

2280. potencia - potence / power
Estos parlantes tienen mucha potencia - These speakers have a lot of power

2281. toros - bulls
Esto solía ser una plaza de toros - This used to be a bullring

2282. puro - pure
Quiero respirar aire puro - I want to breathe pure air

2283. elegir - to choose
Debemos elegir un regalo para tu madre - We have to choose a gift for your mother

2284. facultad - faculty / power / capability
Leandro tiene la facultad de tomar decisiones - Leandro has the power to make decisions

2285. ocupa - he/she/it occupies / takes care of
Inés se ocupa de los niños - Ines takes care of the children
2286. patio - patio
La casa tiene un patio precioso - The house has a beautiful patio
2287. recuperar - to recover / make up for
Quiero recuperar el tiempo perdido - I want to make up for lost time
2288. corta - short (feminine)
Escribí una novela corta - I wrote a short novel
2289. pase - that I/he/she/it passes / you pass (imperative)
Esperemos que pase la tormenta - Let's wait for the storm to pass
2290. necesarios - needed (plural)
Para hacer la tortilla, son necesarios ocho huevos - To make the omelette, eight eggs are needed
2291. responder - to answer / to respond / to reply
¿Puedes responder la pregunta que te hice? - Can you answer my question?
2292. reuniones - reunions / meetings
He tenido tres reuniones a lo largo del día - I have had three meetings throughout the day
2293. daño - damage / hurt
Nadie se ha hecho daño - No one got hurt
2294. trabaja - he/she/it works / you work (imperative)
Mi madre trabaja en una fábrica - My mother works in a factory
2295. promoción - promotion
Conseguí un descuento por una promoción - I got a discount because of a promotion
2296. ingredientes - ingredients
¿Tenemos todos los ingredientes para el pastel? - Do we have all the ingredients for the cake?
2297. descubrir - to discover
No puedes descubrir lo que ya estaba descubierto - You can't discover what had already been discovered

2298. viviendas - households / houses
En este barrio solo hay viviendas - In this neighborhood there are only houses

2299. señal - signal
¿Tu teléfono tiene señal? - Do you have phone signal?

2300. clínica - clinic
Trabajo en una clínica de fertilidad - I work in a fertility clinic

2301. tradicionales - traditional
Quiero probar los platos tradicionales - I want to try the traditional dishes

2302. loco - crazy (masculine)
Mi padre quiere ir caminando hasta el Machu Picchu, ¡está loco! - My father wants to walk up to the Machu Picchu, he's crazy!

2303. paseo - walk / stroll
Demos un paseo por la playa - Let's take a walk on the beach

2304. arena - sand
La arena está caliente - The sand is hot

2305. consideración - consideration
Ten en consideración los sentimientos de tu hermana - Consider your sister's feelings

2306. deberán - they will have to
Los niños deberán comer en la mesa pequeña - Children will have to eat at the small table

2307. esquema - scheme
¡Es una estafa! ¡Un esquema piramidal! - Is a scam! A pyramid scheme!

2308. creado - created (masculine)
He creado un nuevo trago - I have created a new cocktail

2309. utilizado - used (masculine)
¿Has utilizado el transporte público de esta ciudad? - Have you used public transportation in this city?

2310. establecido - established
Han establecido una cuarentena total - They have established a total quarantine

2311. concierto - concert
Iremos a un concierto esta noche - We will go to a concert tonight

2312. manifestación - manifestation / demonstration
Hay una manifestación frente al ayuntamiento - There is a demonstration in front of the town hall

2313. enfermos - sick / ill (plural)
Mis hermanos están enfermos con gripe - My brothers are sick with the flu

2314. rechazo - rejection
He recibido una carta de rechazo de la universidad - I received a letter of rejection from the university

2315. salido - stepped out / left / gone out (masculine)
Matías no ha salido de la casa en todo el día - Matías has not left the house all day

2316. dejan - they leave / let
Mis padres no me dejan conducir su coche - My parents won't let me drive their car

2317. consciente – conscious / aware
¿Eres consciente de lo que ha sucedido? - Are you aware of what has happened?

2318. propone - he/she/it proposes
Lautaro le propone matrimonio a Marta - Lautaro proposes to Marta

2319. manifiesto - manifesto
¿Has leído el Manifiesto Comunista? - Have you read the Communist Manifesto?

2320. publicado - published (masculine)
Han publicado un artículo muy interesante en el periódico de hoy - They have published a very interesting article in today's newspaper

2321. ejemplos - examples
¿Podrías darme algunos ejemplos? - Could you give me some examples?

2322. llamaba - he/she/it called
¿Cómo se llamaba tu empresa? - How was your company called?

2323. barco - ship / vessel / boat
Vamos a ir hasta Ecuador en barco - We are going to Ecuador by boat

2324. usar - to use
Debes usar guantes - You must wear gloves

2325. signo - sign
¿De qué signo eres? - Which sign are you?

2326. afecta - affects
Esto nos afecta a todos - This affects us all

2327. árbol - tree
El niño trepa el árbol - The boy climbs the tree

2328. riqueza - richness / wealth
La riqueza del país está en sus recursos minerales - The country's wealth is in its mineral resources

2329. difusión - dissemination
Trabajo en la difusión de estadísticas - I work in the dissemination of statistics

2330. quiera - I/he/she/it wants (subjunctive)
El que quiera puede venir - Whoever wants can come

2331. disciplina - discipline
Debes tener mucha disciplina - You must have a lot of discipline

2332. vemos - we see / watch
¿Vemos una película? - Shall we watch a movie?

2333. felicidad - happiness
La felicidad de nuestros clientes es fundamental - The happiness of our clients is essential

2334. mejora - improvement
Deberíamos ver una mejora en los próximos días - We should see an improvement in the next few days

2335. dirige - he/she/it runs / directs / manages

Mi madre dirige una firma de abogados - My mother runs a law firm

2336. correr - to run

Salgo a correr todas las mañanas - I go out for a run every morning

2337. dimensión - dimension

Ahora comprendemos la verdadera dimensión del problema - Now we understand the true dimension of the problem

2338. petición - request / petition

Los vecinos firmaron una petición - The neighbors signed a petition

2339. transformación - transformation

Karina sufrió una verdadera transformación - Karina underwent a true transformation

2340. notable - notable / considerable / remarkable

Juliana hace un esfuerzo notable para que todo sea perfecto - Juliana makes a remarkable effort to make everything perfect

2341. pista - clue

¡Encontré una pista! - I found a clue!

2342. realizada - realized / made (feminine)

Esta mesa fue realizada con madera de roble - This table was made with oak wood

2343. aplicar - to apply

Debes aplicar tus conocimientos a tu trabajo - You must apply your knowledge to your work

2344. cena - dinner

¡Hay tacos para la cena! - There are tacos for dinner!

2345. eléctrica - electric (feminine)

Quiero comprar una guitarra eléctrica - I want to buy an electric guitar

2346. enviado - sent (masculine)

Le he enviado un mensaje a Jorge - I sent Jorge a message

2347. modos – modes / ways
Hay varios modos de ver las cosas - There are several ways of seeing things

2348. fortuna - fortune
Ese coche debe costar una fortuna - That car must cost a fortune

2349. conflictos - conflicts
El político se oponía a los conflictos armados - The politician was opposed to armed conflicts

2350. infancia - childhood
Este era mi libro favorito en la infancia - This was my favorite childhood book

2351. permitió - he/she/it allowed
La señora me permitió usar su teléfono - The lady allowed me to use her phone

2352. campesinos - farmers / country people / peasants
En esta zona solo hay campesinos - In this area there are only farmers

2353. tercero - third (masculine)
Somos cuatro hermanos; yo soy el tercero - We are four brothers; I am the third one

2354. desea - he/she/it wishes (present) / you wish (formal) / that you want (subjunctive)
¿Qué desea, señor? - What do you want, sir?

2355. obligación - obligation
Todos tenemos la obligación de pagar impuestos - We all have an obligation to pay taxes

2356. oriente - east
Muchos inmigrantes llegaron desde el oriente - Many immigrants came from the east

2357. colección - collection
Mi abuelo tiene una colección de estampas - My grandfather has a collection of stamps

2358. eficaz - effective

La campaña publicitaria fue muy eficaz - The advertising campaign was very effective

2359. exceso - excess

El exceso de ejercicio también es malo - The excess of exercise is also bad

2360. evidencia - evidence

Hay evidencia en contra del acusado - There is evidence against the accused

2361. poderes - powers

El niño tenía poderes mágicos - The boy had magical powers

2362. demostrar - to demonstrate

¿Has podido demostrar tu hipótesis? - Have you been able to prove your hypothesis?

2363. muestran - they show

Los bailarines muestran su talento a la audiencia - Dancers show their talent to the audience

2364. protagonista - the main character / the lead / the protagonist

Seré el protagonista de la obra escolar - I will be the lead of the school play

2365. alcanza - it is enough

¿Nos alcanza el dinero para comprar regalos? - Do we have enough money to buy gifts?

2366. recuerdos - memories

Tengo buenos recuerdos de Costa Rica - I have fond memories of Costa Rica

2367. montaña - mountain

Mi tía escaló esa montaña - My aunt climbed that mountain

2368. dictadura - dictatorship

En este país hubo una dictadura hace tiempo - In this country there was a dictatorship long ago

2369. observa - he/she/it observes

El gato observa los pájaros - The cat observes the birds

2370. indígenas - *native (feminine, plural)*
Las comunidades indígenas no viven aisladas - Native communities do not live in isolation

2371. pasan - *they go through / they pass / they happen*
A veces pasan cosas inesperadas - Sometimes unexpected things happen

2372. claridad - *clarity*
Cristina habla con mucha claridad - Cristina speaks with a lot of clarity

2373. estuviera - *I/he/she/it were (subjunctive)*
Si estuviera en España, sería feliz - If I were in Spain I would be happy

2374. consulta - *query / question*
Tengo una consulta para el abogado - I have a query for the lawyer

2375. financiero - *financial*
El equipo financiero presentó el nuevo plan comercial - The financial team presented the new business plan

2376. inflación - *inflation*
La inflación aumentó el mes pasado - Inflation increased last month

2377. senado - *senate*
El senado discutió el asunto durante horas - The Senate discussed the matter for hours

2378. tropas - *troops*
Las tropas regresaron a la base - The troops returned to the base

2379. mexicana - *Mexican (feminine)*
Me gusta mucho la comida mexicana - I really like Mexican food

2380. correspondientes - *corresponding (plural)*
Debes colocar las cartas en los buzones correspondientes - You must put the letters in the corresponding mailboxes

2381. levantó - *he/she/it lifted / got up*
Cuando Josefina se levantó, ya todos habían desayunado - When Josefina got up, everyone had already had breakfast

2382. vuelo - flight

El vuelo partirá en veinte minutos - The flight will depart in twenty minutes

2383. imperio - empire

El imperio ocupaba más de la mitad de Europa - The empire occupied more than half of Europe

2384. gana - he/she/it wins

Cuando jugamos a las escondidas, Irene siempre gana - When we play hide and seek, Irene always wins

2385. agente - agent / officer

Ricardo es agente de la policía - Ricardo is a police officer

2386. respuestas - answers

Tengo las respuestas a tus preguntas - I have the answers to your questions

2387. civiles - civil (plural) / civilians

Deben garantizarse los derechos civiles - Civil rights must be guaranteed

2388. pierde - he/she/it loses

Julia nunca pierde - Julia never loses

2389. moderno - modern

Me gusta el arte moderno - I like modern art

2390. homenaje - tribute / homage

Varios cantantes harán un homenaje a Prince - Several singers will pay tribute to Prince

2391. establecimiento - settling / establishment

Hay un nuevo establecimiento comercial en la ciudad - There is a new commercial establishment in town

2392. crea - he/she/it creates

El artista crea una nueva obra todos los días - The artist creates a new work every day

2393. fiestas - parties

No me gustan las fiestas - I don't like parties

2394. números - numbers

Sé los números en español hasta el veinte - I know Spanish numbers up to twenty

2395. controlar - to control

Es difícil controlar las cometas - Kites are difficult to control

2396. tratando - trying to

Estoy tratando de encontrar empleo - I'm trying to find a job

2397. intenta - he/she/it tries

Susana intenta reservar una habitación - Susana tries to book a room

2398. circulación - circulation

La circulación de automóviles es muy alta a esta hora - Car circulation is very high at this time

2399. reserva - booking / reservation

Tengo una reserva para tres noches - I have a reservation for three nights

2400. silla - chair

Necesitamos otra silla - We need another chair

Chapter 9 – Words 2401-2700

2401. franceses - French (plural)
Mis abuelos eran franceses - My grandparents were French

2402. escribió - he/she/it wrote
Carla escribió todo en su diario - Carla wrote everything in her diary

2403. virtud - virtue
Nuria tiene la virtud de escuchar sin interrumpir - Nuria has the virtue of listening without interrupting

2404. satisfacción - satisfaction
Siento mucha satisfacción cuando viajo - I feel a lot of satisfaction when I travel

2405. huevos - eggs
¿Quieres unos huevos revueltos? - Do you want some scrambled eggs?

2406. vos - you (Argentina, Uruguay)
¿Vos vas a venir también? - Are you coming too?

2407. descenso - decrease / descent
Tripulación, prepárese para el descenso - Crew, prepare for descent

2408. terrorismo - terrorism
El terrorismo es un tema tabú en esta región - Terrorism is a taboo subject in this region

2409. chico - boy / small (masculine)
Mi coche es muy chico - My car is very small

2410. segura - sure (feminine)
¿Estás segura de que tenemos que ir a la terminal 2? - Are you sure we have to go to Terminal 2?
2411. contó - he/she/it told
Luciana me contó un secreto - Luciana told me a secret
2412. líderes - leaders
Habrá varios líderes importantes en la reunión - There will be several important leaders at the meeting
2413. lentamente - slowly
Lentamente, Fiona se puso de pie - Slowly, Fiona stood up
2414. historias - stories / histories
Contamos historias junto a la hoguera - We told stories by the bonfire
2415. acompañado - accompanied (masculine)
Isidro fue a la fiesta acompañado por su novia - Isidro went to the party accompanied by his girlfriend
2416. décadas - decades
Me mudé a esta ciudad hace dos décadas - I moved to this city two decades ago
2417. reconoció - he/she/it acknowledge / recognize
Tu madre no me reconoció - Your mother didn't recognize me
2418. hago - I do / I make
¿Qué hago ahora? - What do I do now?
2419. apartado - apart / set aside (masculine)
He apartado la sección de deportes para ti - I have set aside the sports section for you
2420. feria - fair
Esta mañana fuimos a la feria de antigüedades - This morning we went to the antique fair
2421. rueda - wheel
La rueda de la bicicleta está desinflada - The bicycle wheel is flat
2422. usuarios - users
Hay millones de usuarios en redes sociales - There are millions of users on social networks

2423. útil - *useful*

Este libro de español es muy útil - This Spanish book is very useful

2424. cumplimiento - *compliance / fulfillment*

El campamento es muy estricto con el cumplimiento de las normas - The camp is very strict with the fulfillment of the norms

2425. transición - *transition*

La transición al nuevo sistema informático fue muy difícil - The transition to the new computer system was very difficult

2426. campeón - *champion*

Mi equipo es el nuevo campeón del mundo - My team is the new world champion

2427. verse - *to see themselves / to find themselves / to be*

Los acusados podrían verse en problemas - Defendants could be in trouble

2428. anteriormente - *previously*

Hemos hablado de este asunto anteriormente - We have discussed this matter previously

2429. defender - *to defend*

La policía debe defender a la población - The police must defend the people

2430. cuáles - *which*

¿Cuáles son nuestras bicicletas? - Which ones are our bikes?

2431. hecha - *done (feminine)*

La tarta ya está hecha - The cake is already done

2432. remedio - *medicine*

A veces es peor el remedio de la enfermedad - Sometimes the remedy is worse than the disease

2433. ponen - *they put*

Los viajes ponen las cosas en perspectiva - Travelling puts things in perspective

2434. debo - *I have to*

Debo estudiar más - I must study harder

2435. procedimientos - procedures

Debes seguir los procedimientos adecuados - You must follow the proper procedures

2436. gritos - shouts

Hay gritos en las calles - There are shouts in the streets

2437. círculo - circle

Sentémonos en un círculo - Let's sit in a circle

2438. norteamericanos - North American

Nosotros somos norteamericanos - We are North American

2439. rojas - red (feminine, plural)

¿Has visto mis sandalias rojas? - Have you seen my red sandals?

2440. dirigido - directed / led (masculine)

La jefa siempre ha dirigido la empresa con responsabilidad - The boss has always led the company with responsibility

2441. delitos - crimes

Jamás hemos cometido delitos - We have never committed crimes

2442. avenida - avenue

Vivimos en aquella avenida - We live on that avenue

2443. obtuvo - he/she/it obtained / got

Jaime obtuvo lo que buscaba - Jaime got what he was looking for

2444. matar - to kill

Debemos matar las malas hierbas del jardín - We must kill the weeds in the garden

2445. cortes - cuts

Ha habido cortes en el presupuesto - There have been cuts in the budget

2446. grados - degrees

El poste está colocado a noventa grados - The pole is placed at ninety degrees

2447. previamente - previously

Previamente, deberíamos hacer un plan - Previously, we should make a plan

2448. publicación – publication / post

Lorenzo hizo una publicación en Instagram - Lorenzo made an Instagram post

2449. aprendizaje - learning

El aprendizaje en línea está en etapa experimental - Online learning is in the experimental stage

2450. motor - engine

Apaga el motor - Turn off the engine

2451. crítico - critical (masculine)

Iñaki es muy crítico - Iñaki is very critical

2452. señores - sirs / misters / gentlemen

Señores, hagan silencio por favor - Gentlemen, please be quiet

2453. muchacha - girl

Giselle es una muchacha muy dulce - Giselle is a very sweet girl

2454. rumbo - course

Tenemos que cambiar el rumbo - We have to change course

2455. trato - treatment / agreement / deal

Hagamos un trato - Let's make a deal

2456. arquitectura - architecture

Estoy estudiando Arquitectura en la universidad - I am studying Architecture at university

2457. querer - to want to

No basta con querer, hay que hacer - It's not enough to want, you have to act

2458. encargado - manager / in charge (masculine)

Tiago es encargado de un bar - Tiago is in charge of a bar

2459. pensé - I thought

Siempre pensé que Mendoza era una ciudad de Chile - I always thought Mendoza was a city in Chile

2460. distrito - district

En el Distrito Federal de México hay muchos millones de personas - In the Federal District of Mexico there are many millions of people

2461. rápida – quick / fast
Mi bicicleta es muy rápida - My bike is very fast
2462. campeonato - championship
¡Hemos ganado el campeonato! - We have won the championship!
2463. maestros - teachers
Los maestros hicieron huelga - Teachers went on strike
2464. reformas - reformations
Hicieron varias reformas en la Constitución - They made several reformations to the Constitution
2465. explotación - exploitation
La explotación de los recursos debe hacerse con mesura - The exploitation of resources should be done in moderation
2466. católica - catholic
Mi abuela es muy católica - My grandmother is very Catholic
2467. contenidos - contents
Soy redactor de contenidos digitales - I'm a digital content writer
2468. sustancias - substances
No puedes pasar sustancias peligrosas por la aduana - You cannot pass dangerous substances through customs control
2469. regresar - to go back / to return
Debes regresar mañana - You must return tomorrow
2470. formado - formed
Linda y Albertino han formado una pareja - Linda and Albertino have formed a couple
2471. creía - I/he/she/it believed / used to believe / thought (indefinite past)
Yo creía que pagarían por adelantado - I thought they would pay in advance
2472. juzgado - judged (masculine)
Te he juzgado antes de conocerte - I've judged you before I met you

2473. famoso - famous
Creo que ese es un cantante famoso - I think that's a famous singer

2474. avance - advance
¿Podrías darme un avance de mi salario? - Could you give me an advance on my salary?

2475. particulares - particular / individual (plural)
Los correos electrónicos son particulares y privados - Emails are individual and private

2476. usa - he/she/it uses
¿Tu hijo usa la pelota que le regalé? - Does your son use the ball I gave him?

2477. cerrar - to close
¿Podrías cerrar la puerta? - Could you close the door?

2478. aprobación - approval
Estamos esperando la aprobación del director - We are waiting for the director's approval

2479. llamadas - calls
Recibimos varias llamadas de queja - We received several complaint calls

2480. termina - he/she/it ends
¿A qué hora termina el recital? - What time does the recital end?

2481. borde - border / edge / verge
Juana está al borde de las lágrimas - Juana is on the verge of tears

2482. fenómenos - phenomena
Hubo varios fenómenos extraños en los últimos días - There were several strange phenomena in the past few days

2483. metro - meter
Mido un metro y sesenta y cinco centímetros - I am one meter and sixty-five centimeters tall

2484. corrientes - currents / ordinary (plural)
Hubo cambios en las corrientes oceánicas - There were changes in the ocean currents

2485. dedicado - dedicated (masculine)
Eduardo me ha dedicado un poema - Eduardo has dedicated a poem to me

2486. creen - they believe / think
Mis padres creen que pasaré la Navidad solo en mi casa - My parents think I will spend Christmas alone in my house

2487. continente - continent
América es un continente, no un país - America is a continent, not a country

2488. ventajas - advantages
¿Cuáles son las ventajas de contratar una agencia de viajes? - What are the advantages of hiring a travel agency?

2489. clásico - classic
Esta película es un clásico - This movie is a classic

2490. orquesta - orchestra
La orquesta está lista para tocar - The orchestra is ready to play

2491. oye - hey
Oye, ¿tienes hora? - Hey, do you have the time?

2492. analizar - to analyze
Hay que analizar los datos con cuidado - You have to analyze the data carefully

2493. cuentan - they tell
Los niños le cuentan al maestro lo que hicieron durante el fin de semana - The children tell the teacher what they did during the weekend

2494. diarios - newspapers / daily (plural)
La noticia está en todos los diarios - The news is in all the newspapers

2495. dueño - owner
Soy dueño de un apartamento – I'm the owner of an apartment

2496. actitudes - attitudes
Román tiene actitudes nuevas que no me gustan - Román has new attitudes that I don't like

2497. bajar - to go down
Voy a bajar a la cocina, ¿quieres algo de beber? - I'm going down to the kitchen, do you want something to drink?
2498. telefónica - telephone / phone (adjective, feminine)
Tuve una conversación telefónica con mi prima - I had a phone conversation with my cousin
2499. gustaría - I / you (formal) / he/she/it would like
¿Le gustaría algo de comer? - Would you like something to eat?
2500. cerrado - closed (masculine)
El restaurante está cerrado los lunes - The restaurant is closed on Mondays
2501. descubierto - uncovered / discovered (masculine)
Los científicos han descubierto la cura - Scientists have discovered the cure
2502. urbano - urban
Este automóvil es ideal para un entorno urbano - This car is ideal for an urban setting
2503. deportivo - sports / sporting (adjective)
Hay un evento deportivo en el estadio - There is a sporting event at the stadium
2504. viendo – seeing / watching
Estoy viendo una serie sobre detectives - I'm watching a series about detectives
2505. órgano - organ
El corazón es un órgano - The heart is an organ
2506. asociaciones - associations / organizations
Hay cerca de una docena de asociaciones juveniles en la ciudad - There are about a dozen youth associations in the city
2507. instalación - installation
El ayuntamiento prohibió la instalación de un club en este barrio - The city council prohibited the installation of a club in this neighborhood

2508. hombros - *shoulders*
Debes ponerte loción solar en los hombros - You should put sun lotion on your shoulders

2509. introducción - *introduction*
Solo leí la introducción del libro - I only read book introduction

2510. demostrado - *demonstrated / shown*
Gabriela me ha demostrado que estoy equivocado - Gabriela has shown me that I am wrong

2511. determinados - *determined / certain (masculine, plural)*
En determinados momentos, siento dolor en la espalda - At certain times, I feel pain in my back

2512. mostrar - *to show*
Le voy a mostrar la ciudad a mi familia - I'm going to show the city to my family

2513. atmósfera - *atmosphere*
La atmósfera está muy contaminada - The atmosphere is heavily polluted

2514. fronteras - *frontiers / borders*
Las fronteras están cerradas - The borders are closed

2515. moreno - *brown / tanned*
Lucas ha vuelto muy moreno de las vacaciones - Lucas has returned very tanned from his holidays

2516. sabido - *known*
Es sabido que hubo fraude - It is known that there was a fraud

2517. diga - *I say / he/she/it says (subjunctive) / you say (imperative)*
¿Qué quieres que le diga a Andrea? - What do you want me to say to Andrea?

2518. vender - *to sell*
Vamos a vender nuestra casa - We are going to sell our house

2519. dejaba - *I/he/she/it left / let / used to leave (imperfect past)*
Mi madre no me dejaba comer golosinas - My mother wouldn't let me eat sweets

2520. polémica - scandal / controversy
Hubo una polémica en la televisión - There was a controversy on television

2521. vacaciones - vacations
Me tomaré vacaciones desde la semana que viene - I will take a vacation starting next week

2522. vidas - lives
Los cinturones de seguridad salvan vidas - Seat belts save lives

2523. mediados - mid-
Nos veremos a mediados de abril - We will see each other in mid-April

2524. subir - to go up / to climb / to get on / to ride
¿Quieres subir a la montaña rusa? - Do you want to ride the roller coaster?

2525. iniciar - to start / to begin
Vamos a iniciar una partida de Scrabble - Let's start a Scrabble game

2526. droga - drug
El tabaco es una droga legal - Tobacco is a legal drug

2527. asegurar - to assure
Te puedo asegurar que será la mejor comida de tu vida - I can assure you that it will be the best meal of your life

2528. entusiasmo - enthusiasm
El entusiasmo de Alma es inigualable - Alma's enthusiasm is unmatched

2529. prestigio - prestige
Tu marca de ropa tiene mucho prestigio - Your clothing brand has a lot of prestige

2530. centrales - central
Los bancos centrales regulan la economía - Central banks regulate the economy

2531. edificios - buildings
En el gran incendio se quemaron varios edificios - Several buildings were burned in the great fire

2532. *contestó - he/she/it answered / replied / responded to*
Jazmín nunca contestó mi mensaje - Jasmine never answered my message

2533. *extraña - he/she/it misses*
Olivia extraña a su prima - Olivia misses her cousin

2534. *signos - signs*
No creo que los signos del zodíaco signifiquen algo - I don't think the zodiac signs mean anything

2535. *permitir - to allow*
La presidenta no va a permitir esto - The president is not going to allow this

2536. *sensibilidad - sensibility / sensitivity*
Patricio tiene una gran sensibilidad - Patrick has a great sensitivity

2537. *lógico - logical (masculine)*
Es lógico que te sientas frustrada - It is logical that you feel frustrated

2538. *terminado - ended / finished (masculine)*
¿Has terminado tu tarea? - Have you finished your homework?

2539. *bar - bar*
Vamos al bar - Let's go to the bar

2540. *comenzaron - they started / began*
Los pájaros comenzaron a volar - The birds began to fly

2541. *ciudadano - citizen*
Soy argentino, pero también soy ciudadano español - I am an Argentinian, but I am also a Spanish citizen

2542. *actuaciones - performances*
Se anunciaron nuevas actuaciones de la banda - New performances by the band were announced

2543. *particularmente - particularly*
Esa ciudad fue particularmente afectada por el temporal - That city was particularly affected by the storm

2544. *especialistas - specialists*
Ellos dos son especialistas en microbiología - They are both specialists in microbiology

2545. canciones - songs
Anoche cantamos canciones junto a la fogata - Last night we sang songs by the campfire

2546. golpes - punches / blows
Recibí varios golpes mientras jugaba al rugby - I received several blows while playing rugby

2547. pertenece - it belongs
Esta cartera pertenece a alguien llamado Sergio Gutiérrez - This wallet belongs to someone named Sergio Gutiérrez

2548. legislación - legislation
La nueva legislación entró en vigencia - The new legislation went into effect

2549. delegación - delegation
Una delegación de la Organización Mundial de la Salud llegó a Gaza - A delegation from the World Health Organization arrived in Gaza

2550. anoche - last night
Anoche soñé que nos íbamos a vivir a España - Last night I dreamed that we were moving to Spain

2551. dignidad - dignity
Debes mantener tu dignidad - You must maintain your dignity

2552. unidas - united / close / joined (feminine, plural)
Estamos unidas en este momento de adversidad - We are united in this moment of adversity

2553. citado – quoted / cited
Este artículo es citado por todos los expertos - This article is cited by all the experts

2554. conveniente - convenient
Es conveniente que esperes un rato antes de hacer ejercicio – It is convenient to wait a while before exercising

2555. empresario - businessman
El señor Martínez es un importante empresario - Mr. Martínez is an important businessman

2556. llaman - they call
Mis abuelos me llaman todos los sábados - My grandparents call me every Saturday

2557. presos - prisoners
Los presos fueron puestos en libertad sin cargos - The prisoners were released without any charges

2558. expansión - expansion
La expansión de la empresa fue un éxito - The expansion of the company was a success

2559. radical - radical
Internet generó un cambio radical en las relaciones sociales - The Internet generated a radical change in social relations

2560. advirtió - he/she/it warned
El juez advirtió al abogado por tercera vez - The judge warned the lawyer a third time

2561. tomando - taking
Estoy tomando la medicina que me recetó el médico - I am taking the medicine the doctor prescribed

2562. comenzar - to start / to begin
Los Juegos Olímpicos van a comenzar en breve - The Olympic Games are going to start soon

2563. conforme - according / pursuant to
Conforme a lo dispuesto por el tribunal, deberá pagar una multa - Pursuant to court order, you must pay a fine

2564. detenidos - arrested (masculine, plural)
Los infractores fueron detenidos - The offenders were arrested

2565. deseos - wishes / desires
Tus deseos son órdenes - Your wishes are my command

2566. impulso - impulse / urge
Tengo el impulso de decirte que te amo - I have the urge to tell you that I love you

2567. dispone - he/she/it provides
El juez dispone que el niño vivirá con su madre - The judge provides that the child will live with his mother

2568. necesarias - needed / necessary (feminine, plural)
Las leyes son necesarias - Laws are necessary
2569. esquina - corner
Hay una tienda en la esquina - There is a store on the corner
2570. productores - producers
Mis tíos son productores de tomates - My uncles are tomato producers
2571. ponerse - to put oneself / to wear
Inés quiere ponerse su vestido rosa - Inés wants to wear her pink dress
2572. destaca - he/she/it stands out / highlights
El profesor destaca los buenos resultados del experimento - The teacher highlights the good results of the experiment
2573. mantuvo - he/she/it maintained
El policía mantuvo el orden - The policeman maintained the order
2574. cola - tail
El gato tiene una cola larga y peluda - The cat has a long, furry tail
2575. tuviera - he/she/it had (subjunctive)
Si tuviera mucho dinero, iría a un hotel de lujo - If I had a lot of money, I would stay in a luxury hotel
2576. inmediata - immediate
La ministra ordenó la movilización inmediata de los recursos - The minister ordered the immediate mobilization of resources
2577. mexicanos - Mexican (masculine, plural)
Los mexicanos aman la buena comida - Mexicans love good food
2578. socios – associates / partners
Ellos dos son mis socios - Those two are my partners
2579. bajas - low / short (feminine, plural)
Las ventas en junio han sido muy bajas - Sales in June have been very low

2580. informes - reports
He leído los informes policiales - I have read the police reports

2581. jefes - bosses
Mis jefes estaban muy satisfechos con la presentación - My bosses were very satisfied with the presentation

2582. argumento - argument
Ese argumento no tiene sentido - That argument doesn't make sense

2583. cultivo - culture / crop
El cultivo se arruinó por la inundación - The crop was ruined by the flood

2584. vivía - I/he/she/it lived / used to live (imperfect past)
En aquella época, yo vivía en Costa Rica - At that time, I lived in Costa Rica

2585. opiniones - opinions
Las opiniones no son datos - Opinions are not data

2586. reloj - clock / watch
Creo que mi reloj está roto - I think my watch is broken

2587. habido – there have been
Jamás ha habido tanta gente en este restaurante - There have never been so many people in this restaurant

2588. riesgos - risks
¿Comprendes los riesgos de la inversión? - Do you understand the risks of this investment?

2589. meta - goal
Tengo una nueva meta para este año - I have a new goal for this year

2590. laboratorio - laboratory / lab
Este laboratorio no experimenta con animales - This laboratory does not experiment with animals

2591. comunicaciones - communications
El piloto transmitió las comunicaciones a la torre de control - The pilot transmitted the communications to the control tower

2592. a medias - fifty-fifty / half

Repartiremos las ganancias a medias - We will divide the profits in half

2593. escolar - scholar

El año escolar comienza en marzo en el hemisferio sur - The scholar year begins in March in the southern hemisphere

2594. danza - dance

Esa es una danza tradicional mexicana - That's a traditional mexican dance

2595. terrible - terrible

El incendio fue terrible - The fire was terrible

2596. notas - notes / grades

¿Obtuviste buenas notas este año? - Did you get good grades this year?

2597. entero - entire / whole (masculine)

¡Me comí el pollo entero! - I ate the whole chicken!

2598. suave - soft

Tu suéter es muy suave - Your sweater is very soft

2599. activa - active (feminine)

Jimena es una chica muy activa - Jimena is a very active girl

2600. dirigida - directed / addressed (feminine)

La carta está dirigida a tu padre - The letter is addressed to your father

2601. eje - axis

Las ruedas giran en torno al eje - Wheels turn around the axis

2602. variedad - variety

Hay mucha variedad de vegetales en esta región - There is a lot of variety of vegetables in this region

2603. fácilmente - easily

Con tu teléfono puedes hacerlo fácilmente - With your phone you can do it easily

2604. canción - song

Esta canción está inspirada en eventos reales - This song is inspired in true events

2605. cantidades – quantities / amounts

Consumí grandes cantidades de chocolate - I consumed large amounts of chocolate

2606. orientación - orientation / direction

Las palomas tienen un gran sentido de la orientación - Pigeons have a great sense of direction

2607. fotos - photos / pictures

¿Podrías enviarme las fotos del viaje? - Could you send me the photos of the trip?

2608. definir - to define

Debemos definir nuestra relación - We must define our relationship

2609. masas - masses / mass

Ella estudia la psicología de masas - She studies mass psychology

2610. tabaco - tobacco

El tabaco es muy dañino - Tobacco is very harmful

2611. aventura - adventure

El viaje fue una verdadera aventura - The trip was a real adventure

2612. próximas - next (feminine, plural)

En las próximas horas te llamaremos - In the next few hours we will call you

2613. pude - I could (past)

No pude leer el libro que me regalaste - I couldn't read the book you gave me

2614. llegaba - I/he/she/it arrived / used to arrive (imperfect past)

Marcos siempre llegaba tarde - Marcos always arrived late

2615. conocidos - acquaintances / known

No son mis amigos, son conocidos - They are not my friends, they are acquaintances

2616. raíces - roots

Las raíces del árbol crecen bajo la tierra - Tree roots grow underground

2617. gravedad - gravity
En el espacio no hay gravedad - There's no gravity in space
2618. blancos - targets / white (masculine, plural)
Mis zapatos blancos están sucios - My white shoes are dirty
2619. municipio - city hall / municipality
El municipio lanzó fuegos artificiales - The municipality launched fireworks
2620. arroz - rice
Me encanta el arroz - I love rice
2621. potencial - potential
Leandro tiene mucho potencial - Leandro has a lot of potential
2622. islas - islands
Nadie vive en estas islas - No one lives on these islands
2623. goles - goals
Mi equipo metió cinco goles - My team scored five goals
2624. oportunidades - opportunities
No dejes pasar oportunidades como esta - Do not miss opportunities like this one
2625. estuvieron - they were
Mamá y Papá estuvieron muy ocupados - Mom and Dad were very busy
2626. caballero - gentleman
Octavio es todo un caballero - Octavio is quite a gentleman
2627. colocar - to place
Voy a colocar tu regalo en mi mesa de luz - I will place your gift on my bedside table
2628. comentarios - comments
No emitiré comentarios sobre este asunto - I will not comment on this matter
2629. profundidad - depth
La piscina tiene una profundidad de un metro y medio - The pool is one and a half meters Deep

2630. comprensión - *understanding / comprehension*
El alumno logra la comprensión de los textos - The student achieves comprehension of the texts

2631. panorama - *landscape*
El panorama es desolador - The landscape is bleak

2632. revolucionario - *revolutionary*
Fue un acto revolucionario - It was a revolutionary act

2633. síntesis - *synthesis*
Debo hacer una síntesis del capítulo 4 - I must make a synthesis of chapter 4

2634. buscando - *searching / looking for*
Flavio está buscando a su perro - Flavio is looking for his dog

2635. dependencia - *dependence*
Raúl quiere un empleo, no soporta la dependencia de sus padres - Raúl wants a job, he cannot bear the dependence on his parents

2636. primavera - *spring*
En primavera, quiero viajar a Ecuador - In spring I want to travel to Ecuador

2637. aumenta - *he/she/it increases*
El empresario aumenta el salario de sus empleados - The employer increases the salary of his employees

2638. manifiesta - *he/she/it manifests / expresses*
Daniela manifiesta su temor - Daniela expresses her fear

2639. fruto - *fruit*
El melón es un fruto muy dulce - The melon is a very sweet fruit

2640. brillante - *brilliant*
Camila es brillante - Camila is brilliant

2641. fechas - *dates*
¿Recuerdas las fechas patrias importantes? - Do you remember the important national dates?

2642. torre - *tower*
Desde la torre de control ven todo - From the control tower they see everything

2643. oscuridad - darkness / dark
No puedes trabajar en la oscuridad - You can't work in the dark
2644. anuncio - announcement
¡Tengo un anuncio importante! - I have an important announcement!
2645. intelectuales - intellectuals
Odio a esos intelectuales que se creen mejor que el resto - I hate those intellectuals who think they are better than the rest of us
2646. ampliación - extension / expansion
Los activistas propusieron una ampliación de las reservas naturales - Activists proposed an expansion of nature reserves
2647. conservación - conservation
Ana María trabaja en la conservación de obras de arte - Ana María works in the conservation of works of art
2648. inicia - he/she/it starts / begins
Este año, Martín inicia la universidad - This year, Martín starts university
2649. alcanzó - he/she/it reached / fulfilled
Silvina alcanzó sus objetivos - Silvina fulfilled her goals
2650. demuestra - he/she/it demonstrates
Esta investigación demuestra que las vacunas funcionan - This research demonstrates that vaccines work
2651. salas - rooms
Tenemos varias salas de conferencias - We have several conference rooms
2652. vital - vital
El aire es vital para las plantas - Air is vital for plants
2653. pudieron - they could / were able to
Los rehenes pudieron escapar - The hostages were able to escape
2654. carreras - races / careers
No me interesan las carreras de caballos - I'm not interested in horse races

2655. sabor - flavour / taste
Me encanta el sabor del plátano - I love the taste of the banana
2656. combate - combat
No quiero entrar en un combate - I don't want to enter a combat
2657. efectivamente - effectively / sure enough
Efectivamente, Andrea tenía razón - Sure enough, Andrea was right
2658. lágrimas - tears
Estas son lágrimas de felicidad - These are tears of happiness
2659. disminución - decrease
Habrá una disminución de los beneficios - There will be a decrease in profits
2660. plantea - he/she/it poses
El profesor plantea un problema a los alumnos - The teacher poses a problem to the students
2661. provincial - provincial
El gobierno provincial sigue las leyes nacionales - The provincial government follows national laws
2662. miraba - I/he/she/it looked
Nicolás miraba el paisaje - Nicolás looked at the landscape
2663. situado - located (masculine)
El País Vasco está situado en el norte de España - The Basque Country is located in the north of Spain
2664. caballos - horses
A Clara le encantan los caballos - Clara loves horses
2665. proteínas - proteins
Debes consumir proteínas - You must consume proteins
2666. biblioteca - library
En la biblioteca encontrarás todo lo que necesites - In the library you will find everything you need
2667. recientes - recent (plural)
Los eventos recientes lo cambiaron todo - Recent events changed everything

2668. afuera - *outside*
El perro está jugando afuera - The dog is playing outside

2669. tasas - *rates*
El banco aumentó sus tasas hipotecarias - The bank increased its mortgage rates

2670. levanta - *he/she/it rises / gets up*
Luciana se levanta temprano por la mañana - Luciana gets up early in the morning

2671. cuarta - *fourth (feminine)*
Es la cuarta vez que vengo a Chile - It is the fourth time that I've come to Chile

2672. taza - *mug*
Daniel me regaló una taza - Daniel gave me a mug

2673. conclusiones - *conclusions*
Las conclusiones del informe son muy claras - The conclusions of the report are very clear

2674. necesitan - *they need*
Estas familias necesitan un lugar donde vivir - These families need a place to live

2675. negativa - *negative*
La respuesta del público fue negativa - The public response was negative

2676. dieta - *diet*
Isabel está haciendo una dieta por su diabetes - Isabel is going on a diet because of her diabetes

2677. alcanzado - *reached / attained*
Hemos alcanzado nuestro objetivo anual - We have reached our annual goal

2678. andar - *to go / to walk*
¿Puedes andar o estás cansada? - Can you walk or are you tired?

2679. destacó - *he/she/it highlighted / pointed out / stood out*
El orador destacó la puntualidad de los presentes - The speaker highlighted the punctuality of those present

2680. *pilar - pillar*
La justicia es un pilar de la democracia - Justice is a pillar of democracy

2681. *flor - flower*
Esteban me regaló una flor - Esteban gave me a flower

2682. *suficientes - sufficient / enough (plural)*
Estas bebidas son suficientes, no necesitamos más - These drinks are enough, we don't need more

2683. *existentes - existing (plural)*
Debemos aprovechar los recursos existentes - We must take advantage of existing resources

2684. *utilizan - they use*
Los granjeros utilizan agua del arroyo para regar - The farmers use water from the stream to irrigate

2685. *ceremonia - ceremony*
La ceremonia está por comenzar - The ceremony is about to begin

2686. *abogados - lawyers*
Mi esposo y yo somos abogados - My husband and I are lawyers

2687. *mantienen - they keep / remain*
Los pasajeros mantienen la calma - The passengers remain calm

2688. *castellano - Castilian*
El español también es llamado "castellano", porque viene de Castilla - Spanish is also called "Castilian," because it comes from Castilla

2689. *vivido - lived*
Nunca he vivido en otro país - I have never lived in another country

2690. *representan - they represent*
Los políticos representan a la gente - Politicians represent the people

2691. *cámaras - cameras*
Tengo dos cámaras de fotos, pero he olvidado ambas - I have two cameras, but I have forgotten both

2692. aparecer - to appear / to show up
Mi padre va a aparecer por aquí en cualquier momento - My father will show up around here at any time

2693. dioses - gods
Los mayas creían en muchos dioses - The Mayans believed in many gods

2694. programación - programming
Todos deberíamos aprender un poco de programación - We should all learn a little bit of programming

2695. médica - doctor / medical (feminine)
Mi hija es médica - My daughter is a doctor

2696. opciones - options
Tenemos varias opciones para la cena - We have several options for dinner

2697. permiso - permission
¿Tienes permiso de tu jefe para faltar mañana? - Do you have permission from your boss to miss work tomorrow?

2698. verdes - green (plural)
Julia tiene unos hermosos ojos verdes - Julia has beautiful green eyes

2699. mensajes - messages
Tengo muchos mensajes sin leer - I have many unread messages

2700. participantes - participants
Los participantes deben seguir las reglas del juego - Participants must follow the rules of the game

Chapter 10 – Words 2701-3000

2701. sacó - he/she/it took out / pulled
El jardinero sacó las malas hierbas - The gardener pulled the weeds

2702. profesión - profession
Mi profesión es muy inusual - My profession is very unusual

2703. senador - senator
El senador dio un discurso - The senator gave a speech

2704. convocatoria - announcement / call
La universidad lanzó una convocatoria de propuestas de investigación - The university launched a call for research proposals

2705. largas - long (feminine, plural)
Hay largas filas para entrar en el concierto - There are long lines to enter the concert

2706. afirmar - to affirm
¡No puedes afirmar que eso sea cierto! - You cannot affirm that it is true!

2707. arma - gun / weapon
El policía lleva consigo su arma reglamentaria - The policeman carries his regulatory weapon

2708. americano - American
El continente americano tiene 35 países - The American continent has 35 countries

2709. provincias - provinces
Argentina tiene 24 provincias - Argentina has 24 provinces

2710. cuantos - as many

Te daré cuantos bombones quieras - I will give you as many chocolates as you want

2711. proporción - proportion / ratio

Hay una proporción de dos mujeres por cada hombre en esta ciudad - There is a ratio of two women to one man in this city

2712. rival - rival

El equipo rival ganó el partido - The rival team won the match

2713. angustia - anguish

Siento mucha angustia - I feel a lot of anguish

2714. escasa - sparse / scarce (feminine)

Debemos racionar la escasa comida que tenemos - We must ration the scarce food we have

2715. largos - long (plural)

El viajero estuvo ausente durante largos años - The traveler was absent for long years

2716. destrucción - destruction

Sergio fue testigo de la destrucción del edificio - Sergio witnessed the destruction of the building

2717. europeas - European (feminine, plural)

Las naciones europeas deben permanecer unidas - European nations must remain united

2718. podríamos - we could (conditional)

Podríamos ir al cine esta tarde - We could go to the cinema this afternoon

2719. celebración - celebration

La celebración se extendió hasta las tres de la mañana - The celebration lasted until three in the morning

2720. traje - suit / I brought

Traje algo de beber - I brought something to drink

2721. parecían - they seemed

Los niños parecían cansados - The children seemed tired

2722. jurídico - legal
Le presté a Laura mi diccionario jurídico - I lent Laura my legal dictionary
2723. techo - roof
El pobre hombre no tiene un techo sobre su cabeza - The poor man doesn't have a roof over his head
2724. elevado - elevated / high
El terreno está muy elevado - The terrain is very high
2725. financiera - financial (feminine)
La especulación financiera es dañina para la economía - Financial speculation is harmful to the economy
2726. utilizando - using
Amanda está utilizando el secador que le regalé - Amanda is using the hairdryer that I gave her
2727. cubrir - to cover
Deberíamos cubrir la piscina antes de que llueva - We should cover the pool before it rains
2728. descanso - rest / break
Tómate un descanso - Take a break
2729. percepción - perception
La percepción humana no es perfecta - Human perception is not perfect
2730. bosque - forest
La cabaña está junto a un bosque - The cabin is next to a forest
2731. continuidad - continuity
No hay continuidad entre las dos partes del libro - There is no continuity between the two parts of the book
2732. británico - British
Tienes acento británico - You have a British accent
2733. financiación - financing
Ya conseguimos la financiación para el proyecto - We already obtained the financing for the Project

2734. bienestar - well-being
Solo me importa el bienestar de mi familia - I only care about the well-being of my family

2735. afectados - affected (masculine, plural)
Los grandes empresarios no se vieron afectados por la crisis - Businessmen were not affected by the crisis

2736. consejero - adviser / counselor
El consejero emitió su opinión - The counselor issued his opinion

2737. dé - he/she/it gives (subjunctive)
No creo que el clima nos dé problemas - I don't think the weather will give us trouble

2738. diría - I/he/she/it would say
Normalmente diría que sí, pero hoy estoy cansado - Normally I would say yes, but today I'm tired

2739. descubrimiento - discovery
¿En qué año sucedió el descubrimiento de la pólvora? - In what year the discovery of gunpowder happened?

2740. escándalo - scandal
¡Fue un verdadero escándalo! - It was a real scandal!

2741. estancia - stay
Pasamos una agradable estancia en Mallorca - We had a pleasant stay in Mallorca

2742. seguros - safe (masculine, plural)
Aquí estamos seguros - Here we are safe

2743. argumentos - arguments
No me importan tus argumentos, no cambiaré de opinión - I don't care about your arguments, I won't change my mind

2744. espero - I wait / I hope
Espero que podamos vernos pronto - I hope we can see each other soon

2745. deportes - sports
Me gustan los deportes acuáticos - I like water sports

2746. informa - he/she/it informs

El periodista informa que ha habido un accidente - The journalist informs that there has been an accident

2747. preparado - prepared / ready (masculine)

Estoy preparado para la expedición - I am ready for the expedition

2748. negó - he/she/it denied

Rita negó los rumores - Rita denied the rumors

2749. añadir - to add

Ahora debes añadir un huevo - Now you must add an egg

2750. corona - crown

Mi sobrina tiene una corona de plástico - My niece has a plastic crown

2751. cabezas - heads

Los niños golpearon sus cabezas accidentalmente - The kids accidentally bumped their heads

2752. cadáver - dead body / corpse

La serie comienza con el descubrimiento de un cadáver - The series begins with the discovery of a corpse

2753. iguales - equal / same (plural)

¡Nuestros teléfonos son iguales! - Our phones are the same!

2754. pendiente - pending

Tengo un asunto pendiente con Gastón - I have a pending issue with Gastón

2755. relacionados - related

Los eventos artísticos siempre están relacionados con su contexto histórico - Artistic events are always related to their historical context

2756. abuelo - grandfather

Mi abuelo ama leer historietas - My grandfather loves reading comic books

2757. decirle - to tell him/her

¿Puedes decirle a Catalina que venga? - Can you tell Catalina to come?

2758. normalmente - normally

Normalmente iría, pero hoy no tengo ganas - Normally I would go, but today I don't feel like it

2759. oficinas - offices

La empresa tiene oficinas en el centro - The company has offices in the city center

2760. revisión - revision / review

Debo terminar la revisión de estos documentos - I must finish the review of these documents

2761. frecuentes - frequent (plural)

Los terremotos son frecuentes en esta zona - Earthquakes are frequent in this area

2762. institucional - institutional

El gobierno inició una reforma institucional - The government started an institutional reform

2763. cae - he/she/it falls

El globo cae lentamente - The balloon falls slowly

2764. previa - previous / prior (feminine)

¿Tiene una cita previa? - Do you have a prior appointment?

2765. ricos - rich

Mis vecinos son ricos - My neighbors are rich

2766. símbolo - symbol

Ella se convirtió en un símbolo de la moda - She became a fashion symbol

2767. sostiene - he/she/it holds / argues

La investigadora sostiene que la hipótesis es falsa - The researcher argues that the hypothesis is false

2768. capa - layer

La capa de ozono se está recuperando - The ozone layer is recovering

2769. temporal - temporary

Tengo un trabajo temporal - I have a temporary job

2770. vigilancia - vigilance / surveillance
Debemos mejorar el sistema vigilancia - We must improve our surveillance system

2771. mínima - minimum (feminine)
La jubilación mínima no es suficiente - Minimum retirement is not enough

2772. columna vertebral - spine
Debes mejorar tu postura para cuidar tu columna vertebral - You must improve your posture to take care of your spine

2773. ves - you see
¿Ves ese colibrí? - Do you see that hummingbird?

2774. ofrecen - they offer
Mis jefes me ofrecen un mejor salario, pero más responsabilidad - My bosses offer me a better salary, but more responsibility

2775. acababa - I/he/she/it had just... (verb)
Julieta acababa de salir de la ducha cuando sonó el teléfono - Juliet had just got out of the shower when the phone rang

2776. determinada - determined / certain (feminine)
No puedes tomar más que una cantidad determinada de café por día - You cannot drink more than a certain amount of coffee per day

2777. salsa - sauce
No me gusta la salsa agridulce - I don't like sweet and sour sauce

2778. ruta - route / road
Frenamos en la ruta para comer algo - We stopped on the road to eat something

2779. cursos - courses / classes
Me anoté en unos cursos de cocina - I signed up for some cooking courses

2780. huesos - bones
Te vas a romper todos los huesos si te caes de ahí - You're going to break all your bones if you fall out of there

2781. permitido - permitted / allowed
El perro no tiene permitido estar dentro de la casa - The dog is not allowed to be inside the house

2782. difíciles - difficult
Se acercan días difíciles - Difficult days are coming

2783. amiga - friend (feminine)
Tengo una amiga que vive en Panamá - I have a friend who lives in Panama

2784. observación - observation
Gregorio hizo una observación muy pertinente - Gregorio made a very pertinent observation

2785. escritores - writers (masculine)
Los escritores no ganan mucho dinero - Writers don't make a lot of money

2786. asumir - to assume
Debemos asumir que la electricidad no volverá por varias horas - We must assume that the electric power will not return for several hours

2787. sufrido - suffered
Rosa ha sufrido mucho ya - Rosa has suffered a lot already

2788. setenta - seventy
Mi abuela cumplió setenta años - My grandmother turned seventy

2789. dejaron - they left
Los fugitivos dejaron la ciudad - The fugitives left the city

2790. guía - guide
El guía nos recordó que bebamos agua - The guide reminded us to drink water

2791. haría - I/he/she/it would do
No sé qué haría si no te tuviera - I don't know what I would do if I didn't have you

2792. nervioso - nervous (masculine)
Lisandro está muy nervioso - Lisandro is very nervous

2793. vivos - alive (plural)
Todos mis abuelos están vivos - All my grandparents are alive
2794. dimensiones - dimensions
Incluso la lucha económica tiene dimensiones medioambientales - Even economic struggle has environmental dimensions
2795. atender - to attend / to serve / to answer
Debo atender esta llamada - I must answer this call
2796. contratos - contracts / agreements
¿Los nuevos empleados ya firmaron los contratos? - Have the new employees already signed the contracts?
2797. bandera - flag
La bandera de Perú es roja y blanca - The flag of Peru is red and white
2798. quedarse - to stay
Las mascotas deben quedarse dentro cuando llueve - The pets must stay indoors when it rains
2799. regular – regular / regulate
El Estado puede regular la economía - The state can regulate the economy
2800. presupuestos - budgets
Debemos ajustar nuestros presupuestos - We must adjust our budgets
2801. rendimiento - performance
El rendimiento de la fábrica ha aumentado - Factory performance has increased
2802. igualdad - equality
Bianca lucha por la igualdad de género - Bianca fights for gender equality
2803. tocar - to touch / to play
Quiero tocar una canción - I want to play a song
2804. jurídica - legal (feminine)
Necesito asesoría jurídica - I need legal advice

2805. confusión - confusion
Creo que hubo una confusión con nuestras maletas - I think there was a confusion with our suitcases

2806. sufrir - to suffer
La empresa va a sufrir pérdidas - The company will suffer losses

2807. descripción - description
La descripción del artículo me convenció de comprarlo - The item description convinced me to buy it

2808. ilusión - illusion / dream
Su ilusión es que sus hijos tengan acceso a una buena educación - Her dream is that her children have access to a good education

2809. bajos - low (plural)
Vengo de una familia de bajos recursos - I come from a low-income family

2810. actriz - actress
La actriz fue invitada a la ceremonia - The actress was invited to the ceremony

2811. perfil - profile
Coincides con el perfil que estamos buscando - You match the profile we are looking for

2812. malos - bad / evil (masculine, plural)
Helena tiene malos modales - Helena has bad manners

2813. consideró - he/she/it considered
La directora consideró que la reunión se estaba tornando demasiado larga - The director considered that the meeting was getting too long

2814. posiblemente - possibly
Posiblemente lloverá mañana - It will possibly rain tomorrow

2815. tiro - shot
¡Buen tiro! - Good shot!

2816. colonia - colony
Este pueblo solía ser una colonia galesa - This town used to be a Welsh colony

2817. premios - awards
Estoy viendo la ceremonia de premios - I am watching the award ceremony

2818. espectadores - spectators
Los espectadores aplaudieron - The spectators applauded

2819. dedo - finger
Me rompí un dedo mientras jugaba al baloncesto - I broke a finger while playing basketball

2820. determinadas - determined / certain (feminine, plural)
Hay determinadas cosas que no puedes decir en una cena formal - There are certain things you cannot say at a formal dinner

2821. humo - smoke
Sale humo de la chimenea - There is smoke coming out of the chimney

2822. sujetos - subjects
Los sujetos encuestados aseguraron estar insatisfechos - The surveyed subjects claimed to be dissatisfied.

2823. oeste - west
Debes caminar un par de kilómetros hacia el oeste para encontrar la playa - You have to walk a couple of kilometers to the west to find the beach

2824. de espaldas - backwards / to have the back to
Lucrecia estaba de espaldas a la ventana - Lucrecia had her back to the window

2825. gira - tour
La banda se fue de gira - The band went on tour

2826. hoja - leaf / paper sheet
La hoja seca cayó del árbol - The dry leaf fell from the tree

2827. integrantes - members
Los integrantes de la banda discutieron - The members of the band argued

2828. rural - rural
Me gusta el paisaje rural - I like the rural landscape

2829. nariz - nose
Me pica la nariz - My nose itches

2830. esencia - essence
La música está en la esencia de esta cultura - Music is at the essence of this culture

2831. cura - cure / priest
Los científicos trabajan en encontrar la cura a la enfermedad - Scientists work to find a cure for the disease

2832. reducido - reduced
Aseguran que se han reducido las emisiones de gases - They claim that gas emissions have been reduced

2833. perfecto - perfect
El día está perfecto - The day is perfect

2834. intentó - he/she/it tried
Oscar intentó llamarte - Oscar tried to call you

2835. básicos - basic (plural)
Conozco los verbos básicos del español - I know the basic Spanish verbs

2836. enemigos - enemies
No tengo enemigos, por suerte - I have no enemies, luckily

2837. muestras - shows / samples / you show
¿Por qué no les muestras la ciudad? - Why don't you show them the city?

2838. insistió - he/she/it insisted
Mi madre insistió en que te invite - My mother insisted that I invite you

2839. letra - letter
La letra *ñ* solo existe en el español - The letter ñ only exists in Spanish

2840. pescado - fish
¿Te gusta el pescado? - Do you like fish?

2841. automóvil - car
Mi automóvil se rompió - My car broke down

2842. testigos - witnesses
Hay testigos del accidente - There are witnesses to the accident
2843. toneladas - tons
Las ballenas pesan toneladas - Whales weigh tons
2844. fama - fame
No me interesa la fama - I'm not interested in fame
2845. impedir - to prevent
Debes impedir que el problema empeore - You must prevent the problem from getting worse
2846. eliminar - to eliminate / to delete
¿Puedes eliminar ese archivo? - Can you delete that file?
2847. facilidad - ease
Silvana cocina con facilidad - Silvana cooks with ease
2848. templo - temple
Ayer visitamos un antiguo templo olmeca - Yesterday we visited an ancient Olmec temple
2849. reservas - reserves
No debemos agotar las reservas de agua - We must not exhaust our water reserves
2850. iglesias - churches
Me gustan las iglesias del período colonial - I like the churches of the colonial period
2851. privadas - private (feminine, plural)
Nuestras conversaciones son privadas - Our conversations are private
2852. logra - he/she/it achieves
Santino siempre logra lo que se propone - Santino always achieves what he sets out to do
2853. necesariamente - necessarily
Beber alcohol no es necesariamente malo - Drinking alcohol is not necessarily bad
2854. ofreció - he/she/it offered
Juan Manuel se ofreció para llevarme a casa - Juan Manuel offered to take me home

2855. electorales - electoral (plural)

Las campañas electorales son muy costosas - Electoral campaigns are very expensive

2856. existir - to exist

Las hadas no pueden existir - Fairies cannot exist

2857. ópera - opera

¿Quieres ir a la ópera esta noche? - Do you want to go to the opera tonight?

2858. emocionado - excited

Me sentí muy emocionado cuando escuché la canción - I was very excited when I heard the song

2859. ser testigo – to witness

Fui testigo del incendio - I witnessed the fire

2860. maneras - ways

Hay varias maneras de ver el asunto - There are several ways to view the matter

2861. datos - data

El periodista reveló datos impactantes - The journalist revealed shocking data

2862. ácido - acidic / acid

Este zumo de limón está muy ácido - This lemon juice is very acidic

2863. banca - bank

Puedes ver cuánto dinero tienes en tu banca electrónica - You can see how much money you have in your electronic bank

2864. formal - formal

Nos invitaron a una cena formal - We were invited to a formal dinner

2865. canto - singing

Estoy tomando clases de canto - I'm taking singing lessons

2866. identificación - identification

La policía está trabajando en la identificación del sospechoso - Police are working on the identification of the suspect

2867. directiva - directive
Esta nueva directiva va a trabajar más duro – This new directive is going to work harder

2868. relativamente - relatively
El libro es relativamente breve - The book is relatively short

2869. preparar - to prepare
Debo preparar el almuerzo para mañana - I must prepare lunch for tomorrow

2870. blancas - white (feminine, plural)
Quiero comprar sillas blancas para el comedor - I want to buy white chairs for the dining room

2871. destacar - to highlight
Quiero destacar el trabajo de mis colegas - I want to highlight the work of my colleagues

2872. núcleo - core
El café es el núcleo de nuestra cultura - Coffee is the core of our culture

2873. frases - phrases
Estoy leyendo un libro de frases en español - I'm reading a phrasebook in Spanish

2874. hiciera - I/he/she/it did / made (subjunctive)
No matter how much effort she made, she always failed the exam – No importa cuanto esfuerzo hiciera, ella siempre suspendía el examen

2875. sencillo - simple
El texto no es sencillo - The text is not simple

2876. colectiva - collective
Varios artistas hicieron una canción colectiva - Various artists made a collective song

2877. femenino - feminine
¡Ese es un modo feminino de lucir tu pelo largo! - That's a feminine way to wear your hair long!

2878. cristal - crystal
La princesa vivía en un palacio de cristal - The princess lived in a crystal palace
2879. seco - dry
El arroyo está seco - The stream is dry
2880. débil - weak
Se sintió muy débil después del accidente - He felt very weak after the accident
2881. cebolla - onion
No me gusta la cebolla - I do not like onion
2882. consigue - he/she/it achieves / gets
Ruth siempre consigue lo que quiere - Ruth always gets what she wants
2883. religiosa - religious (feminine)
Mi familia es muy religiosa - My family is very religious
2884. pérdidas - losses
Las pérdidas no fueron muy graves - The losses were not very serious
2885. realizan - they make / hold
Los habitantes locales realizan un festival todos los años - Local people hold a festival every year
2886. plato - dish / plate
El pulpo a la gallega es mi plato preferido - Galician octopus is my favorite dish
2887. curiosidad - curiosity
Siento mucha curiosidad por ver cómo termina la película - I am very curious to see the end of the movie
2888. instancia - instance
Esta es la instancia final - This is the final instance
2889. monte - mount / mountain
Quiero escalar ese monte - I want to climb that mount
2890. ética – ethics / ethical (feminine, singular)
Dicen que el médico cometió una falta ética - They say the doctor committed an ethical fault

2891. química - chemistry
Federico es doctor en química - Federico is a doctor in chemistry
2892. hablado - spoken / talked
¿Has hablado con mamá? - Have you talked to mom?
2893. permita - he/she/it allows (subjunctive)
Necesito una tienda de campaña que me permita acampar en la montaña - I need a tent that allows me to camp in the mountain
2894. merece - he/she/it deserves
Carlos merece un aumento - Carlos deserves a raise
2895. salen - they go out
Mis amigas salen a bailar esta noche, ¿quieres ir? - My friends are going out dancing tonight, do you want to join them?
2896. cientos - hundreds
Tengo cientos de correos sin leer - I have hundreds of unread emails
2897. desarrollado - developed
Han desarrollado un nuevo sistema operativo - They have developed a new operating system
2898. daños - damages / damage
Debemos prever los posibles daños - We must anticipate possible damage
2899. romper - to break
¡Vas a romper el vidrio! - You're going to break the glass!
2900. alternativas - alternatives
Tenemos varias alternativas para la cena - We have several alternatives for dinner
2901. mediodía - noon
Saldremos al mediodía - We will leave at noon
2902. externa - external (feminine)
La deuda externa aumentó - External debt increased
2903. galería - gallery
Estamos tomando un café en la galería - We are having coffee in the gallery

2904. fotografías - pictures / photographs

Debes enviarme las fotografías del viaje - You must send me the pictures of the trip

2905. hablan - they speak

Mis amigos hablan inglés, español y francés - My friends speak English, Spanish and French

2906. legales - legal (plural)

Tengo problemas legales para quedarme en el país - I have legal problems to stay in the country

2907. desarrolla - he/she/it develops

Daniel desarrolla sistemas para una gran empresa - Daniel develops systems for a large company

2908. habíamos - we had

Habíamos acordado encontrarnos en el parque - We had agreed to meet in the park

2909. salto - jump

La rana dio un salto - The frog jumped

2910. perros - dogs

Tengo tres perros - I have three dogs

2911. plazas - squares

Hay muchas plazas en la ciudad - There are many squares in the city

2912. responsabilidades - responsibilities

Silvina tiene muchas responsabilidades - Silvina has many responsibilities

2913. ataques - attacks

La escritora sufrió varios ataques de la prensa - The writer suffered several attacks from the press

2914. positiva - positive (feminine)

La reseña de la película fue positiva - The movie review was positive

2915. tranquilo - relaxed / calm (masculine)

¡Quédate tranquilo! - Stay calm!

2916. toca - he/she/it touches
El niño toca todos los juguetes - The child touches all the toys

2917. costumbres - customs
Quiero conocer las costumbres locales - I want to know the local customs

2918. adultos - adults
Mis hijos ya son adultos - My children are already adults

2919. aparentemente - apparently
Aparentemente, el problema está resuelto - Apparently the problem is solved

2920. acusado - accused (masculine)
El acusado se declaró inocente - The accused pleaded not guilty

2921. incluyendo - including
Me gustan todas sus películas, incluyendo la primera - I like all his movies, including the first one

2922. odio - hate
El odio no es bienvenido en esta empresa - Hate is not welcome in this company

2923. contactos - contacts
Tengo muchos contactos en el mundo editorial - I have many contacts in the publishing world

2924. bomba - bomb
La noticia fue una verdadera bomba - The news was a real bomb

2925. reacciones - reactions
Nos interesa conocer las reacciones de los espectadores - We are interested in knowing the reactions of the spectators

2926. estar de vuelta – to be back
Mi madre está de vuelta en España - My mother is back in Spain

2927. estábamos - we were
Estábamos de vacaciones, por eso no vi tu correo - We were on vacation, that's why I didn't see your email

2928. desaparición - disappearance

¿Cómo explicas la desaparición de la tarta que estaba en el refrigerador? - How do you explain the disappearance of the cake that was in the refrigerator?

2929. rincón - corner

El gato está durmiendo en un rincón - The cat is sleeping in a corner

2930. gris - grey

El cielo está gris - The sky is grey

2931. hacemos - we do

¿Qué hacemos hoy? - What do we do today?

2932. intercambio - exchange

Jessica hizo un intercambio académico en Uruguay - Jessica went on an academic exchange in Uruguay

2933. créditos - credits

Hay una escena adicional después de los créditos - There is an additional scene after the credits

2934. característica - characteristic

La comida picante es característica de esta región - Spicy food is characteristic of this region

2935. heridos – wounded / injured

No hubo heridos en el accidente - There were no injured people in the accident

2936. deberían - they should

Mis alumnos deberían hablar menos en clase - My students should talk less in class

2937. dirigió - he/she/it directed

El cineasta dirigió una película de terror - The filmmaker directed a horror movie

2938. sentirse - to feel

Es normal sentirse cansado después de una caminata de tantas horas - It is normal to feel tired after such a long walk

2939. harina - flour

Hay que comprar harina - We need to buy flour

2940. dinámica - dynamic
Cada grupo tiene una dinámica particular - Each group has a particular dynamic

2941. garantizar - to guarantee
Puedo garantizar que todo saldrá bien - I can guarantee that everything will be fine

2942. tarjeta - card
¿Aceptan tarjeta de crédito? - Do you accept credit cards?

2943. consenso - consensus
Hubo consenso entre los jueces - There was consensus among the judges

2944. financieros - financial (masculine, plural)
El país tiene problemas financieros - The country has financial problems

2945. llamados - calls
La secretaria atendía los llamados - The secretary answered the calls

2946. por consiguiente - therefore
Por consiguiente, la reunión se canceló - Therefore, the meeting was canceled

2947. secretos - secrets
Celina tiene secretos - Celina has secrets

2948. debían - they had to
Los niños debían ir a la escuela - The children had to go to school

2949. dispuestos - willing to (masculine, plural)
Están dispuestos a llegar a un acuerdo - They are willing to reach an agreement

2950. pensado - thought
Mejor pensado, deberíamos volver antes de que anochezca - On second thought, we should go back before it gets dark

2951. surge - it arises
Cada tanto surge algún problema - Every now and then a problem arises

2952. existía - he/she/it existed
En aquella época no existía la televisión - At that time television didn't exist

2953. espectador - spectator / viewer
El espectador disfrutó la obra de teatro - The spectator enjoyed the theatre play

2954. precisa - precise / accurate (feminine)
Sofía es muy precisa cuando habla - Sofia is very accurate when she speaks

2955. jurado - jury
El jurado encontró al acusado culpable - The jury found the defendant guilty

2956. agencias - agencies
Envié mis fotos a varias agencias - I sent my photos to several agencies

2957. convencido - convinced
Martín está convencido de que tiene razón - Martín is convinced that he is right

2958. oreja - ear
El explorador apoyó la oreja contra el suelo - The explorer leaned his ear against the ground

2959. alemana - German (feminine)
Nora es alemana, pero habla español - Nora is German, but she speaks Spanish

2960. chicos - children / kids / small (masculine, plural)
Los chicos están jugando en el parque - The kids are playing in the park

2961. ochenta - eighty
El artista tiene ochenta años, pero sigue pintando - The artist is eighty years old, but he continues to paint

2962. botella - bottle
Compra una botella de champán para esta noche - Buy a bottle of champagne for tonight

2963. femenina - feminine
"Sartén" puede ser una palabra femenina o masculina en español - "Frying pan" can be a feminine or masculine word in Spanish

2964. examen - test / exam
El examen es mañana - The test is tomorrow

2965. ambiental - environmental
La contaminación ambiental es un problema serio - Environmental pollution is a serious problem

2966. pasaron - they happened / spent
Laura y Carmen pasaron el verano en Ibiza - Laura and Carmen spent the summer in Ibiza

2967. contaba - I/he/she/it counted / told
Mi abuelo siempre contaba historias de su infancia - My grandfather always told stories from his childhood

2968. barrios - neighbourhoods
Este es uno de los barrios más bellos de la ciudad - This is one of the most beautiful neighborhoods in the city

2969. llevaron - they took / brought
Los pescadores llevaron mariscos al mercado - The fishermen brought seafood to the market

2970. invitados - guests / invited (masculine, plural)
Hemos sido invitados a una fiesta - We have been invited to a party

2971. entrenador – trainer / coach
Pablo es entrenador de un equipo de fútbol - Pablo is a coach of a soccer team

2972. risa - laugh
Los chistes de Abel me causan mucha risa - Abel's jokes make me laugh a lot

2973. circunstancia - circumstance
Esta es una circunstancia excepcional - This is an exceptional circumstance

2974. tendencias - tendencies / trends
Las tendencias del mercado son claras - Market trends are clear
2975. etapas - stages
El curso tiene cuatro etapas - The course has four stages
2976. roca - rock / stone
Debajo de la roca hay una lombriz - There is an earthworm under the rock
2977. comparación - comparison
El profesor nos pidió una comparación entre los dos textos - The professor asked us for a comparison between the two texts
2978. provoca - he/she/it provokes / causes
El sedentarismo provoca problemas en la salud - Sedentary lifestyle causes health problems
2979. vieron - they saw / watched
Los niños vieron una película - The children watched a movie
2980. prevención - prevention
La prevención es más barata que la cura - Prevention is cheaper than curing
2981. dama - lady
Sandra era una dama de la alta sociedad - Sandra was a lady of the high society
2982. líquido - liquid / fluid (masculine)
El coche necesita líquido de frenos - The car needs brake fluid
2983. estarán - they will be
Mis padres estarán muy contentos con la noticia - My parents will be very happy with the news
2984. decidir - to decide
Debemos decidir a dónde ir a comer - We must decide where to go to eat
2985. calmado - calm
El océano está calmado - The ocean is calm
2986. suficientemente - sufficiently / enough
Los chicos son suficientemente grandes para quedarse solos en casa un rato - The kids are old enough to be home alone for a while

2987. comentario - comment

Alguien dejó un comentario en tu publicación - Someone left a comment on your post

2988. garantía - guarantee

El producto tiene una garantía por tres meses - The product has a guarantee of three months

2989. protagonistas - main characters / leads / protagonists

Me siento identificado con los protagonistas del libro - I feel identified with the protagonists of the book

2990. temprano - early

Nuestro vuelo parte mañana temprano - Our flight departs early tomorrow

2991. artística - artistic (feminine)

El museo organizó una jornada artística para niños - The museum organized an artistic day for children

2992. obreros - workers

Los obreros de la fábrica hicieron una huelga - The factory workers went on strike

2993. quinto - fifth (masculine)

Mayo es el quinto mes del año - May is the fifth month of the year

2994. imprescindible - essential

Alberto fue imprescindible durante todo el proyecto - Alberto was essential throughout the project

2995. retrato - portrait

El pintor hizo un retrato del rey - The painter made a portrait of the king

2996. cero - zero

Las temperaturas son inferiores a cero durante el invierno - Temperatures are below zero during the winter

2997. desaparecido - disappeared / gone / missing (masculine)

Mi teléfono ha desaparecido - My phone is gone

2998. temperaturas - temperatures

Estamos viviendo las temperaturas más altas en años - We are experiencing the highest temperatures in years

2999. baile - dance

Te veré en el baile de fin de año - I'll see you at the end of the year dance

30000. curioso - curious (masculine)

Eres muy curioso - You are very curious

Conclusion

Congratulations! You have reached the end of this 3.000-word journey, which actually took us more than 50.000 words to complete.

Spanish is not as hard as some people think, but it's not the easiest language in the world either. Verbs are conjugated in complex ways and, rather than memorizing grammar rules, sometimes the easiest way to learn those tricky conjugations is practicing, practicing and practicing some more.

Through these words and sentences, by now, you should have a clear idea of how to use the most frequent words in the Spanish language. This will help you not only to communicate but to truly engage with Spanish speakers, to be able to really know the Spanish and Latin American cultures, to make friends, to solve problems, and even maybe to fall in love...

We hope that you found this book very useful and that once you start immersing yourself in the Spanish-speaking world, you will find that you have improved your language skills.

Don't hesitate in moving forward! Travelling and putting these words and sentences to use is the best way to keep them alive. Learning a language, unfortunately, is not like riding a bicycle: you *do* forget how to do it if you don't do it constantly!

This means that, if you want the time you spent learning Spanish to be a good investment, you have to keep on practicing every day:

read books, watch movies, read the news, follow social media referents who post in Spanish.

And, specially, if you can, travel and make some Spanish-speaking friends. You will not regret it!